Fair Trade For All

Fair Trade For All

HOW TRADE CAN PROMOTE DEVELOPMENT

Joseph E. Stiglitz and **Andrew Charlton**

OXFORD
UNIVERSITY PRESS

OXFORD
UNIVERSITY PRESS

Great Clarendon Street, Oxford OX2 6DP

Oxford University Press is a department of the University of Oxford.
It furthers the University's objective of excellence in research, scholarship,
and education by publishing worldwide in

Oxford New York

Auckland Cape Town Dar es Salaam Hong Kong Karachi
Kuala Lumpur Madrid Melbourne Mexico City Nairobi
New Delhi Shanghai Taipei Toronto

With offices in

Argentina Austria Brazil Chile Czech Republic France Greece
Guatemala Hungary Italy Japan Poland Portugal Singapore
South Korea Switzerland Thailand Turkey Ukraine Vietnam

Oxford is a registered trade mark of Oxford University Press
in the UK and in certain other countries

Published in the United States
by Oxford University Press Inc., New York

British Library Cataloguing in Publication Data
Data available

Library of Congress Cataloging in Publication Data
Data available

Typeset by Newgen Imaging Systems (P) Ltd., Chennai, India
Printed in Great Britain
on acid-free paper by
Clays Ltd., St Ives plc., Suffolk

ISBN 0-19-929090-3   978-0-19-929090-1

Foreword

⚓

By the end of the twentieth century trade liberalization had become part of the mantra of political leadership of both the left and the right in the advanced industrial countries. President Clinton had hoped that a new round of trade negotiations, which was to have been launched at the Seattle meeting of the WTO in December 1999, would be his final achievement in helping create a new world of trade liberalization, capping the successful creation of NAFTA and the completion of the Uruguay Round. Perhaps the new round would be remembered as the Seattle Round, or even better, as the Clinton Round, as previous rounds had been named after the city where they were started (e.g. the Torquay Round of 1951 and the Tokyo Round of 1973–9) or the official who came to be identified with the talks (e.g. the Dillon Round of 1960–1 and the Kennedy Round of 1964–7).

As Chief Economist of the World Bank, I was greatly worried about the imbalances of the Uruguay Round, and sensitive to the fact that it had not delivered on the promises that had been made to the developing countries. In an address to the WTO in Geneva, I documented those imbalances and called for a Development Round to redress them.[1] Just days before the WTO meeting convened in Seattle (in an address at Harvard University) I predicted that unless redressing those imbalances was at the top of the agenda, the developing countries would reject another round of trade negotiations. As it turned out, Seattle was a watershed. The riots and protests on the streets during the conference were the most public manifestation of a shift in the debate about trade and trade liberalization—and of a more significant shift in the relationship between the developed and the developing world.

[1] See Stiglitz (1999*b*, *c*).

At the turn of the millennium, there was a new sense of collective responsibility for the challenges faced by poor countries, and also a recognition of the inequities created by previous rounds of trade negotiations. The advanced industrial countries responded to the events at Seattle and the broader public support for a new approach to international issues. At Doha, in November 2001, they agreed to an agenda that they *claimed* reflected the concerns of the developing countries.

But a year and a half later it was clear that the developed countries were, by and large, reneging on the promises they had made at Doha. It appeared that even if progress were made in agriculture, it would be slow—it might even be years before subsidies were cut back to the 1994 levels. Until just before the meeting in Cancún, in September 2003, the United States was the only country still holding out on an agreement to make life-saving medicines available, but even after it caved in to pressure it appeared as if it were demanding severe restrictions on the availability of such medicines. The terms it was forcing on developing countries—and even on Australia—in bilateral agreements made clear that there was no intent to make it easy for countries to have, say, generic drugs at affordable prices.

Not one of the trade ministers of the developed countries will defend the inequities of, say, the agricultural provisions. When an earlier version of this report was presented at the UN, at the invitation of the President of the General Assembly, and when it was presented at the WTO in Geneva, no one, not even the representatives of the United States, challenged the charges that we made against the gross inequities of the previous rounds, or even the inequities of some of the proposals then under discussion. But the trade ministers say in private, 'What are we to do? Our congresses and parliaments have tied our hands. We cannot tame the special interests. We live in democracies, and that is part of the price one has to pay for democracy. We are doing the best we can.'

At Cancún, for perhaps the first time, there was sufficient transparency that journalists could cover what was going on. There were quick reports back to national capitals about daily developments in the negotiations. In effect, the democracies of the developing countries replied: 'We too live in democracies. Our democracies are demanding that we sign a fair agreement. If we return with another agreement as unfair as the last, we will be voted out of office. We too have no choice.' So the choice for the world was between a fair agreement reflecting the sentiments of a broad majority of the populations in both developed and less developed countries, or another unfair agreement, reflecting the special interests in developed countries. It was clear that the developing countries were on far higher moral ground than were the developed countries.

In the aftermath of the failure of Cancún, the Commonwealth countries—a group of nations with a historical association to the United Kingdom—asked us to undertake a study of the Development Round. The 52 Commonwealth countries consist of developed countries (the UK, Canada, Australia, South Africa, and New Zealand), and large developing countries (India, Pakistan, Nigeria, Malaysia) and many small countries (including Saint Kitts, Fiji, Cyprus). Thus the Commonwealth provides a unique forum in which the vital issues affecting the relationship between developing and developed countries can be discussed in a spirit of openness and understanding.

The Commonwealth posed the question: 'What would a true development round—one reflecting the interests and concerns of the developing world, one which would promote their development—look like?' Our answer was that it would look very different from that embodied in the agenda that was set forth in Doha, and even more different from how matters had evolved subsequently. We came to the conclusion that the so-called 'Development Round' did not deserve its epithet. This book puts the recommendations of that report within the broader context of trade policy, development, and the WTO.

There are some people that will criticize the content and motivation of this book. There is certainly a concern that by pointing out the unfairness of global trade rules, this book will cause governments and vested interests in developing countries to blame outsiders for their problems rather than engage in difficult internal reform. But like the result of any analysis, information can be misused, and the only protection is to be as clear as one can about the assumptions underlying the analysis. While it is true that developing countries could do more for themselves, and that many of their problems are only marginally related to constraints on external market access, that is no excuse for an international trade regime that makes life more difficult for the developing countries. The fact that the truth might lead individuals to unhappiness as they realize how poorly they have been treated can hardly be an argument for *not* engaging in analysis and disseminating results. There is, of course, the risk that recalcitrance in the North and unrealistic expectations in the South could lead to a stalemate. But this book, by showing that there is in fact a rich agenda ahead, provides a variety of channels through which progress can occur.

Most of the book is an incidence analysis. It describes the policies that would do the most to integrate the developing countries into the world trading system, to give them new trading opportunities, and to help them to capitalize on those opportunities. It is premised on the hope that a better understanding of the effects of trade agreements will help mobilize public opinion in both developed and less developed countries; that it will strengthen the case for negotiators in the hard bargaining that marks any round of trade negotiations; and that it will help bring about reforms in the procedures and in the institutions of the WTO which will enhance transparency and more equitable outcomes. As the old aphorism has it, *knowledge is power*. It is our hope that the information provided by this book might play a small role in shaping the outcome of trade negotiations.

We should clarify what this book is, and what it is not. It is a review of the theoretical and empirical evidence—much of the detail of which is located in the Appendices—concerning the impact of provisions of previous trade agreements and proposed new agreements on the well-being and development of the developing countries. On the basis of that review we delineate a set of priorities for a 'true' Development Round. The book itself does not undertake any original analyses of these impacts, though we comment on the assumptions, strengths, and weaknesses of studies already in the literature.

If there is a successful conclusion to the Doha Round—or to any subsequent round of trade discussions—developing countries will need substantial assistance to enable them to adapt to the resulting changes, and to take advantage of any resulting new opportunities. Thus, the second question we address is: 'What kind of assistance should be provided by the advanced industrial countries?' But before addressing that question, we needed to ask prior ones: 'Why is such assistance so important? Why are the costs of adjustment for developing countries higher, and their ability to bear those costs so much lower, than for developed countries?' It is our hope that by making it clear why assistance is so important if trade liberalization is to bring its potential benefits to developing countries, we can further increase the resolve of developed countries to live up to the commitments they have already made to provide additional assistance to the developing countries. Just as the developed countries appear to have fallen markedly short of their commitments to the developing countries and to each other that they made at Doha in November 2001, to make the current round of trade negotiations a Development Round, at least some of the developed countries appear to have fallen markedly short of the commitments in financial assistance that they made at Monterrey in March 2003. These were commitments based on the noblest of ambitions, to create a fairer globalization and to increase the well-being of the world's poorest. It is our hope that this book may, in some small way, contribute to the achievement of these ambitions.

Joseph Stiglitz
2005

Preface

⌬

This book goes to press as the world moves towards the WTO's 6th Ministerial Meeting in Hong Kong in December 2005. This is the first Ministerial Meeting since the 5th Ministerial in Cancun, Mexico, collapsed in failure and recriminations in 2003. Progress since Cancun on the central issues in dispute, including agriculture, has been slow, and there has been growing pessimism about the potential outcomes of the Hong Kong negotiations. The optimists hope not only for an agreement, but one which is more than just a face-saving gesture, such as a pro-forma commitment to continue discussions and a reiteration of the lofty goals set at Doha.

The document which launched this round of talks—The Doha Declaration—was full of noble ambition. It promised to rectify the imbalances of previous rounds of trade agreements, that had left, for instance, developed country tariffs against developing country products far higher than those against developed countries. The world has come to recognize the imperative of reducing poverty in the Third World. It has agreed upon a set of targets—the Millennium Development Goals. And it has increasingly come to recognize the importance of opening up trade opportunities for the developing countries—and providing them assistance to grasp these opportunities—if these targets are to be met. It was accordingly totally appropriate that at Doha the trade ministers agreed to make the Round of trade negotiations they were then launching a *development round*, one which would help, not hinder, the developing countries in achieving those aspirations. The rest of the world cannot solve the problems facing developing countries—their success will depend largely on their own efforts—but it should not tilt the playing field against them, which, as we have shown, in many respects, it has been doing.

Part of the problem has been that discussions on reforming the global trading system have been approached as a pure matter of bargaining—and in the bargaining, the poor and the weak, the developing countries, almost inevitably come out short. Even had the agenda that had been set out in Doha been more fully accomplished, it would have been a far cry from a *true* development agenda. But what has been emerging since then clearly does not deserve that epithet. The irony is that both the North and the South as a whole could benefit from a *fair* and *development-oriented* agenda.

This book has made it clear that, regardless of the outcome of Hong Kong, we have a long way to go if we are to establish a global trading regime which represents *fair trade for all*. We should, however, be content with nothing less.

Acknowledgements

This book has been written by Joseph Stiglitz and Andrew Charlton, on behalf of the Initiative for Policy Dialogue (IPD), a network of some two hundred economists and development researchers throughout the developed and developing world who are committed to furthering the understanding of the development process and policies that would enhance development. This project was managed by the IPD Managing Director, Shari Spiegel, and assisted by the IPD Program Coordinator, Shana Hofstetter, and the Publications Manager, Kira Brunner. The original report, which forms the core of Chapters 5, 8, and 9, was written at the request of and with the support of the Commonwealth Secretariat. It was reviewed at a meeting of the IPD Trade Task Force, chaired by Dani Rodrik of Harvard and Andres Rodriguez-Clare of the Inter-American Development Bank (both acting in a personal capacity), in New York in March 2004. There were subsequent presentations in Washington in the spring of 2004, on the fringes of the IMF and World Bank meetings and at a meeting held at the Institute for International Economics, with comments presented by Supachai Panitchpakdi, the Director General of the WTO. In May 2004 it was presented in Brussels at the Annual Bank Conference on Development Economics—Europe, sponsored by the World Bank; and in September 2004 it was presented at the United Nations at the invitation of the President of the General Assembly, and at the WTO in Geneva, and at the Commonwealth Finance Ministers' meeting in Saint Kitts. We wish to acknowledge the helpful comments of the participants in those presentations, many of which have been incorporated into this book. We are also indebted to David Vines, Simon Evenett, Andrew Glyn, Sarah Caro, the publisher at Oxford University Press, Anya Schiffrin for invaluable help with many areas of the production and publicity, Dan Choate and Josh Goodman for their editiorial assistance, and several anonymous reviewers who provided useful comments on the manuscript.

We would also like to acknowledge the financial support of the Ford Foundation, the Macarthur Foundation, the Mott Foundation, the Canadian International Development Agency (CIDA), and the Swedish International Development Cooperation Agency (SIDA) for their financial support for the Initiative for Policy Dialogue. In particular, the IPD Trade Task Force is supported by a grant from CIDA.

Joseph Stiglitz and Andrew Charlton

2005

Contents

List of Tables

List of Figures

ⵌ

Glossary

African, Caribbean, and Pacific (ACP) countries Group of African, Caribbean, and Pacific countries which have received special treatment from the European Union through a series of agreements, including the Lomé Convention and the Cotonou Agreement.

Agreement on Agriculture WTO agreement which focuses on improving market access and reducing trade-distorting domestic support payments and export subsidies in agriculture.

anti-dumping duties Specific import duties imposed by importing countries on goods which are dumped by foreign exporters and cause injury to producers of competing products.

anti-globalization A political stance of opposition to the perceived negative aspects of globalization.

Appellate Body The WTO's judicial body that hears appeals to the findings of dispute settlement panels.

Cairns Group A group of countries which lobby together for agricultural liberalization, including Argentina, Australia, Bolivia, Brazil, Canada, Chile, Colombia, Costa Rica, Fiji, Guatemala, Indonesia, Malaysia, New Zealand, Paraguay, the Philippines, South Africa, Thailand, and Uruguay.

competition policy Policies designed to protect and stimulate competition in markets by outlawing anti-competitive business practices such as cartels, market sharing, or price fixing, the body of laws of a state which encourage competition by restricting practices which remove competition from the market, such as monopoly and cartels.

compulsory license Authorization for a government or company to make and sell a product (such as a life-saving drug) without the permission of the patent holder on the grounds of public interest.

Cotonou Agreement A treaty signed in Cotonou, Benin, in June 2000 which sets out the relationship between the European Union and the ACP countries on foreign aid, trade, investment, human rights, and governance; Replaces the Lomé Convention.

countervailing duty A means to restrict international trade in cases where imports are subsidized by a foreign country and harm domestic producers.

development box Measures proposed to give developing countries special flexibility within WTO rules for the purpose of ensuring food security, protecting farmer livelihoods, and reducing poverty.

Dispute Settlement Body The General Council of the WTO, composed of representatives of all member countries, convened to administer rules and procedures established in various agreements. It has the authority to establish panels, oversee implementation of rulings and recommendations, and authorize suspension of concessions or other obligations under various agreements.

Doha Declaration Statement made at the fourth WTO ministerial conference in Doha, Qatar, launching the Doha Round.

dumping The export of goods at a price less than their normal value, generally at less than in the domestic market or third-country markets, or at less than production cost.

enabling clause The 1979 decision of the GATT to give developing countries 'differential and more favorable treatment, reciprocity and fuller participation'. One of the so-called framework agreements, it enables WTO members to accord such treatment to developing countries without giving it to other contracting parties.

Everything but Arms (EBA) The name given by the EU to the package it offered to the least developed countries in 2001, which is expected to eliminate quotas and tariffs on all of their exports—except arms.

externality A side-effect or consequence (of an industrial or commercial activity) which affects other parties without this being reflected in the cost of the goods or services involved; a social cost or benefit.

G33 A group actually consisting of 42 developing countries of the WTO. They are: Antigua and Barbuda, Barbados, Belize, Benin, Botswana, China, Republic of the Congo, Côte d'Ivoire, Cuba, Dominican Republic, Grenada, Guyana, Haiti, Honduras, India, Indonesia, Jamaica, Kenya, Korea, Mauritius, Mongolia, Montserrat, Mozambique, Nicaragua, Nigeria, Pakistan, South Panama, Peru, the Philippines, Saint Kitts, Saint Lucia, Saint Vincent and the Grenadines, Senegal, Sri Lanka, Suriname, Tanzania, Trinidad and Tobago, Turkey, Uganda, Venezuela, Zambia, and Zimbabwe.

General Agreement on Tariffs and Trade (GATT) An organization established in 1947 to agree on common rules for tariffs and to reduce trade restrictions through a series of negotiating rounds. The Uruguay Round, completed in 1994, created the World Trade Organization, which superseded the GATT in 1995.

General Agreement on Trade in Services (GATS) WTO agreement concluded at the end of the Uruguay Round. It provides a legal framework for trade in services, and the negotiated, progressive liberalization of regulations that impede this. It covers areas such as transport, investment, education, communications, financial services, energy and water services, and the movement of persons.

Generalized System of Preferences (GSP) A program to grant trade advantages (such as reduced tariff levels) to particular developing countries.

government procurement Purchase of goods and services by governments and state-owned enterprises.

green box Income support and subsidies that are expected to cause little or no trade distortion. The subsidies have to be funded by governments but must not involve price support. Environmental protection subsidies are included. No limits or reductions are required for such income support or subsidies.

Green Room Closed meetings during which developed countries negotiated with selected countries as part of non-transparent bargaining tactics during the GATT and WTO proceedings.

import quota A form of protectionism used to restrict the import of goods by limiting the legal quantity of imports.

import substitution A trade and economic policy based on the premise that a developing country should attempt to substitute locally produced substitutes for products which it imports (mostly finished goods). This usually involves government subsidies and high tariff barriers to protect local industries and hence import substitution policies are not favored by advocates of absolute free trade. In addition import substitution typically advocates an overvalued currency, to allow easier purchase of foreign goods, and capital controls.

GLOSSARY

infant industry protection Protection of a newly established domestic industry.

Jubilee 2000 An international coalition which called for cancellation of unpayable third world debt by the year 2000.

market access The extent to which a country permits imports. A variety of tariff and non-tariff trade barriers can be used to limit the entry of products from other countries.

market failure A case in which a market fails efficiently to provide or allocate goods and services, therefore requiring state intervention.

Mercosur A trading zone consisting of Brazil, Argentina, Uruguay, and Paraguay, founded in 1995. Its purpose is to promote free trade and movement of goods, peoples, skills, and money between these countries.

Millennium Development Goals (MDGs) Goals which governments committed themselves at the UN General Assembles in 2000 to achieving by 2015: namely, eradicating extreme poverty and hunger; achieving universal primary education; promoting gender equality and empowering women; reducing child mortality; improving maternal health; combating HIV/AIDS; malaria, and other diseases; ensuring environmental sustainability; and developing a global partnership for development.

mode of supply WTO term to identify how a service is provided by a supplier to a buyer.

most-favored-nation (MFN) treatment A country extending to another country the lowest tariff rates it applies to any other country. All WTO contracting parties undertake to apply such treatment to one another under Art. I of the GATT. When a country agrees to cut tariffs on a particular product imported from one country, the tariff reduction automatically applies to imports of that product from any other country eligible for most-favored-nation treatment.

national treatment Treating foreign producers and sellers the same as domestic firms.

necessity test Procedure to determine whether a policy restricting trade is necessary to achieve its intended objective.

non-tariff barriers (NTBs) A catch-all phrase describing barriers to international trade other than tariffs.

Organization for Economic Co-operation and Development (OECD) Group of industrial countries that 'provides governments a setting in which to discuss, develop and perfect economic and social policy'.

parallel imports Products made and marketed by the patent owner (or trademark or copyright owner) in one country and imported into another country without the approval of the patent owner.

Pareto efficiency The criterion which stipulates that for change in an economy to be viewed as socially beneficial, it should make no one worse off while making at least one person better off.

patent A grant from a government to a firm conferring the exclusive privilege of making or selling some new invention.

Poverty Reduction Strategy Paper (PRSP) A document describing a country's macroeconomic, structural and social policies and programmes to promote growth and reduce poverty, as well as associated external financing needs. Initiated by the boards of the World Bank and International Monetary Fund (IMF), PRSPs are expected to be prepared by governments through a participatory process involving civil society and development partners, including the World Bank and IMF, and are required for countries seeking to obtain concessional lending and debt relief under the enhanced Heavily Indebted Poor Countries (HIPC) initiative.

predatory pricing Action by a firm to lower prices so much that rival firms are driven out of business, after which the firm raises prices to exploit its resulting monopoly power.

production subsidy A payment perhaps implicit, by government, to producers encouraging and assisting their activities and allowing them to produce at lower cost or to sell at a price lower than the market price.

protocol of accession Legal document recording the conditions and obligations under which a country accedes to an international agreement or organization.

Quad countries Canada, the EU, Japan, and the US.

quota Measure restricting the quantity of a good imported or exported. Quantitative restrictions include quotas, non-automatic licensing, mixing regulations, voluntary export restraints, and prohibitions or embargos.

Rules of Origin Criteria for establishing the country of origin of a product. Often based on whether production (processing) leads to a change in tariff heading (classification) or in the level of value added in the country where the good was last processed.

safeguard action or measure Emergency protection to safeguard domestic producers of a specific good from an unforeseen surge in imports.

sanitary and phytosanitary measures Border control measures necessary to protect human, animal, or plant life or health.

second-best argument for protection An argument for protection to partially correct an existing distortion in the economy when the first-best policy for that purpose is not available.

Singapore Issues The topics discussed by four working groups set up during the WTO Ministerial Conference of 1996 in Singapore, namely investment protection, competition policy, transparency in government procurement, and trade facilitation. Disagreements, largely between largely developed and developing economies, prevented a resolution of these issues, despite repeated attempts to revisit them, notably during the 2003 Ministerial Conference in Cancún, Mexico, where no progress was made.

single undertaking Provision that requires countries to accept all the agreements reached during the Uruguay Round negotiations as a single package, rather than on a case-by-case basis.

special and differential treatment The principle in the WTO that developing countries be accorded special privileges, either exempting them from some WTO rules or granting them preferential treatment in the application of WTO rules.

tariff A government-imposed tax on imports.

tariff binding Commitment not to increase a rate of duty beyond an agreed level. Once a rate of duty is bound, it may not be raised without compensating the affected parties.

tariff equivalent The level of tariff that would be the same, in terms of its effect, as a given non-tariff barrier.

tariff escalation An increase in tariffs as a good becomes more processed, with lower tariffs on raw materials and less processed goods than on more processed versions of the same or derivative goods: for example, low duties on fresh tomatoes, higher duties on canned tomatoes, and higher yet on tomato ketchup.

tariffication Conversion of non-tariff barriers to their tariff equivalents.

tariff peak A single, particularly high, tariff on a good.

tariff rate quotas (TRQs) The quantitative level of imports of agricultural products (quotas) above which higher tariffs are applied.

terms of trade Ratio of the price of a country's export commodities to the price of its import commodities. An improvement in a nation's terms of trade is good for that country in the sense that it has to pay less for the products it imports, that is, it has to give up fewer exports for the imports it receives.

trade diversion Trade displacement, as a result of trade policies that discriminate among trading partners, of more efficient (lower-cost) sources by less efficient (higher-cost) sources. Can arise when some preferred suppliers are freed from barriers but others are not.

trade liberalization Reduction of tariffs and removal or relaxation of non-tariff barriers.

Trade-Related Aspects of Intellectual Property Rights (TRIPS) Agreement WTO agreement which sets down minimum standards for most forms of intellectual property regulation within all member countries of the WTO.

Trade-Related Investment Measures (TRIMS) Agreement WTO agreement aimed at eliminating the trade-distorting effects of investment measures taken by members. It does not introduce any new obligations, but merely prohibits TRIMS considered inconsistent with the provisions of GATT 1994 for both agricultural and industrial goods.

Uruguay Round The last round under the GATT, which began in Uruguay in 1986 and was completed in 1994 after nearly eight years of negotiations. It created the World Trade Organization.

value added Additional value created at a particular stage of production, i.e. the value of output minus the value of all inputs used in production.

voluntary export restraint An agreement between importing and exporting countries in which the exporting country restrains exports of a certain product to an agreed maximum within a certain period.

World Trade Organization An International organization which administers multilateral agreements defining the rules of international trade between its member states. The WTO replaced the General Agreement on Tariffs and Trade; its primary mission is to reduce international trade barriers.

WTO-plus Trade agreements that go beyond what the WTO multilateral trade regime requires. Regional trade agreements sometimes contain WTO-plus elements.

1
Introduction: The Story so Far

In November of 2001, trade ministers from 140 nations gathered in Doha, Qatar, to seek to give the World Trade Organization (WTO) a historic new mandate. The WTO's previous ministerial meeting in Seattle, USA, in 1999 had ended in failure and brought protests and violence to the city. Now they were meeting in the midst of a global recession, just two months after the shocking attacks on the United States of 11 September 2001. On the evening of 14 November, after several days of negotiations, and more than 18 hours after their original deadline, the ministers announced that they had reached a landmark agreement to launch a new round of trade talks. The agreement—the Doha Declaration—outlined a framework for a wide-ranging new round of multilateral negotiations. The top US trade negotiator, Robert Zoellick, was jubilant. 'We have sent a powerful signal to the world,' he said, adding that a new trade round would deliver 'growth, development and prosperity'.[1] Zoellick's claim that a new round of trade liberalization would deliver prosperity to the world was plausible, but he was perhaps too optimistic about the ensuing negotiations.

The purpose of this book is to describe how trade policies can be designed in developed and developing countries with a view to integrating developing countries into the world trading system and to help them to benefit from their participation. This book starts from the presumption that trade can be a positive force for development.

---

[1] Quoted in 'Seeds Sown for Future Growth', *The Economist*, 15 Nov. 2001.

In the right circumstances, policies which reduce tariffs and other barriers to the movement of goods and services can facilitate trade between nations and deliver welfare gains. However, we also point out that while increased trading opportunities are good for developing countries, liberalization needs to be managed carefully—the task is much more complex than the simple prescriptions of the Washington Consensus, which blithely exhorts developing countries to liberalize their markets rapidly and indiscriminately.[2]

In the run-up to the Doha meeting, the expectations of the developing country members of the WTO had been tempered by negative experiences from previous rounds of trade negotiations. Many developing countries had feared that the large industrialized countries would use their superior bargaining power to force through agreements which would disadvantage the developing countries. These fears seemed to be realized in the Uruguay Round. After the round was completed and an agreement had been signed, developing countries felt that they had not been fully aware of the cost of the obligations they had agreed to, and they felt that the liberalization in developed countries had fallen short of their expectations. Developing countries gained less than they had hoped on such issues as the speed with which textile protection would be reduced and the extent of tariff and subsidy reduction on agricultural goods in developed countries. The developed countries walked away from Uruguay with a large share of the gains, and many developed countries were predicted to be left worse off as a result of the round. After the Uruguay Round, many developing countries were reluctant to embark upon a new round of trade negotiations which might lead to another imbalanced agreement.

However, at the turn of the millennium there was renewed optimism. A new global consensus seemed to be developing to confront the economic challenges faced by the poorest nations which gained prominence in international affairs through a series of new initiatives. In trade, the Cotonou Agreement, led by the European Union, and

---

[2] The Washington Consensus is a set of policies believed by some economists to be the formula for promoting economic growth in developing countries. These policies include privatization, fiscal discipline, trade liberalization, and deregulation. In the 1990s these policies were vigorously advocated by several powerful economic institutions located in Washington, including the International Monetary Fund, the World Bank, and the US Treasury.

the US African Growth and Opportunity Act (AGOA) granted exporters from the poorest countries in the world free access to the richest markets in the world. At the same time, grassroots movements—including the worldwide Jubilee 2000 campaign devoted to debt cancellation for the poorest countries and the World Social Forum—gained unprecedented publicity and momentum for their causes. In addition, world leaders signed landmark treaties which placed the plight of poor countries at the heart of the global agenda. At the United Nations Millennium Summit in New York in September 2000, world leaders adopted the Millennium Development Goals (MDGs);[3] at the International Conference on Financing for Development, held in Monterrey, Mexico in March 2002, the advanced industrial countries committed themselves to helping provide the finance for development priorities of poor countries; and the Johannesburg Summit on Sustainable Development in September 2002 established an action plan to ensure sustainable global development.

The WTO conference at Doha reflected the new determination to address development problems collectively in multilateral forums. It was a hopeful milestone for developing nations and they emerged from it with some optimism. Several of their concerns were incorporated into the agreement made at Doha, which explicitly focused on the promotion of economic development and the alleviation of poverty in poor countries. This 'Doha Round'—the ninth of a series of such negotiations, and the first since the formalization of trade negotiations under the WTO[4]—came to be commonly referred to as the 'Development Round'.

Unfortunately, in the years since it was launched, the Doha Round has not delivered on its development mandate in several important respects. First, there has been little progress on the issues of interest to developing countries. In particular, developing countries are interested in agreements to reduce tariffs on the goods that they can

[3] The Millennium Development Goals are the United Nations targets for reducing poverty, hunger, disease, illiteracy, environmental degradation, and discrimination against women by 2015. The targets address extreme poverty in its many dimensions—income poverty, hunger, disease, lack of adequate shelter, and exclusion—while promoting gender equality, education, and environmental sustainability. They are also basic human rights—the rights of each person on the planet to health, education, shelter, and security.
[4] The first round, held in Geneva in 1947, resulted in the General Agreement on Tariffs and Trade (GATT), which was formally replaced by the WTO in 1995.

export competitively. These are mainly labor-intensive goods, i.e. goods that are produced cheaply in countries with low wage rates and abundant unskilled labor.

A second problem with the so-called 'Development Round' is that the new issues that were initially put on the agenda primarily reflect the interests of the advanced industrial countries and have been strongly opposed by many developing countries. The most prominent new issues in the Doha Round emerged from the decision by WTO member countries at the 1996 Singapore Ministerial Conference to establish three new working groups: on trade and investment, on competition policy, and on transparency in government procurement. They also instructed the WTO Goods Council to consider ways of simplifying trade procedures, an issue sometimes known as 'trade facilitation'. Because these four issues were introduced to the agenda at the Singapore ministerial meeting, they are often called the 'Singapore Issues'. These issues have been opposed by developing countries, who are skeptical of new multilateral obligations which could restrict existing developmental domestic policy options and which might require large implementation costs.

Less than two years after the Doha Declaration, it had become clear that the Round was seriously off track. In September 2003, the WTO convened another ministerial meeting in Cancún, Mexico, with the special task to 'take stock of progress in the [Doha Development Agenda] negotiations, provide any necessary political guidance and take decisions as necessary'.[5] After four days the meeting ended abruptly without agreement on any of the main issues. The apparently irreconcilable conflict between developed and developing countries which produced failure at Cancún led to calls for a reassessment of the direction of global trade negotiations. Many of the participants in the Cancún meeting felt that Europe and the United States had reneged on the promises that had been made at Doha, emblematized by the lack of progress on agriculture.

There were mutual recriminations about who was to blame for the failure at Cancún. There was even disagreement about who would

---

[5] This is spelt out in para. 45 of the declaration that ministers issued at the previous ministerial conference in Doha in November 2001.

suffer the most. The United States and Europe were quick to assert that it was the developing countries who were the ultimate losers.[6] But many developing countries had taken the view that no agreement was better than a bad agreement, and that the Doha Round was rushing headlong (if any trade agreement can be described as 'rushing') into one which, rather than redressing the imbalances of the past, would actually make them worse. Though *some* progress had been made in addressing the concerns about the manner in which the negotiations were conducted, the failure to address these concerns fully[7] generated the further worry that the developing countries would, somehow, be strong-armed in the end into an agreement that was disadvantageous to them. There were also threats, especially by the United States, that it would effectively abandon the multilateral approach, taking up a bilateral approach. It differentiated between the 'can do' countries and others, and suggested that the 'can do' countries would benefit from a series of bilateral agreements. The smaller developing countries recognized that in these bilateral discussions their bargaining position was even weaker than it was in the multilateral setting. Several of the bilateral trade agreements made since Cancún have shown that these worries were justified. On the other hand, the United States has not succeeded in establishing a bilateral trade agreement with any major developing country.

This book takes a step back from these disputes. It attempts to support progress in the current round by asking what a true Development Round of trade negotiations would look like, one that reflects the interests and concerns of the developing countries and is designed to promote their development. What would an agreement based on principles of economic analysis and social justice—not on economic power and special interests—look like? Our analysis concludes that the agenda would look markedly different from that which has been at the center of discussions for the past

---

[6] See the op-eds in *The Financial Times* and the *New York Times* e.g. Robert B. Zoellick, 'America Will Not Wait for the Won't-Do Countries', *The Financial Times*, 22, Sept. 2003, 23.

[7] Most notable in this regard was the request by a number of developing countries that the Cancún draft be prepared on the basis of views and inputs at open-ended consultations, and where there was no consensus, to indicate clearly the differing positions or views. The proposal was rejected by a coalition of developed countries.

two years, and that the fears of the developing countries that the Doha Round of trade negotiations would disadvantage them (were the demands of the developed countries acceded to) were in fact justified.

In Chapter 2 we describe the conceptual foundations for the policy proposals in this book, starting with the theoretical proposition that trade liberalization is, in general, welfare-enhancing. We then show that for some countries, particularly the least developed countries, the assumptions on which this proposition is based are not entirely applicable. The problems of poverty, inequality, and incomplete risk and capital markets lead the experience of these countries to diverge from the predictions of the simple neo-classical models. These problems cause the experience of liberalization to vary across countries depending on their individual characteristics. There is a difference between trade openness (the state of having low barriers to imports) and trade liberalization (the process of reducing those barriers). Trade liberalization is supposed to deliver gains as resources are transferred from protected sectors, in which a country does not have comparative advantage, to those sectors where it is more efficient and where it can export more successfully. But in developing countries the lack of resources (labor and other production inputs) available to new industries is not usually the constraint which prevents the growth of new export sectors.[8] Developing countries have vast reserves of resources, particularly labor, which are already unemployed or underemployed. Thus trade liberalization is not required to 'free up' these resources for use in new industries. Unless complementary policies are used to ease the other constraints which prevent the advancement of export sectors, liberalization, by removing the protection given to domestic industries, may just leave the workers and other resources used in formerly protected industries idle in the short run.

Chapter 3 addresses the need for a Development Round. It examines some elements of the experience of developing countries in previous trade negotiations and briefly reviews some of the potential gains available from further liberalization. Chapter 4 is a brief review

---

[8] Other constraints on the ability of developing countries to develop successful export industries might include technological backwardness, workforces too small to generate economies of scale, high trade and transport costs, poor infrastructure, weak government institutions, and a lack of skilled labor.

of the Doha Round so far, and the extent to which it has lived up to the expectations of developing countries. It makes clear that there is a huge discrepancy between the Development Round trade agenda, both as it was formulated at Doha and as it has evolved since, and a *true* Development Round agenda that would do much more to integrate the developing countries into the world trading system and to remove the barriers which curtail the benefits they receive from their participation. Such an agenda would promote growth in developing countries and work to reduce the huge disparity that separates them from the more advanced industrial countries.

Chapter 5 outlines our proposals for the principles that should be adopted in a Development Round of trade negotiations. The primary principle of the Doha Round must be to ensure that the agreements promote development in poor countries. To make this principle operational the WTO needs to foster a culture of robust economic analysis to identify pro-development proposals and promote them to the top of the agenda. In practice this means establishing a source of impartial and publicly available analysis of the effects of different initiatives on different countries and groups within countries. This should be a core responsibility of an expanded WTO Secretariat. On the basis of this analysis, any agreement that differentially hurts developing countries or provides disproportionate benefits to developed countries should be presumptively viewed as unfair and as being against the spirit of the Development Round.

The agreements must enshrine both *de jure* and *de facto* fairness. This means ensuring that developing countries are not prevented from unlocking the benefits of free trade because of a lack of institutional capacity. In this regard, developing countries will require special assistance to enable them to participate equally in the WTO.

The principle of fairness should also be sensitive to countries' initial conditions. Chapter 6 discusses special treatment for developing countries which is needed to recognize that adjustment to new trading rules involves particularly high costs for those developing countries whose institutions are weakest and whose populations are most vulnerable. Prescriptive multilateral agreements must not be allowed to run roughshod over national strategies to deal with idiosyncratic development problems.

Chapters 7–10 present pro-development priorities that should form the core of the Doha Round agreements. Much of the recent discussion has focused on agriculture, but there is much more to a true Development Round. Primary attention should be given to market access for goods produced by developing countries. There is an urgent need to reduce protection on labor-intensive manufactures (textiles and food processing) and unskilled services (maritime and construction services). Priority should also be given to the development of schemes to increase labor mobility—particularly the facilitation of temporary migration for unskilled workers. As tariff barriers have come down, developed countries have increasingly resorted to non-tariff barriers; these need to be circumscribed. The proposals in these chapters are motivated by empirical analysis of the gains and costs of liberalization. For ease of exposition the analysis of this evidence is presented separately in Appendices 1 and 2. Chapter 11 considers the terms on which non-members are able to accede to the WTO.

Chapter 12 takes a brief look at some institutional reforms that might facilitate a more transparent and democratic negotiating process, and ones which might more likely result in agreements that are both fair and in the general interests of the world. A fair agreement is unlikely to be produced through an unfair process. In particular, greater transparency and openness are required to create a more inclusive bargaining process.

Chapter 13 considers the potentially costly process of adjustment to the kind of new trading regime envisioned in this book. In one sense, adjustment costs can be thought of as the price to be paid for the benefits of multilateral trade liberalization. It is these adjustment costs together with the trade benefits that determine the net effect of trade reform for each country. The Doha Round has placed renewed emphasis on the importance of sharing the *benefits* of trade reform fairly among developed and developing countries. However, there has been less attention to the distribution of adjustment costs among countries. The fact that implementation and adjustment costs are likely to be larger in developing countries, unemployment rates are likely to be higher, safety nets weaker, and risk markets poorer, are all facts that have to be taken into account in trade negotiations.

For some of the smallest and poorest states, the adjustment costs of trade liberalization may significantly outweigh the benefits available.

If the Development Round is to bring widespread benefits to people living in developing countries—and if there is to be widespread support for the continuing agenda for trade reform and liberalization—the developed world must make a stronger commitment than it has in the past to giving assistance to the developing world. Assistance is required not only to help bear the often large costs associated with trade reform, but also to enable developing countries to avail themselves of the new opportunities provided by a more integrated global economy.

2
Trade Can Be Good for Development

International trade can have a significant positive effect on economic growth and development.

In the eighteenth century, technological breakthroughs put Britain on the path to becoming the first truly 'modern' economy. Between 1870 and 1950 Britain's population nearly tripled. Towns like Birmingham, Liverpool, and Manchester grew into huge cities, average incomes grew more than twofold, and the share of farming fell from just under a half to less than a fifth of total production. There were many social, political, and geographical factors that caused the Industrial Revolution, but Britain's trade with her neighbors and colonies played a decisive role in fueling the new industrial activity and spreading prosperity to other countries. Before long British cities became the workshops of the world, importing vast quantities of food and raw materials, and exporting manufactured goods to America, Asia, and Africa.

Meiji Japan's rapid industrialization in the early twentieth century was also the result of a combination of domestic and international factors. The Meiji rulers established stable political institutions and they were quick to adopt the Western technology they had seen during the Iwakura missions to Europe and the United States in the 1870s. They established a new education system for all young people, sent students to the United States and Europe, and emphasized modern science, mathematics, technology, and foreign languages.

The government built railroads, improved the road network, and pursued land and financial sector reforms. The availability of trading opportunities was also vitally important. It is hard to imagine the Meiji industrialization occurring if Japan had not been able to import vast quantities of machinery, transport equipment, and other capital goods from the West in exchange for exports of cheap cloth, toys, and other labor-intensive consumer products. And this trade would have been impossible if it were not for the steady flow of food and cheap raw materials arriving in Japan from its colonies in Taiwan and Korea.

Similarly, international trade played a major role in the industrial development of North America and Australia in the nineteenth century, and of the East Asian 'Tiger' economies, India, and China at various points in the second half of the twentieth century. These examples, together with the many instances where growth did not occur, show that trade was necessary for sustained industrial development, but it was not sufficient. Trade liberalization created opportunities for economic development, but other factors determined the extent to which those opportunities were realized.

This chapter lays the foundations for the policies that we propose later in the book. The notion that trade—free trade, unencumbered by government restrictions—is welfare-enhancing is one of the most fundamental doctrines in modern economics, dating back at least to Adam Smith (1776) and David Ricardo (1816). But the subject has always been marked by controversy because the issue facing most countries is not a binary choice of autarky (no trade) or free trade, but rather a choice among a spectrum of trade regimes with varying degrees of liberalization.

Almost every country today imposes some trade restrictions and taxes. Since World War II, the world has been moving gradually towards reducing tariffs and restrictions on trade. Some of the developed countries that have been the most ardent advocates of trade liberalization have been somewhat duplicitous in their advocacy. They have negotiated the reduction of tariffs and the elimination of subsidies for the goods in which they have a comparative advantage, but are more reluctant to open up their own markets and to eliminate their own subsidies in other areas where the developing countries have an advantage. As a result we now have an international trade regime which, in many ways, is disadvantageous to the developing countries. In a world in which many see global poverty—by some estimates there are more than 2 billion people living on less than a dollar a day—as the world's most pressing problem, this is especially disturbing. It seems obvious that if the developed countries truly wanted to promote development in the Doha Round they should reduce their tariffs and subsidies on the goods of interest to the developing countries.

But many of the developed countries' negotiators have turned this argument on its head. They suggest that the reduction of one's own tariffs is beneficial, and hence the developing countries would be helping themselves by liberalizing in the WTO, irrespective of the actions of the developed countries. On this basis they argue that the developing countries should accept almost any offer that is put on the table.

If matters were so easy a pro-development trade agenda would be trivial—the developing countries should simply unilaterally open up their markets, and the faster they do so, the better. In this book we argue that matters are not so easy and that a pro-development agenda is more complex.

This chapter provides the conceptual framework for the policies that we propose for the Doha Round. In the first section we take a quick look at the interpretations and misinterpretations of the contrasting trade policies and growth experiences of Latin America and East Asia. In the second section we examine the theory behind the claims that trade is good for welfare and good for growth. In the third, we turn to the difficulties confronting the empirical studies and explain why they remain such a subject of controversy. In the final two sections we discuss the policy implications of the theoretical analysis and empirical evidence, and we consider the way forward. In each section, we develop our theme that trade liberalization can promote development, but that the results of different trade policies have varied across countries; and the evidence suggests that the benefits of liberalization depend on a host of factors. Thus the implementation of trade liberalization needs to be sensitive to national circumstances. The sequencing of liberalization is important, and there is much that can be done in conjunction with trade liberalization (by developing and developed countries alike) to ensure that developing countries are provided with meaningful new trading opportunities, and that they are able to benefit from them.

The lessons of East Asia and Latin America

The post-World War II world has seen several grand experiments in trade policy. The import substitution policies of Latin America and the export-oriented strategies of several East Asian countries are of particular interest. In both cases several countries undertook similar policies at similar times and saw broadly similar results. Economists have attempted to draw trade policy lessons from these experiences, but the conclusions have been contentious because each country pursued a multifaceted economic policy agenda from which it is difficult to isolate the contribution of trade policy alone to their economic success or failure.

The success of East Asia

The success of East Asia begins with Japan, which within a few decades after World War II had raised itself to the second largest economy in the world. It experienced sustained growth rates beyond those previously seen anywhere in the world. Japan's success was followed first by South Korea, Taiwan, Hong Kong, and Singapore; and then by Thailand, Indonesia, and Malaysia, and finally by China.

East Asia's growth over more than three decades was remarkable. In particular Japan and the other countries in East Asia refuted two of the classic propositions of development. First, they showed that inequality was not necessary to growth, whereas previously it had been widely believed that only through inequality could the requisite high savings rates be generated (Lewis 1955). Second, these countries proved that the initial stages of development did not have to be associated with an increase in inequality (*contra* Kuznets

1955). Instead the new prosperity was widely shared among its population and millions were lifted out of poverty. For example in Malaysia and Thailand, the incidence of poverty declined from almost 50 per cent in the 1960s to less than 20 per cent by the end of the century.

There were important differences among the polices pursued by the East Asian countries. Korea and Japan's industrial model focused on large domestic corporate conglomerates and actively restricted flows of foreign direct investment (FDI), which made up less than 5 per cent of GDP in the period 1987–92. By contrast Singapore and Malaysia both developed policies to attract large foreign multinational corporations and encourage clusters of activity to develop around them. FDI in these countries reached more than 30 per cent of GDP by 1992. However, at a deeper level, the Asian countries shared much in common. They had high rates of investment in physical and human capital, rapid growth of agricultural productivity, and declining fertility.

But it is the role of the state in Asia's growth miracle which has created the most controversy. Adherents of the orthodox view believe that East Asia's free market philosophy was the main source of its success. They stress the prevailing stability-oriented macroeconomic policies, including responsible government monetary and fiscal policy, low inflation, and the maintenance of an appropriate real exchange rate. They also stress the reliable legal framework, which promoted stability, investment, and competition.

These factors were certainly conducive to growth, but they are far from the whole story. In other respects the Asian countries' economic policies certainly did not fit the orthodox framework. Their economic model included a strong role for the public sector. They clearly did not believe in free and unfettered markets. At the core of success had to be well-functioning firms and markets, but government played a critical role. Governments acted as catalysts which helped markets by providing the requisite physical and institutional infrastructure, by remedying market failures, and by promoting savings and technology. Noland and Pack (2003) trace Japan's industrial policies back to the Meiji Restoration of the mid-nineteenth century, and the state-led development under the slogans 'shokusan-kogyo' (industrialization) and 'fukoku-kyohei' (a wealthy nation and a strong army). They point out that the economic terms of the treaties forced on Japan by the Western powers encouraged the development of state intervention. The rather onerous treaties required Japan to reduce its tariffs, and consequently encouraged Japanese policy-makers to formulate alternative ways of providing support to their domestic industries, including subsidized credit from state banks. These policy tools survived into the last decades of the twentieth century.

In the modern context, there are many examples of government selectively intervening in particular industries, although the consequences of these interventions is controversial. For example, the Japanese government initially cultivated heavy industries in the post-war period. The steel, aluminum, car, and shipbuilding industries all received support after the war and in subsequent decades more advanced industries, including electronics and semi-conductors, were supported as the government expanded credit to large firms for the purpose of fostering investment.

In many countries trade policy in particular did not follow the orthodox free trade prescriptions. The governments of many Asian countries pursued a two-track policy of protection for industries not ready to compete internationally and promotion for export-ready industries. For example, governments intervened in many industries by providing credit through banks supported in one way or the other by government, restricting competition from imports, constraining new domestic competitors, and developing export marketing institutions.

These elements of the East Asian policies certainly did not fit the orthodox 'laissez-faire' economic model. But there is controversy about the role of these industrial and trade policies, with both those who argue for and against government interventions claiming that East Asia supports their case. Proponents of laissez-faire economic policies contend that the industrial policies were irrelevant or even harmful. Some economists argue that total-factor productivity growth in the sectors which were supported by government policies that have been the beneficiary of industrial policy has not been particularly strong. But the methodologies for calculating total-factor productivity are notoriously weak, especially at the sectoral level. In addition, to the extent that industrial policies in one sector led to improved productivity in other sectors (so-called 'spillover effects'), the benefits of these policies would not be entirely captured by sectoral total-factor productivity. Still other economists argue that growth would have been even stronger had government not engaged in these industrial policies. But this is a particularly unpersuasive counterfactual, since no country has ever achieved faster sustained growth than the countries of East Asia (Stiglitz 1996).

Although there is debate about the role of industry policy in Asia's success, there can be no doubt that the policies pursued by these countries were broader than (and in some cases clearly violated) the strict free-market prescriptions of the Washington Consensus. Whatever one's beliefs about the desirability of active industry policy, there can be no doubt that there is ongoing controversy and debate about the role of trade policy, industry policy, and controls on capital flows (including regulation of foreign direct investment). There can also be no doubt that the successful cases of development over the last fifty years have pursued inventive and idiosyncratic economic policies. To date, not one successful developing country has pursued a purely free market approach to development.

In this context it is inappropriate for the world trading system to be implementing rules which circumscribe the ability of developing countries to use both trade and industry policies to promote industrialization. The current trend to force a narrow straitjacket of policy harmonization on developing countries is simply not justified by the available evidence. Economists have learned much about the process of economic development, but there is still a lot that we do not know, and in these areas developing countries should be given the freedom to develop their own policy strategies tailored to their own idiosyncratic circumstances.

Latin America and import substitution

In the years following the Second World War, Latin America tried a quite different economic strategy than East Asia did. Like many third world countries, several Latin American governments took heart from the recent experiences of the richer countries. Many of the countries that had fought in the Second World War had achieved centrally planned growth in heavy industries as they mass-produced munitions, ships, aircraft, machinery, and chemicals for the war effort. Developing countries had also witnessed the 'big bang' of Stalinist industrialization in the Soviet Union during the 1930s. The Soviet Union experienced rapid capital accumulation and double-digit economic growth rates while the more liberal Western capitalist economies floundered in the Great Depression. The apparent industrial successes of wartime planning and the Soviet planned economies conspired to convince many developing countries that there was a large role for government in managing the industrialization process.

These observations were supported by development economists who believed that the problems in developing countries were structural and required radical government intervention to overcome. Arthur Lewis (1955) proposed that economic development required coordination because 'various sectors must grow in the right relationship to each other or they cannot grow at all'. He advocated a form of managed industrialization simultaneously occurring across many sectors to achieve 'balanced growth'. Other economists combined this idea with economies of scale and concluded that the problem of underdevelopment could only be broken by a 'big push' of new investments across many sectors which would reinforce each other. Paul Rosenstein-Rodan (1961) suggested that attempts at economic development which were too narrowly focused on a small number of sectors would run into the problem of inadequate demand, which would ultimately constrain growth.

The prevailing economic wisdom was thus that economic development required industrialization and the development of vibrant manufacturing industries, and that industrialization would not happen on its own. At the time, developing countries' production consisted mainly of agricultural goods. Since most of the manufactured goods consumed in these countries were imported, they came to the conclusion that the path to success lay in encouraging domestic firms to produce the consumer goods that had previously been acquired from abroad. Accordingly many developing countries embarked on 'import substitution' policies. It was argued that they should import only 'essential' capital goods. Not only would scarce foreign exchange thereby be directed to where it had the highest social returns, but the resulting demand for locally produced goods (because other imports were restricted) would promote industrialization. Moreover, only through protection could their industries compete with the well-established firms of Europe and the United States.

In Brazil in 1951 the government of Getúlio Vargas established a system of import licensing to give priority to imports of fuel and capital goods. They subsequently augmented this with a multiple exchange rate system, whereby priority imports were brought in at a favorable rate, while imports of goods that were deemed to be domestically producible, were hit with higher exchange rates. Later, trade policy was added to the mix when the Tariff Law of 1957 increased protection for domestically produced goods. In the 1950s, 1960s, and 1970s similar import substitution policies were pursued by developing countries across the world, including Chile, India, Ghana, Peru, Brazil, Mexico, Argentina, Ecuador, Pakistan, Indonesia, Nigeria, Ethiopia, Zambia, and others.

Of course, the idea that these developing countries should attempt to use trade policy to actively promote industries in which they are uncompetitive is anathema to the simple logic of comparative advantage that David Ricardo had elucidated more than a century before. The reason so many countries rejected comparative advantage in the context of their economic development strategies lay in the prevailing belief that the concept of comparative advantage was insufficient because it was too static. Developing countries did not want to rely on the primary commodity exports that were compatible with their existing capabilities because they saw them as having limited long-term growth prospects and falling terms of trade. Instead they believed that comparative advantage could be developed over time toward more 'desirable' industries with the help of active industrial and trade policies.

Latin American countries grew rapidly in the decades of import substitution. But then, in the early eighties, one country after another found itself in difficulty; they defaulted on their debt, and the continent entered 'the lost decade', during which growth halted and the region's income per person actually fell. Economic growth rates, which had averaged 6 per cent for the region in the 1970s, fell to almost zero in the 1980s.

The contrast between Latin America's stagnation in the 1980s and South-East Asia's remarkable growth led many commentators to draw conclusions about the relative effectiveness of their trade policies. This stark regional contrast did not appear to be attributable to resource endowments or global factors, and thus it appeared that the difference must lie in the policies each region pursued. In this regard, many economists believed that the major important differences between the two groups of countries were the policies of integration, openness, and free trade, i.e. import substitution in Latin America versus export promotion in Asia. The neo-liberal view was that Latin America's problem was too much state intervention in developing national industries, which caused them to be inefficient and uncompetitive and required too much government spending, which ultimately caused runaway inflation. The IMF and the World Bank, in particular, championed the view that import substitution was one of the main causes of stagnation in Latin American countries.

Import substitution rested on the controversial belief that temporary industry support from government could promote long-term development—often referred to as the 'infant industry' argument. This analysis argues that there is some dynamic element to industrial development which, when combined with a market failure, can justify temporary government intervention. One branch of the argument suggests that firms may need to go through an initial period of learning before they are able to compete successfully with more established foreign firms. However, critics argued that if a firm eventually becomes profitable, then it should be able to finance its learning phase through private capital markets (assuming that effective capital markets exist), and if the benefits of this learning stay wholly within the firm then there is no case for government intervention. Only some imperfection in the capital market justifies government action and, even then, the best policy (if available to developing countries) would be to improve the capital market rather than impose trade distortions.

Another branch of infant industry theory argues that pioneering firms bring benefits to the economy when they may invest in providing workers with new knowledge and skills that can be appropriated by other firms when workers move or start their own firm. Or alternatively, pioneering firms may generate new knowledge which becomes a public good available to all subsequent firms. However, the infant industry argument was criticized by Robert Baldwin (1969), who argued that, even when market imperfections existed, temporary industry protection might be futile. It might not provide an incentive for firms to acquire more knowledge than they otherwise would. Also, by subsidizing domestic production, infant industry protection might encourage later entrants to bring their investments forward, which could actually make the pioneer firm worse off. Baldwin showed how some of the simplistic arguments against free trade were theoretically flawed; but as later discussion makes evident, some compelling arguments remained.

However, an alternative to the neo-liberal view argues that Latin America's failure had less to do with import substitution and more to do with exogenous factors independent of domestic policies. The combined effects of a global recession and the policy response of the developed countries had a deleterious effect on the region. According to the South Centre (1996: 42) Latin American countries simultaneously experienced four kinds of shocks: 'a demand shock to developing country exports; a consequent fall in commodity prices and a terms of trade shock; an interest rate shock; and a capital supply shock'.

This alternative view puts the blame for the lost decade not so much on the import substitution strategy, but on the debt policy of Latin American countries combined with unfortunate global circumstances. These countries borrowed heavily during the seventies, enabling them to avoid the global recession which followed upon the oil price shock. But by the end of the 1970s the region's foreign debt had exploded and debt service payments reached US$33 billion per year—nearly one-third of the region's export earnings. Latin American countries were left to bear the risk of interest rate fluctuations; when the US Federal Reserve raised interest rates to unprecedented levels, many countries were pushed over the brink. Among the evidence for this interpretation is the fact that all of these countries, both those in which there were relatively large problems with the import substitution program and those in which there were not, went into default, and at about the same time, shortly after the increase in American interest rates. If the underlying problem had been the import substitution strategy, then presumably the unwinding of that strategy would have taken place differently in different countries. Yet not one single Latin American country experienced much growth during the 1980s, regardless of their policy differences.

This alternative view suggests that it was Latin America's open capital markets rather than its relatively closed trade policy which led to the lost decade. In the 1970s Latin American countries operated the most open capital markets in the developed world—evidenced by their high share of global FDI flows. In terms of financial liberalization, Latin America was far more open than South East Asia, where controls over foreign capital flows were strict. Latin America's reliance on foreign capital flows and foreign direct investment are what made it particularly vulnerable to global economic shocks.

Thus, just as there are alternative interpretations of the role of trade and industrial policy in East Asia's success, there are alternative views on the role of trade and industrial policy in Latin America's failure. Certainly the import substitution policies were far from perfect and there were some bad investments and some corruption. But what Latin America and East Asia show is that the process of successful liberalization is considerably more complex than the neo-liberal Washington Consensus would suggest. The Asian countries pursued complex economic development policies which combined government intervention with export promotion and controls on the volume and quality of capital inflows. Moreover they sequenced their liberalization and paid attention to social policy, including education and equality, as well as investing heavily in infrastructure and technology.

Mexico

In 1994, Mexico entered the North American Free Trade Agreement (NAFTA), a far-reaching trade liberalization agreement with its northern neighbors, the United States and Canada. If ever there were an opportunity to demonstrate the value of free trade for a developing country, this was it. NAFTA gave Mexico access to the largest economy in the world, which was right next door.

After ten years, Mexico's experience of trade liberalization under NAFTA has been mixed. Certainly there have been several benefits. Trade liberalization has stimulated trade, with Mexico's exports growing at a rapid annual rate of around 10 per cent per year through much of the 1990s. Foreign direct investment has also significantly increased. And NAFTA played a critical role in Mexico's recovery from the Tequila Crisis of 1994–5 (Lederman, Menendez, Perry *et al.* 2000).

On the other hand, growth during the first decade of free trade was slower than it had been in earlier decades (prior to 1980), mean real wages at the end of the decade were lower, and some of the poorest had been made worse off as subsidized American agricultural products flooded the market and lowered the price received for their domestic production. Inequality and poverty both increased under NAFTA and by the end of the decade, Mexico was losing to China many of the jobs that had been created since the signing of NAFTA. Even the manufacturing sector, which had seen significant output growth, has experienced a net loss in jobs since NAFTA took effect.

Three lessons emerged from Mexico's experience which are of particular relevance to our discussion in later chapters on how trade and trade liberalization may affect development. The first is that trade liberalization by itself clearly does not ensure growth, and its impacts may well be swamped by other factors. Mexico suffered from low levels of innovation—low research and development expenditures and low levels of patenting activity compared with the economies of East Asia. It also has weak institutions, including poor regulatory effectiveness and high levels of corruption.

Second, one of the reasons that Mexico did poorly in competition with China was that China was investing heavily in infrastructure and education. Mexico's limited tax revenues, exacerbated by the loss of tariff revenue, was one reason why it did not make the necessary investments.

Third, NAFTA was not really a free trade agreement. America retained its agricultural subsidies. NAFTA pitted the heavily subsidized US agribusiness sector against peasant producers and family farms in Mexico. US farmers export many of their products into Mexico at costs far below those of the local market, driving down prices for local farmers. Moreover, America continued to use what were effectively non-tariff barriers to keep out some of Mexico's products. These policies had deleterious effects on rural livelihoods. One-fifth of Mexico's workers are employed in the agricultural sector and 75 per cent of Mexico's poverty is found in rural areas. While some large Mexican agribusiness sectors have expanded their exports, much of Mexico's rural sector is in crisis. Local farms are threatened by cheap imports from the US, falling commodity prices, and reduced government support. Four-fifths of the population of rural Mexico lives in poverty, and more than half are in extreme poverty.

Mexico's experience with NAFTA provides a cautionary tale. The goal of economic integration should be to raise living standards, but it is clear that trade liberalization by itself is not sufficient to achieve this. There is no doubt that trade and investment are vitally important for economic growth but the real challenge is to pursue liberalization in a manner which promotes sustainable development, in which those at the bottom and middle see incomes rising.

Trade liberalization, welfare, and growth

The intuition behind the notion that trade is welfare-enhancing is simple. Imagine two people exchanging goods with each other. They would voluntarily trade their goods if and only if they both benefit from doing so. Thus government intervention to prohibit, restrict, or tax their trade restricts their ability to realize welfare gains from such mutually beneficial exchange.

However, trade among countries is somewhat more complex. In the basic economic model, trade is beneficial because it allows each country to specialize in the goods that they produce relatively efficiently. This principle of 'comparative advantage', established by the nineteenth-century economist David Ricardo, is the core of trade theory and is the foundation of its normative implication in favour of free trade.

In addition to the gains from specialization according to comparative advantage, trade may deliver benefits and costs through four other channels. Trade liberalization opens foreign markets, expanding the demand for domestic firms' goods and enabling them to serve a larger market and realize gains from economies of scale. Trade liberalization may make available a range of inputs at lower prices, lowering costs of production. Liberalization may also introduce more competition from foreign firms to the domestic economy, which may result in improvements to the efficiency of local production. Finally, trade liberalization may, through various channels, affect the rate of economic growth.

Most of the traditional arguments for free trade are, however, based not on growth but on efficiency, i.e. liberalization leads to a change in the level of welfare rather than any change in the long-run rate of growth. The basic results were formalized in modern economics by Paul Samuelson (1938), who showed that free trade is superior to autarky, and later (1962) that it is also superior to any intermediate regime of trade restrictions.

However, the underlying assumptions which yield that conclusion are highly restrictive, and often fail to capture relevant features of developing countries' economies. The standard argument in favor of trade liberalization is that it improves the average efficiency in a country. Imports from foreign producers may destroy some inefficient local industries, but competitive local industries are supposed to be able to absorb the slack as they expand their exports to foreign markets. In this way, trade liberalization is supposed to allow resources to be redeployed from low-productivity protected sectors into high-productivity export sectors. But that argument assumes that resources will be fully employed in the first place, whereas in most developing countries unemployment is persistently high. One does not need to redeploy resources to put more resources into the export sector; one simply needs to employ hitherto unused resources. In practice trade liberalization often harms competing local import industries, while local exporters may not automatically have the necessary supply capacity to expand. So liberalization often seems to result in labour temporarily going from low-productivity protected sectors to zero-productivity unemployment. Unfortunately, most of the models which attempt to address questions of welfare gains from trade liberalization assume full employment, and therefore provide no answers to this key question: the impact of liberalization in economies with underemployed resources. But the issue of unemployment is not just a theoretical problem. Concern that trade liberalization will lead to increased unemployment is perhaps the most important source of opposition to liberalization. And the concerns are particularly relevant in countries where there is no unemployment insurance and weak social safety nets.

A second assumption of the model underlying the conclusion that trade liberalization is welfare-enhancing is the existence of perfect risk markets. But there is high volatility in international markets, risk markets are highly imperfect, and trade policy can reduce exposure to risk (Dasgupta and Stiglitz 1977). Without trade, producers are insulated from the full force of output fluctuations by built-in insurance: if there is a reduction in the quantity of output firms can produce, then they can charge a higher price for it. Thus their incomes vary less than output. Trade may weaken this automatic insurance, since in small economies prices will be determined on the world market and will be unrelated to domestic output. Because their incomes will be more variable, risk-averse firms will invest less in some sectors with high returns but high variability; and as the economy moves into lower-return, less variable activities, total output will decline. Under quite plausible conditions, one can show that free trade is Pareto-inferior to autarky—everyone is worse off—which is just the opposite result to that of the conventional wisdom (Newbery and Stiglitz 1984). These market failures underline the importance of sequencing. It makes a great deal of difference, for instance, whether trade liberalization occurs before or after risk markets or social insurance programs have been created. But imperfections of risk markets are inherent, a consequence of imperfect and costly information.

One of the strengths of the market economy is that prices provide all the coordination that is required, i.e. there is no need for a central planner. But in developing countries, markets are often absent or, even when present, often do not work well, and prices accordingly are not able to perform this critical function. The problem, in some sense, is intrinsic. The process of economic development entails the creation of whole new industries. But some industries are dependent on inputs from other, 'intermediate' industries, for example, the car industry is dependent on the steel industry for fabricated metals. Intermediate goods industries will not be created until the final goods industries that use those intermediate goods are created; but the final goods industries cannot be created until the intermediate goods that they require are available. It is too much to expect markets for goods not yet produced to function well! Curiously, these arguments have been used both to support and to criticize trade interventions. In one sense, trade helps countries get around the need for planning. A country does not need to develop its own intermediate goods industries if it can import intermediate goods. In addition an open developing country does not need to rely on its own local demand. It can take advantage of the global market to attain the requisite economies of scale in tradeable goods. However, many of the key intermediate inputs are non-tradeables, so there is still a need for coordination, especially if there are significant scale economies in the non-tradeables. This, in turn, provides one of the critical arguments for trade restrictions: to get the necessary scale, one may have to restrict competition from foreign producers.[1] The existence of these market failures suggests a need for government intervention. The appropriate form for the intervention needs to take into account limitations on the information available to government and the nature of the (irremediable) market failures.

The need for government revenue can also, in some circumstances, provide a rationale for trade taxes. One corollary of the classic Diamond–Mirrlees production efficiency theorem (1971) is that it is optimal in a small open economy for the government to raise revenue from tax on the net demand of households rather than from border taxes (see Dixit and Norman 1980). But the conditions under which this is true are very restrictive, and especially do not hold in most

---

[1] Especially, as suggested above, in the presence of capital market imperfections.

developing countries (Dasgupta and Stiglitz 1972). In many developing countries, moreover, tariffs are the main source of government revenue, and where this is the case, the optimal tariff structure may not be uniform (Dasgupta and Stiglitz 1974). Max Corden (1974) argues that, particularly in developing countries, the collection costs associated with trade taxes are likely to be much smaller than those of income and commodity taxes. Where this is true, trade taxes might be the best revenue-raising device. Recently international institutions have been encouraging developing countries to reduce their trade taxes in favour of indirect commodity taxation such as a value-added tax (VAT). However, many developing countries have large informal sectors which are beyond the reach of indirect taxation. In these circumstances, M. Shahe Emran and Joseph Stiglitz (2004) have shown that a switch from trade to indirect taxes may be welfare-reducing.

Trade liberalization will also affect inequality. Opening up to trade does not make everyone in a country better off. Instead it changes the distribution of income and creates winners and losers. The standard economic argument is that the net gains from trade liberalization are positive so the gainers can compensate the losers and leave the country better off overall. Unfortunately, such compensation seldom occurs. These distributional consequences are an important practical consideration. They provide much of the political opposition to trade liberalization. And they become more salient in global international trade regimes which are viewed to be 'unfair'.

Moreover the standard theory assumes that taxes and subsidies to compensate the 'losers' from trade liberalization are costless. But there may be large inefficiencies associated with redistributive schemes. Once the distributional consequences are taken into account, trade liberalization may not be Pareto-superior; it may not be possible to make everyone better off. Concerns about inequality may place a limit on the desirability of liberalization in situations, especially where a market distortion creates a link between the distribution and allocation of resources. Sudhir Anand and Vijay Joshi (1979) describe the situation (fairly common in developing countries) where workers in the urban sector receive a higher wage than those in the rural sector,[2] giving the

---

[2] While in their model the wage differential is simply given exogenously, efficiency wage theory (e.g. Shapiro and Stiglitz 1984) provides an explanation for such differentials.

government an incentive to intervene to increase employment in the urban industries. Anand and Joshi show that, under fairly general conditions, a Pareto-efficient outcome cannot be achieved using wage subsidies alone. In their model the rigid factor price creates an unavoidable trade-off between efficiency and equality even when the standard best-policy instrument is available and can be financed by lump-sum taxation. They conclude that '[d]epartures from technical efficiency may be called for as part of the rational response by governments to the limitations they face in carrying out desirable income distribution policies'.

Ricardo Hausmann and Dani Rodrik (2004) demonstrate another type of market failure based on information externalities. They emphasize the importance of entrepreneurship in developing countries. These entrepreneurs are engaged in a process of 'discovering' which economic activities will be successful in their country. Hausmann and Rodrik point out that successful (and failed) entrepreneurs provide information to the market which is of great social value yet is poorly remunerated. If the entrepreneur fails in his venture, he bears the full cost of the failure: if he is successful he shares the discovery with others who enter the new industry. 'The entrepreneurs who figured out that Colombia was good terrain for cut flowers, Bangladesh for t-shirts, Pakistan for soccer balls, and India for software generated large social gains for their economies', but could keep very few of these gains to themselves. Thus 'it is no great surprise that low-income countries are not teeming with entrepreneurs engaged in self-discovery' (Rodrik 2004). Coordination failures may occur when the profitability of new industries depends on the simultaneous development of upstream and downstream industries, or when new industries are characterized by scale economies and have non-tradeable inputs (Rodrik 1996).

While most of the economic theory of trade liberalization has focused on static welfare gains, the long-term effects of trade liberalization are determined by its effect on the economy's rate of growth. Recent models of endogenous growth have important implications for the theoretical relationship between free trade and economic growth, although their results are not fully understood, and their policy consequences remain to be thoroughly established.

There are several possible arguments for why increased trade may lead to faster sustained growth rates. One argument is that larger markets will lead to larger returns to investments in R & D. This would suggest that a global regime with free trade will be associated with higher overall growth rates. A similar argument is that, with learning by doing, there are strong spillovers within a country (i.e. the learning in one firm spills over to other firms) but not across countries. Here, accordingly, the pace of innovation is related to the scale of production within the country: if there is more specialization, there will be more learning. A third argument focuses on the fact, again noted earlier, that with a larger market, there can be a larger variety of inputs, which can sustain not only more efficient production but a faster pace of innovation.

These theories suggest the importance of knowledge, learning, and human capital. One possible implication for policy (though not necessarily trade policy) is that countries may benefit by promoting more technologically dynamic sectors. Research by Dani Rodrik and others suggests that developing countries may need to 'embed private initiative in a framework of public action that encourages restructuring, diversification, and technological dynamism beyond what market forces on their own would generate' (Rodrik 2004). For example, the theory of comparative advantage told South Korea, as it emerged from the Korean War, that it should specialize in rice. But Korea believed that even if it were successful in increasing the productivity of its rice farmers, it would never become a middle- or high-income country if it followed that course. It had to change its comparative advantage, by acquiring technology and skills. It had to focus not on its comparative advantage today, but on its long run, its dynamic comparative advantage. And government intervention was required if it was to change its comparative advantage.

The existence of these market failures or learning externalities may suggest a need for government intervention, but they do not, by themselves, justify trade policy as the best instrument. Research into policy choices has been developed into a general theory of distortions (see Corden 1957) which generally show that tariffs and other introduced trade distortions are usually the nth-best policy instrument, after various types of subsidies including training, employment, output, and knowledge diffusion subsidies (if those are available). But often, in poor and backward developing countries, these instruments may not be immediately practical or affordable. This underlines the importance of sequencing. Even if trade policy is the nth best instrument, trade liberalization should not occur until one of the $n - 1$ preferred alternatives is feasible and successfully implemented.

However, in many cases the market failure might be endemic or not readily able to be countered by government action. Much of the earlier literature on correcting market distortions made the critical error of treating the distortion almost as if it was an accidental mistake, which government could easily correct. For example, if markets were imperfect because wages were rigid, the solution was to make wages more flexible, i.e. if the reason for the rigidity was government minimum wages, there was an obvious answer— eliminate the minimum wage. To take another example, if there were capital market failures, the solution was to create perfect capital markets. These direct interventions to correct market failures were preferred to indirect government action, including trade and industrial policies.

But both wage rigidities and capital market imperfections can arise from information imperfections (Stiglitz 2002) and these might be difficult to correct with direct action. So long as it is costly to acquire information, there is no easy way of eliminating these market imperfections. To be sure, government too faces information (and other) constraints; but the nature of those constraints, as well as the objectives, differs between the government and private firms. Optimal interventions may thus involve trade and industrial policies, as the discussion below makes clear.

Consider, for instance, the infant industry argument for protection presented earlier. Critics of the infant industry argument contend that if a firm will eventually become profitable, then it should be able to finance its learning phase through private capital markets, and, accordingly, if the benefits of this learning stay wholly within the firm then there is no case for government intervention. Only some imperfection in the capital market justifies government action, and even then, the best policy, if available to developing countries, would be to improve the capital market rather than to impose trade distortions.

But the modern theory of asymmetric information explains why capital market imperfections are inherent, and not just a happenstance, and why governments cannot simply remedy these capital market imperfections (Stiglitz and Weiss 1981). These capital market imperfections are particularly relevant here, for banks would have to be willing to lend to enable firms to sell below cost, in the hope that by doing so their productivity will increase so much that they will become a viable competitor. It should be obvious that such loans would be viewed, at best, as highly risky. (And banks would likely view themselves at a marked informational disadvantage in judging whether the firm's claims about its future prospects—in spite of large current losses—have credibility.)

Once capital market imperfections are taken into account, then protection may be optimal, as Dasgupta and Stiglitz (1980) show. They argue, in particular, that protection may have advantages over other instruments, e.g. subsidies, when government has limited sources of income and limited ability to target. Interestingly, these are among the reasons that some argue for private production of knowledge, through intellectual property rights, as opposed to public production, through direct government subsidies. The government cannot identify who will be good producers of knowledge, and therefore cannot target the subsidies; the market is a self-selection mechanism. Intellectual property rights increase the returns to private production of knowledge, at a cost—temporary monopoly rights. Protectionism limits competition from abroad, but allows competition from within. By increasing the private returns, it helps to better align private and social returns to innovation. This is even more relevant in the infant economy argument for protection (where learning spillovers extend beyond the industry to the entire economy.)

Theoretical arguments which caution against a full embrace of free trade abound. But the question for policy-makers is not whether these arguments exist, but whether they carry enough weight to be acted upon. In a thoughtful article, two noted proponents of free trade for developing countries, T. N. Srinivasan and Jagdish Bhagwati (1999), review some of the above theory and many other theoretical arguments which caution against the universality of the benefits of free trade. They concede that it is possible to build many theoretical models in which free trade will 'reduce current income and even growth...if market failures are present'. But they challenge inter-preters of this evidence to ask themselves the following question: in formulating policy, 'do we view these models as representing a "central tendency" in the real world or merely "pathologies"?', and they caution policy-makers not to become prisoners of the nihilistic view that 'because anything can be logically shown, nothing can be empir-ically believed and acted upon'. In order to determine whether the case against unconditional trade liberalization for developing coun-tries is important or merely a series of inconsequential theoretical possibilities, it is necessary to turn to the empirical evidence.

Empirical evidence

A number of studies have attempted to show that there is a system-atic relationship between growth and trade and/or trade liberaliza-tion, using cross-country studies. The hypothesis has been that, holding other things constant, countries that have liberalized more or which trade more have grown more.

Our previous discussion suggests that only under certain circum-stances will that be the case. Given the complex and contingent rela-tionship between trade liberalization and economic growth, and the manifold difficulties associated with empirically testing this rela-tionship (discussed briefly below), it comes as no surprise that most economists, even most of those that have no reservations about lib-eralization, accept that the empirical literature has been inconclus-ive (Winters 2003). The economic growth literature has been successful in demonstrating the importance of some variables for economic development, including education, institutions, health, and geography. However, the relationship between trade liberaliza-tion and growth is much more controversial.

The weakness of the evidence in favour of a direct relationship between trade liberalization and economic growth has not prevented some economists from pursuing free trade at full throttle. The IMF's former First Deputy Managing Director, Stan Fischer (2000), boasted that the 'Fund is a powerful voice and actor for free trade' and suggested that this is because 'integration into the world economy is the best way for countries to grow'. The IMF may be right to promote liberalization (by developed and developing countries alike), though that is hardly its mandate, and it would do better focusing on trying to enhance global financial stability. But it should be pointed out that the empirical evidence that it even has a positive effect on growth is mixed, that it almost certainly is not the most important factor in growth, that the theory suggests important caveats, and that the experience of successful countries indicates that the reform process should be managed gradually and carefully. Integration through exports, as in East Asia, has a far more convincing record than integration through rapid liberalization. In short, trade liberalization should be a tailored policy, not a one-size-fits-all.

It is difficult to identify the evidentiary source of the bullishness for unqualified trade liberalization. Certainly there were several studies in the early 1990s which purported to show a positive relationship between trade openness and economic growth (see Dollar 1992; Ben-David 1993; Sachs and Warner 1995), but even these were careful to qualify their results. In the conclusion to their paper, Jeffrey Sachs and Andrew Warner point out several of the important caveats to their study. Their studies focus on trade, not on trade liberalization. Francisco Rodriguez and Dani Rodrik (1999) have persuasively shown that the conclusions of these studies should be interpreted with extreme caution. They found that the indices of openness used in these studies conflated the effects of trade policies with other phenomena. In particular the studies were identifying the negative effects of macroeconomic imbalances, instability, and geographic location, and misattributing them to trade restrictions. Rodriguez and Rodrik pointed out that because of these methodological weaknesses, the policy conclusions drawn from these studies are not strongly supported by the data they present.

To recognize the weakness of the empirical evidence in this field is not to argue that trade protection is good for growth. Rodriguez and Rodrik themselves point out that there is no credible evidence that trade restrictions are systematically associated with higher growth rates in the post-war period. But it does suggest that the relationship between trade liberalization and growth is not simple. Preliminary research being conducted at Columbia University, for instance, suggests that trade liberalization may have positive effects on countries with low unemployment rates, but negative effects on countries with high unemployment rates. More generally, the empirical evidence supports the view that the benefits of trade liberalization depend on a range of other factors which are difficult to observe separately because of measurement problems[3] and other econometric difficulties.[4]

Policy implications

Theory and empirical evidence indicate that trade liberalization can be a positive force for development in poor countries, but that these benefits depend on other, concomitant factors. Given this, we would hope the focus of current economic research to be on how differences across countries affect their experience of liberalization, and we would hope the focus of policy research to be on how trade policies can best be tailored to the particular circumstances of different countries.

But we would hope for a consensus of answers among policy-makers, but we would hope for a consensus of approach. However, international trade negotiations exhibit no such consensus—the acrimonious breakdown of talks at Cancún and Seattle and the ongoing polarization among academics, NGOs, and international institutions are testament to that. There are still those on the right who would press developing countries to move immediately and uncompromisingly towards free trade. And there are still those on the left who believe that the way to help developing countries is to shield them vigorously from the forces of reform and liberalization.

[3] For instance, many of the empirical studies treat trade regimes as a binary variable (i.e. countries are either 'open' or 'closed'), which ignores the subtlety and dynamics of different trade regimes. Studies which analyse trade-weighted average tariff rates will underweight the importance of high tariffs because the quantity of imports in those tariff lines is likely to be low. Many studies ignore non-tariff barriers, and those that include them have a hard time distinguishing which are important and which are not.

[4] For instance, many of the indices used to analyse openness may be endogenously related to other policy or institutional variables which have an independent negative effect on economic growth, making these indices inappropriate variables with which to analyse the direct effect of trade liberalization on growth.

The theoretical and empirical evidence may not speak clearly on all issues, but it certainly rules out the extreme positions on both sides. It is therefore worth asking why these extreme positions have proved so enduring. On the left, the fault probably lies with overzealous altruism. The anti-globalization movement has done much to raise awareness about important international issues, but as is often the case with unstructured social movements, their public message has sometimes become distorted. Unfortunately those within the movement who can attract the most publicity are not always those with the strongest analysis. The unfortunate message from the hard-line activists is that a good round of trade negotiations is one that requires the developing countries to do nothing in the way of reform. They encourage developing countries to look outward to the developed countries as the primary source of and solution to their problems. Unfortunately, unreasonable demands for "reforms" from the developing countries, unsupported by or in some cases counter to historical experiences, strong empirical evidence and theory—reforms which might in fact set development programs back—enhance support for these positions, especially reforms demanded by trade negotiators who otherwise have evidenced little real concern for the developing countries' welfare; this is true even where it is recognized that liberalization of developed countries' trade policies is not a substitute for, but rather than a complement to, developing countries' own internal reforms.

There is a tendency among some in the anti-globalization movement to view the extreme position taken on trade liberalization by many on the right as a revealing testament of their malevolence or wilful disregard for the problems of the world's poorest countries. Of course, at least on the part of the academics who make serious contributions to the debate, there is no such malevolence or disregard. How then can they continue to insist, in the face of the theoretical and empirical evidence, that developing countries pursue rapid and unfettered trade liberalization? One answer is that they are more concerned about government failure than market failure.

Many economists have serious reservations about the ability of officials from developing countries to manage anything but the simplest, most liberal trade policy regime. Alan Winters (2003), Director of the Development Research Group at the World Bank, notes that '[t]here are undoubtedly hundreds of individual cases where a one-off policy intervention would be beneficial, for example where protection would allow learning or training, or generate a terms-of-trade gain, or support a poor family while it learned new skills.' But he rejects the use of such second-best interventions to overcome market failure because, among other things, he believes that developing country officials are not skilled enough to identify and implement them effectively. He says, 'the application of second-best economics needs first-best economists, not its usual complement of third- and fourth-raters'. The same argument was espoused by Anne Krueger, the First Deputy Managing Director of the IMF, in her presidential address to the American Economic Association in 1997. She claimed, 'most [trade] policy implementation is carried out by government officials...[who lack]...the degree of sophistication needed to interpret research results' (Krueger 1997).

This reason for adopting and espousing the simple orthodoxy of free trade is not that such policies are optimal in a standard economic sense, but that any more complicated development strategy would be beyond the capability of the officials of developing countries.

There are many reasons why government interference in the economy may fail. One is that governments are not possessed of full information about market failures; indeed they will often have less information than private agents about particular sectors. This impedes the identification of both the market failure and the (potentially unintended) side effects of any proposed solution. It may be possible to overcome these information problems, but this may be costly, and the government needs to insure that the net gain is larger than for alternative policies. There are many examples of failed trade and industry policy experiments. But, as Dani Rodrik points out, some failures are to be expected. All that needs to be true is that the government intervention delivers social returns on average across a range of projects within each policy. If we observed no failures, the policy would arguably be being carried out in too timid a fashion.

Another important concern linked to government failure is that simple trade regimes are more transparent and less prone to corruption and rent-seeking activities. Less distorting policies usually offer fewer opportunities for corruption.

In our view, the fear of government failure is real, but it is not overriding. Putting aside the condescending attitude towards developing countries evidenced in assertions about 'third- and fourth-raters', the fact is that some developing countries—most notably in East Asia—have arguably been extremely successful in managing trade and industrial policies to promote growth. Concerns about government failures may provide a reason that such policies may be eschewed in the long run, but they do not trump all development objectives, market failures, and adjustment costs in the short run. Policies should be designed to minimize the risk of government failure, for example through carefully designed institutions and policies (see Rodrik 2004) and international technical assistance. The remaining risk should be appropriately weighted within the policymakers' decision-making process.

None of today's rich countries developed by simply opening themselves to foreign trade. As Ha-Joon Chang (2001) has documented, all the developed countries used a wide range of trade policy instruments which should make their WTO ambassadors blush when they sit down to negotiate with today's developing countries. Chang's evidence does not prove that interventionist trade policies were, or are now, the best policies for development, but it does show, at the very minimum, that the risk of government failure can be managed in countries as they develop.

China and India provide more proximate evidence of this fact. Both have successfully integrated into the world trading system, and both have benefited greatly from international trade, yet neither followed orthodox trade and industrial policies. China has been particularly careful to ensure that its economic development strategy is gradually implemented and carefully sequenced. Certainly China has become more open in recent years, and has benefited from doing so, but trade liberalization certainly did not cause China's growth. China began to grow rapidly in the late 1970s, but trade liberalization did not start until the late 1980s, and only took off in the 1990s after economic growth had increased markedly. The Indian story is similar: growth increased in the early 1980s while tariffs were actually going up in some areas and did not begin to come down significantly until the major reforms of 1991–3.

The way forward

Theory teaches us that when markets are perfect, trade-distorting policies will be welfare-reducing, and even when markets suffer from distortions, trade policies may not be the best instruments to overcome them. But, as we have seen, both theory and evidence provide less guidance about policies in a real world marked by market imperfections, many of which are intrinsic, arising whenever information is incomplete and costly and there are costs associated with creating markets.

These concerns are of particular relevance to developing countries. Developing countries certainly do not have perfect markets. Many of their markets are missing or incomplete, particularly markets for insurance and credit. Public goods are undersupplied, coordination failures are rife, and the social benefits of entrepreneurship are larger than the expected private returns. The adjustment costs associated with liberalization would be large and exacerbated by high unemployment and weak social safety nets.

Often there will be better instruments than trade policy with which to overcome these market failures and soften the adjustment costs associated with reform. But poor governments with small public resources have a limited number of instruments at their disposal. Often it would be a mistake for these governments to liberalize their trade regime before they have put compensating policies in place.

Thus, for developing countries, we can put aside the debate about whether the world should move towards free trade. For many of them, the issue is largely about which steps towards liberalization make sense, and pacing and sequencing: what should be done before they liberalize, and how fast the liberalization agenda should be pushed.

There is a middle ground between the extreme positions of the free-traders and the anti-globalizers. This middle ground recognizes that even if one accepts the ultimate desirability of free trade, rushed liberalization may be harmful. Policies in the middle ground need to be found by investigating the effects of market failures on the experience of liberalization in different countries. Developing countries should attempt to promote development by correcting these market failures through policy interventions, including trade policies, if, and only if, they are the best available instruments. Policy-makers should recognize the potential for government failure arising from their interventions. They should neither ignore this risk nor fear it. Instead they should look for ways to overcome it and, where those are not apparent, appropriately weight the risk in their policy-selection process.

Developed countries must do their part. They can help to integrate developing countries into the world trading system and ensure that they benefit from it. As we explain later in the book, developed countries need to reform their own trade policies in ways that open trading opportunities for the developing countries.

The developed countries play the central role in the politics of global trade negotiations and are responsible for much of what happens in the WTO. The developed countries have a responsibility to build the global trade architecture in ways that enhance the participation of the developing countries.

In this book we suggest a policy program within the WTO which would benefit the developing countries. Developed countries are a crucial part of this program because so much of world trade is affected by their policies and because they are the most powerful actors within the WTO. But developed countries are neither the whole problem nor the whole solution. Their trade policies are important, but their reform is a complement to, not a substitute for, reform within developing countries.

3

The Need for a Development Round

⚜

Developing countries and world trade

The current multilateral trade liberalization round, the Doha Round, is the ninth in a series of such negotiations which began in Geneva in 1947. The first eight of these were conducted under the auspices of the WTO's predecessor, the GATT (General Agreement on Tariffs and Trade), which was established on a provisional basis after the Second World War as a draft charter for the proposed International Trade Organization (ITO). The ITO was stillborn—it was never ratified by the US Congress and other national legislatures—but the GATT continued to govern international trade in the form of a multilateral treaty from 1948 to the creation of the WTO in 1995.

The GATT set forth the principles under which the signatories, on a basis of reciprocity and mutual advantage, would negotiate a substantial reduction in customs tariffs and other impediments to trade, and the elimination of discriminatory practices in international trade. As more countries joined, the GATT became a charter governing almost all world trade except for that of the communist countries. Despite its inauspicious beginnings and its provisional nature, the GATT was successful in promoting the liberalization of a considerable proportion of trade and contributed to the substantial

Table 3.1. **The nine trade negotiation rounds under the GATT and WTO**

Year	Place/Name	Subjects covered	Number of countries
1947–8	Geneva	Tariffs	23
1949	Annecy	Tariffs	13
1950–1	Torquay	Tariffs	38
1956	Geneva	Tariffs	26
1960–2	Dillon Round	Tariffs	26
1963–7	Kennedy Round	Tariffs and anti-dumping measures	62
1973–9	Tokyo Round	Tariffs, non-tariff barriers (NTBs), 'framework' agreements	102
1986–3	Uruguay Round	Tariffs, NTBs, rules, services, intellectual property, dispute settlement, textiles, agriculture, creation of WTO	123
2001–	Doha Round	(Under negotiation)	142+

growth of world trade throughout the post-war era.[1] Through its principles of transparency, non-discrimination, and reciprocity, the GATT gave predictability to world trade and provided a reasonably open forum for the mutual exchange of liberalization concessions and the settlement of disputes for almost half a century (Table 3.1).[2]

Developing countries played only a small role in the seven rounds of trade negotiations in the first 20 years of the GATT.[3] To the extent that they participated at all, they campaigned for special treatment. This took the form of preferential access to the rich countries' markets at tariff rates below those applied to other countries (eventually enshrined in the Generalized System of Preferences) and exemptions from GATT rules. Article XVIII in the GATT rules provided developing countries with differential treatment. Among other exceptions, it allowed economies 'which can only support low standards of living and are in the early stages of development' to 'implement

[1] Trade growth was consistently larger than production growth throughout the GATT era.
[2] For a history of the political economy of the GATT see Hoekman and Kostecki (1997).
[3] Developing countries hardly participated at all in the substantive agreements of the Kennedy Round. More than 70 developing countries participated in the Tokyo Round, where the enabling clause was adopted which introduced the concept of special and differential treatment (S&D), but their participation in broader negotiations was limited.

programmes and policies of economic development designed to raise the general standard of living of their people, to take protective or other measures affecting imports'. This recognized the right of developing countries to impose quantitative and other restrictions to protect their infant industries. Because of Article XVIII, developing countries could simultaneously be members of the GATT and evade the obligations imposed on developed countries.

This special status gave developing countries more freedom in determining their own development policies, but it simultaneously allowed them to be marginalized within the substantive negotiations. Even in the absence of their special status, tariff negotiations do not offer many incentives for smaller economies to participate actively, because they have little to offer large markets in reciprocal negotiations. But when exemptions freed developing countries from the requirement of reciprocity, their 'commitments' became almost meaningless because they were at liberty under the special arrangements to raise tariffs or introduce other protection at their own discretion. They therefore had relatively little bargaining power within the GATT rounds because their concessions were of doubtful value. They had no 'skin in the game'.

A passive strategy within the GATT negotiations actually suited some of the largest developing countries (especially China, India, and Brazil) which, until the 1980s, did not see international trade as their primary engine of growth. Instead they pursued policies of 'import substitution' which isolated their economies from the rest of the world. These countries sought economic development from internal sources and they had only a small incentive to pursue progress on multilateral liberalization within the GATT regime.

The developed countries were far more interested in each others' markets than in those of developing countries. Bergsten (1998) describes the history of the post-war multilateral trading system in terms of the power relationships between the rich countries, particularly the EU and US. He argues that the initial creation of the European Common Market in the late 1950s was one of the key motivations for the American initiative to launch the Kennedy Round in the early 1960s. The US wanted to reduce the newly created discrimination against American exports, and also to build the 'new Atlantic partnership' enunciated by President Kennedy.[4] Similarly, the expansion of the European Community to include the United Kingdom and others, with the extension of its discrimination to important new markets, was an important factor in the American decision to insist on the Tokyo Round in the 1970s.[5] Thus the primary concern of developed countries was to gain access to other developed markets and the reform agenda focused on efforts to liberalize those goods traded intensively between developed countries.

Together these factors explain the peripheral role of the developing countries in most of the GATT negotiations. As a consequence, over several rounds of agreements, the world trading system was tailored to the interests of the developed countries, who had, participated intensively in the negotiations. Protection was progressively reduced on the goods of export interest to developed countries, but remained on goods exported intensively by developing countries. It was no surprise that the GATT came to cover trade in all goods except agriculture and textiles—both of interest to developing countries—which were the subject of separate agreements whose provisions were far less liberal than those of the GATT. Textiles were covered by the Multifiber Arrangement (MFA), through which developing countries bargained bilaterally to establish quotas on the quantities of exports that they could export to developed countries. Only developing countries were discriminated against: developed countries did not impose any restrictions on textile imports from other developed countries. Similarly agricultural trade was excluded from the GATT and developed countries still continue to pursue protectionist agricultural policies which distort trade and harm producers in developing countries. As early as the mid-1960s, the world trade system was recognized as being unfair: 'In an important sense the trade policies of the developed countries may be said to discriminate against the less developed countries. While they generally do

---

[4] The Kennedy Round also originated partially in a monetary crisis (see Bergsten 1998). President Kennedy reportedly worried about the balance-of-payments problem and saw access to foreign markets for American exports as a potential solution.

[5] Similarly, the EU decision to launch the 'single market' in 1985, with the implied broadening of discrimination to many new types of economic activity, also added to the US desire to begin the Uruguay Round.

not discriminate against those countries in the form proscribed by the most-favored-nation principle, ... their policies are in effect discriminatory in that the most serious barriers are erected in goods which the less developed countries typically have a comparative advantage in producing—agricultural commodities in raw or processed form, and labor-intensive, technologically unsophisticated consumer goods' (Johnson 1967: 79).

In the 1980s developing countries came to play a larger role in international trade policy. Each of the obstacles to their participation had been reduced. First, the increased importance of developing countries' trade—especially the newly industrialized countries in East Asia—increased the developed countries' interest in their markets and led to calls for them to stop 'free riding' and enter the system. At the same time developing countries placed more stock on the development potential of trade as many of them turned away from import substitution policies. As they did so, policy-makers in newly opened developing countries recognized the importance of participating in trade negotiations. As a result, in contrast to the Kennedy and Tokyo Rounds, developing countries were actively involved in the discussions that led to the Uruguay Round: the large number of accessions or requests for accession to the GATT from such countries at that time (including Mexico and China) indicated that the issues on the table were being taken seriously by a growing number of developing countries.

The Uruguay Round marked a shift in the history of trade negotiations. The largest industrial countries, led by the US, attempted to extend the GATT system to cover services as well as new areas of domestic policy which were deemed to be 'trade-related'. Despite initial resistance from some developing countries, an agenda was agreed at the Uruguayan resort city of Punta del Este in September 1986. The agreement was that developing countries would negotiate on the new issues of services, Trade-Related Aspects of Intellectual Property Rights (TRIPS), and Trade-Related Investment Measures (TRIMS). In return, they would get better market access for their exports of goods. The Uruguay Round, for all its faults and imbalances, was the most ambitious set of trade negotiations ever. It covered reductions in tariff and non-tariff barriers in industrial and agricultural goods, as well as textiles and clothing, and it attempted to extend multilateral rules to new areas, notably services and intellectual property.

Redressing past imbalances

In 1993 the Uruguay Round was finally being brought to a close. Part of the impetus for members to conclude the round was the promise of large welfare gains that had been projected by many researchers (See Table 3.2). In 1992–3, the World Bank, the US Organization for Economic Cooperation and Development, and various other institutions made projections of welfare gains on the order of US$ 200 billion a year.[6] A large share of the gains was predicted to accrue to developing countries.[7]

In hindsight these estimates—particularly in relation to developing countries—were somewhat over-optimistic. It has since been estimated that the vast majority of the gains from the Uruguay Round would accrue to developed countries, with most of the rest going to a relatively few large export-oriented developing countries. Indeed

Table 3.2. **Early estimates of income gains from the Uruguay Round Agreement ($bn)**

Study	World	Developing countries
Harrison, Rutherford, and Tarr (1995)	52.5–188.1	4.8–61.7
Francois, McDonald & Nordstrom (1995)	51.4–251.1	9.0–91.9
GATT Secretariat (1993)	230	65
World Bank (1993)	213	78
Nguyen, Perroni, and Wigle (1993)	212.1	36
OECD (1993)	274.1	89.1
Deardorff (1994)	140–260	–

Source: Epstein (1995).

[6] Indeed after Marrakech, the GATT Secretariat put forward a larger estimate of the minimum gain—US$500 billion per year. For a discussion of the projections see Safadi and Laird (1996). For a survey of the various estimates see Rodrik (1994). See also Martin and Winters eds (1996) and Srinivasan (1998).
[7] In one study the gain to developing countries was estimated at US$90bn, or roughly one third of the US$270bn total gain predicted at the time (OECD 1993).

many of the poorest countries in the world will actually be worse off as a result of the round. Some estimates report that the 48 least developed countries are actually losing a total of US$600 million a year as a result of the Uruguay Round.[8] While some least developed countries will receive net gains, most will be net losers from the round when all of the agreements are fully implemented. A large share of the net losers are among the poorest countries in the world, in particular sub-Saharan Africa, which has been estimated to have lost US$1.2 billion as a result of the round (UNDP 1997:82).

One reason for this was that the modelled scenarios were not fully reflected in actual agreements and the subsequent events.[9] Several reforms which were significant sources of predicted gains did not proceed as had been hoped early in the negotiations. For example, the Agreement on Textiles and Clothing (ATC) was structured to back-load liberalization significantly;[10] the ability of tariff-rate quotas (TRQs) to liberalize agricultural market access was overestimated; and the costs of implementation were almost completely ignored.

In addition the Uruguay Round agenda reflected, in large part, the priorities of developed countries. Market access gains, for example, were concentrated in areas of interest to developed countries and there was only marginal progress on the priorities of developing countries (particularly in agriculture and textiles). The result of this regressive asymmetry was that *after the implementation of Uruguay Round commitments, the average OECD tariff on imports from developing countries is four times higher than on imports originating in the OECD* (Laird 2002). Domestic protection (particularly agricultural subsidies) is also much higher in developed countries, amounting to more than US$300 billion in 2002. The impact of this protection is particularly regressive since producers in the poorest developing countries are those most affected by OECD policies.

---

[8] That is, US$600m in net losses. Some of the least developed countries gained from the round, but the losers lost US$600m more than the sum of the gains.

[9] The models themselves also make assumptions that may not be fully appropriate for less developed countries. See Charlton and Stiglitz (2004).

[10] As we noted, the developed countries were given a decade to remove their textiles quotas; the argument was that the extra time would allow them a smoother adjustment process. In practice, since little if any adjustment has occurred, only the day of reckoning has been postponed. In the United States, the legislation implementing the Uruguay Round, by not adopting a steady phase-out of the quotas, made clear that this postponement was the real motivation.

Only 4 per cent of the exports of developed countries are subsidized by another WTO member, but 6.4 per cent of the exports of middle-income countries are subsidized. By contrast, a much larger share (29.4 per cent) of the exports of the poorest countries (not including China and India) is subsidized by another WTO member.[11]

As well as receiving only a small share of the gains from the Uruguay Round, developing countries accepted a remarkable range of obligations and responsibilities. New trade rules and domestic disciplines were introduced, but they too reflected the priorities and needs of developed countries more than developing countries (e.g. subsidies were permitted for agriculture, but not industrial products). Many of the rules acted to constrain the policy options (such as industrial policies) of developing countries, in some cases prohibiting the use of instruments that had been used by developed countries at comparable stages of their development. Many of the new obligations imposed significant burdens on developing countries. In return the least developed countries were promised financial assistance with implementation costs and extensions of preferential market access schemes. The common feature of these commitments is that they were non-binding on developed countries. As a consequence developing countries found themselves at the mercy of the goodwill of developed countries. As Finger and Schuler (2000) aptly note: 'the developing countries took bound commitments to implement in exchange for unbound commitments of assistance'. Insufficient attention has subsequently been paid to the enormous demands upon developing countries in implementing the outcome from the Uruguay Round. Agreements related to intellectual property, customs valuation, technical barriers to trade, and agricultural food safety have been particular targets of criticism in this regard.[12]

[11] These figures may underestimate the relative effects of subsidies if developing countries' exports are more concentrated in those agricultural products which attract subsidies.

[12] Many developing countries have been unable to meet their Uruguay Round obligations because of these high costs. By January 2000, up to 90 of the WTO's 109 developing country members were in violation of the SPS, customs valuation, and TRIPs agreements. Estimates of the cost of compliance to the Uruguay agreements vary widely depending on the quality of the existing systems and the strength of institutions in each country. Hungary spent more than US$40 million to upgrade the level of sanitation of its slaughterhouses alone. Mexico spent more than US$30 million to upgrade intellectual property laws. Finger (2000) suggests that for many of the least developed countries in the WTO compliance with these agreements is a less attractive investment than expenditure on basic development goals such as education.

Thus in the years after the Uruguay Round was completed, developing countries became increasingly disillusioned with its results. There were continued tariff and non-tariff barriers by the rich countries on developing-country exports and developing countries had to implement their own obligations under the new agreements, such as those on TRIPS, TRIMs, and agriculture. The promised benefits from liberalization had not materialized. In 1999, in response to concerns expressed by many developing countries that the Uruguay Round agreements had produced an unbalanced result, the acting European Trade Commissioner, Sir Leon Brittan, said: 'the only way to address the issue is through a new round of negotiations. Indeed, I would ask all WTO members, including developing countries, whether they are entirely happy with the present trading system. If the answer is no, it is clear that the only way of improving upon that system is in a new round.'[13]

As with previous rounds, the establishment of the Doha Round was rooted in the experience of the past.

Unfinished business from Uruguay

The Uruguay Round left many loose ends. The 1994 Agreement on Agriculture defined a framework in which agricultural protection could be negotiated in the WTO, but it did not deliver significant benefits to developing countries. Martin and Winters (1995) note that the Agreement on Agriculture achieved 'little in terms of immediate market opening'. The most significant element of the agreement was the requirement that non-tariff barriers be converted into tariffs that provide an equivalent level of protection. Since negotiations over tariff reductions are easier than other forms of protection, this 'tariffication' process was supposed to provide a simpler framework for the long-term reform of agricultural trade in the future. However, the Uruguay Round itself actually achieved very little in

---

[13] Statement at the World Trade Organization High Level Symposium on Trade and Development, 17–18 Mar. 1999, reported in *Sustainable Development* 12: 2 (22 Mar. 1999). See also Raghavan (1999).

the way of liberalization. Although some reductions in tariff rates were agreed, countries were able to use the tariffication process to set very high initial tariffs, such that even after the agreed reform, the new binding tariff rates were higher than the prevailing tariff rates that had been in place for some years.

There was similarly little progress in the reduction of subsidies. Indeed the overall level of OECD farm protection was not noticeably reduced. In 1986–8 farm subsidies were equivalent to 51 per cent of all OECD farm production, and fourteen years later, after the implementation of Uruguay commitments, at more than US$300 billion, they still accounted for 48 per cent of all farm production (OECD 2003). Trade-distorting measures of industrialized nations displace the agricultural exports of developing countries. By suppressing world prices, these policies have a direct effect on farm incomes.[14] Moreover there may be long-term effects, as investment is also suppressed in countries whose trade is adversely affected by OECD support.[15]

In non-agricultural goods, there is also scope for further liberalization. The significant liberalization of manufacturing tariffs in developed countries over the last two decades might suggest that there is little to gain from further negotiations on industrial products. However, if this is true to some extent for developed countries, it is certainly not the case for developing countries. While average developed country tariff rates are low, these nations maintain high barriers to many of the goods exported most intensively by developing countries. When weighted by import volumes, developing countries face average manufacturing tariffs of 3.4 per cent on their exports to developed countries, more than four times as high as the average rate faced by goods from developed countries, 0.8 per cent (Hertel and Martin 2000). Moreover aggregate data hides the existence of tariff peaks. In the United States, post Uruguay Round tariff rates on more than half

[14] Estimates of the downward impact on world prices caused by OECD domestic support are between 3.5 and 5% for many agricultural commodities including wheat and other coarse grains and oilseeds (Dimaranan, Hertel, and Keeney 2003).

[15] Diao, Diaz-Bonilla, and Robinson (2003) report that protectionism and subsidies by industrialized nations cost developing countries about US$24bn annually in lost agricultural and agro-industrial income. Latin America and the Caribbean lose about $8.3bn in annual income from agriculture, Asia loses some $6.6bn, and sub-Saharan Africa close to US$2bn. These estimates do not include dynamic effects.

of textile and clothing imports are between 15 and 35 per cent, while in Japan 22 per cent of textile imports face tariffs of 10–15 per cent (UNCTAD 1996).

Similarly in the processed food sector, Canadian, Japanese, and EU tariffs on fully processed food are 42, 65, and 24 per cent respectively. By contrast, the least processed products face tariffs of 3, 35, and 15 per cent in these countries (World Bank 2002). Such tariff escalation serves to discourage the development of food processing in least developed countries since the *effective* tariff rate on 'value added' in food processing is very high. Tariff escalation and tariff peaks are manifestly unfair and have a particularly pernicious effect on development by restricting industrial diversification in the poorest countries.

After the Uruguay Round, there was also a widely held view that the TRIPS Agreement needed to be reviewed, particularly in its application to public health and bio-piracy. Article 71.1 provided for a review of the implementation of the TRIPS Agreement after year 2000, and for possible reviews 'in the light of any relevant new developments which might warrant modification or amendment'. Many developing countries felt that the Agreement as it stood primarily reflected intellectual property rights protection suitable for developed countries, but largely disregarded important factors in developing countries.

International rules for intellectual property rights have potentially huge public health effects and global distributional consequences. Unbalanced rules—and there is a concern that present rules are unbalanced—can impede efforts to close the North–South 'knowledge gap'. Additionally the WTO also has the responsibility to protect indigenous knowledge. While there have been a few dramatic bio-piracy cases,[16] the full impact of expanded patentability remains uncertain. Patent laws need to be changed so that the onus of proof is reversed and companies should give an undertaking that the patent they are seeking is not based on traditional wisdom.

Finally, the Uruguay Round imposed strong restrictions on developing countries' use of industrial policies—policies that had arguably

---

[16] In May 1995 the US Patent and Trademark Office (USPTO) granted to the University of Mississippi Medical Center a patent (no. 5,401,504) for 'Use of Turmeric in Wound Healing'. They revoked the patent after dozens of references to the procedure were found in texts from India.

played an important role both in the development of Western economies in an earlier century[17] and more recently in the East Asian Miracle.[18] But they allowed developed countries to continue to use non-tariff barriers to exclude goods from the developing countries. Developing countries needed more freedom to use industrial policies, and more protection from abuses by developed countries of dumping duties, countervailing duties, safeguard measures, and phytosanitary conditions.

New areas of importance

Services represent an increasingly large share of GDP and trade in both developed and developing countries. With manufacturing dwindling to 14 per cent of US GDP, it was natural for the US to shift the focus of trade liberalization to services.[19] Indeed, the irony was that increasingly, it seemed as if the trade agreements of the past, centered as they were around manufacturing, would, in the future, be of greater benefit to China than to any other country.

But the Uruguay Round focused on the liberalization of those service industries of primary interest to firms in OECD countries (like financial services). There was significantly less attention given to low-skilled labor-intensive services in which developing countries have a comparative advantage.[20] Developing countries have increased their exports of services more than fourfold since 1990, despite the large trade barriers facing many of their most promising industries, such as construction, shipping services, and health services (OECD 2002). In these industries developing countries have legitimate and substantial interest in the outcome of a new round of liberalization.[21]

---

[17] For a discussion, see e.g. Chang (2002).   [18] See e.g. Stiglitz (1996).

[19] Additionally, given the apparent barriers to service trade, there might be large gains from liberalization. (See Brown, Deardorff and Stern (2002). They estimate that the global gains from service liberalization are as high as $400bn. However, these estimates may overstate the benefits from liberalization if many of these barriers are exogenous and not related to economic policy.)

[20] Developing countries are capturing a growing share of trade in services. More than one quarter of the world's top 40 service exporters in 2002 were in developing countries.

[21] As we discuss in the next section, these labor-intensive services are not the ones that have been given priority in the Doha Round so far.

Some of the areas of service sector liberalization that were advanced in the Uruguay Round may well have disadvantaged the developing countries. Financial market liberalization, for instance, may have weakened domestic financial firms, reducing the already scant supply of credit available to domestic small and medium-sized enterprises.

This agenda of 'new issues' and 'unfinished business' is markedly different from the agenda of the Doha Round in spite of the fact that it was supposed to be a development round. The new issues which had been put on the agenda at the Singapore Ministerial Meeting, the so-called 'Singapore Issues',[22] all centered around concerns of the developed countries. There was one issue, competition policy, which in principle could have been of benefit to the developing countries— had dumping duties been brought into the discussion. But the developed countries were adamantly opposed to this.

A new sense of global responsibility for development

On 30, November 1999, the World Trade Organization convened in Seattle, for what was to be the launch of a new round of trade negotiations. The negotiations were unsuccessful, but they were quickly overshadowed by massive and controversial street protests. From 5 a.m. on the morning of the first day of the conference, several hundred activists arrived in the empty streets near the convention center and began to take control of intersections. As the day began, a number of marches began to converge on the convention center from different directions. A group of students marched from the north and

---

[22] As noted earlier, these centered around (1) government procurement; (2) trade facilitation; (3) competition; and (4) investment. The names, however, are somewhat misleading. 'Competition' did not focus, for instance, on anti-trust matters. The developing countries had already expressed their hostility to the initiative by the OECD for a multilateral investment agreement. There was no reason to believe that the WTO provided a venue in which an agreement acceptable to the developing countries could be worked out. In any case, it was clear that this was an initiative of the developed, not of developing countries. Similarly, while developed countries hoped to have greater access to government procurement in developing countries, there was little hope that developing countries could make much inroad into procurement by developed countries, especially in the central area of defense. This too was a developed-country agenda item.

were met by a march of citizens of the developing world who came from the south. There was some violence, although the vast majority of demonstrators were committed to peaceful forms of protest including rallies, teach-ins, and street parties. The scale of the demonstrations—even the lowest estimates claimed there were more than 40,000 people—dwarfed any previous protest associated with global issues of economics and equality.

The protests certainly did not cause the failure of the WTO negotiations at the Seattle meeting. In particular, the negotiators from developing countries were skeptical about the new issues being placed on the agenda for the proposed round. They feared that any compromise on their part on issues to be included in the negotiating agenda would hurt them in the subsequent negotiations. However, even if the effect of the protests on the negotiations is often overstated, the significance of the occasion as the coming-out of the anti-globalization movement in the United States was profound.[23] Over the next two years the movement gained momentum with protests in Melbourne,[24] Prague,[25] Washington,[26] and Genoa.[27] Suddenly the gap between rich and poor was becoming shocking in the public consciousness.

The global protest movement coincided with a significant increase in the activism of civil society organizations and development-focused NGOs such as the Catholic Agency for Overseas Development (CAFOD), Christian Aid, and Oxfam. It also coincided with a surge in international support for alternative development initiatives and popular social movements, such as the Jubilee 2000 campaign to drop the debt burden of the developing countries and the establishment of the World Social Forum. These groups have exerted strong pressure on international political and economic

[23] The anti-globalization movement developed in opposition to the perceived negative aspects of globalization. The term 'anti-globalization' is in many ways a misnomer, since the group represents a wide range of interests and issues and many of the people involved in the anti-globalization movement *do* support closer ties between the various peoples and cultures of the world through, for example, aid, assistance for refugees, and global environmental issues.

[24] More than 5,000 people protested at the Asia-Pacific Summit of the World Economic Forum (Davos Forum) in Melbourne in September 2000.

[25] More than 10,000 people protested in Prague during the IMF, World Bank, and G8 Summit in September 2000.

[26] In April 2000, there were protests at the IMF and World Bank headquarters in Washington.

[27] More than 100,000 people protested at the G8 meeting in Genoa in July 2001.

policy institutions to break the cycle of increasing world poverty, inequality, and economic instability in developing countries.

At the same time developed countries made unprecedented commitments within international institutions to bring development issues to the center of international relations. At the United Nations Millennium Summit in New York in September 2000, world leaders placed poverty eradication at the heart of the global agenda by adopting the Millennium Development Goals (MDGs), which set clear targets for reducing poverty, hunger, disease, illiteracy, environmental degradation, and discrimination against women by 2015. Following this, at the International Conference on Financing for Development, held in Monterrey, Mexico, in March 2002, the advanced industrial countries committed themselves to helping provide the finance for development priorities. The Johannesburg Summit on Sustainable Development in September 2002 attempted to establish an action plan for the tasks to be completed in the coming years in order to ensure sustainable global development.

Together these events signaled a new sense of collective responsibility for the shocking poverty in developing countries and on increasing recognition of the need for global collective action. The addition of development concerns to the new round of WTO negotiations was a natural part of a program of global collective action to reduce poverty. It would have made no sense to exclude trade from the poverty reduction initiatives because, as former US President Jimmy Carter said during the Johannesburg Summit, 'We cost the developing world three times as much in trade source restrictions as all the overseas development assistance they receive from all sources.'

In this context, the Doha Ministerial Declaration adopted on 14 November 2001 contained, in its second article, an affirmation of the new international commitment to development: 'International trade can play a major role in the promotion of economic development and the alleviation of poverty. We recognize the need for all our peoples to benefit from the increased opportunities and welfare gains that the multilateral trading system generates. The majority of WTO members are developing countries. We seek to place their needs and interests at the heart of the Work Programme adopted in this Declaration.'

It is certainly true that this new collective responsibility for the problems of developing countries is in its infancy and has been characterized so far by promises more than results. It is also true that the issues of international equity embodied in the agreements at the Millennium Summit, and followed up at Doha, Monterrey, and Johannesburg, have not been precisely defined, but that does not mean that they are not relevant. For a long time, arguments about equity have held sway in domestic debates, and they should be welcomed into the international arena. Just as the distributional impacts of domestic programs have become an important force in shaping legislation in the democracies of the advanced industrial countries, so too can development and distributional concerns become an important force in the outcome of international bargaining.

4

What has Doha Achieved?

☙

US Trade Representative Robert Zoellick's statements after the Doha Ministerial Conference reflected the prevailing positive mood and the hope for a successful round of negotiations:

Doha lays the groundwork for a trade liberalization agenda that will be a starting point for greater development, growth, opportunity and openness around the world ... we've settled on a program that lays out ambitious objectives for future negotiations on the liberalization of the agriculture market. These objectives represent a cornerstone of our market access priorities for trade and they will create a framework that will help the United States and others to advance a fundamental agricultural reform agenda. On a range of issues, such as agricultural liberalization and reduction of tariffs on non-agricultural goods, we've shown how our interests can converge with the developing world. I believe that we in the United States have an enhanced appreciation for the interests of developing nations in trade.[1]

Despite the expressions of goodwill at Doha, progress on the Development Round has been slow. Part of the problem is that, while the interests of different developing countries differ, the evolving agenda itself was not really designed to reflect the real concerns of developing countries. Throughout 2002 and 2003 it became apparent that many developing countries felt that the Doha Round was moving in the wrong direction on many key issues. They felt that the new round offered them few immediate benefits but carried the risk

[1] 14 Nov. 2001, *Office of the US Trade Representative*. Online speech available at www.ustr.gov

of additional obligations. As a consequence developing countries walked away from the Cancún Ministerial Meeting in September 2003.

Up to that point, Doha had achieved little progress on most of the critical development issues. One of the key disappointments has been agricultural reform, which many developing countries[2] and NGOs[3] viewed as the primary objective of the round. The March 2003 deadline for agreement on agricultural modalities was missed. When the US and EU finally presented a joint paper on agricultural issues in August, the framework was widely criticized by developing countries, correctly in our judgment, for ignoring their interests.[4] On the key issues of market access, domestic support, and export subsidies the text was perceived to fall short of the level of ambition of the Doha mandate; indeed, in some respects, what was offered was a step backward. On domestic support, no specific figures were given for reducing the most trade-distorting support. The text potentially widened the scope for the use of production based financial support (the so-called "Blue Box" support)—a step backwards in terms of liberalization. Also the text did not focus on trade-distorting elements of the "Green Box" measures (permissible forms of subsidy under WTO rules). The framework was critically viewed by the Kenyan Ambassador Ms Amina Chawahir Mohamed, who said that 'the EU–US text falls short of our expectations and as such we find it difficult to accept it as a basis of our further work'.

At the same time, agricultural initiatives within OECD countries seemed to be undermining multilateral efforts. The US Farm Bill in 2002 increased the level of support to US farmers[5] and strengthened

[2] Sec. 7 of 6 June 2003 Communication from Argentina, Bolivia, Botswana, Brazil, Chile, China, Colombia, Cuba, Dominican Republic, Ecuador, El Salvador, Gabon, Guatemala, Honduras, India, Malaysia, Mexico, Morocco, Nicaragua, Pakistan, Paraguay, Peru, Thailand, Uruguay, Venezuela and Zimbabwe (TN/C/W/13), makes it clear that 'Reform of agricultural trade is of central importance for many developing countries' and is *an essential ingredient of the negotiation and its outcome*' (emphasis in original).

[3] Oxfam (2003) argues that 'agriculture is the key to unlocking the Doha development agenda, and without constructive steps on this issue, the broader negotiations cannot really restart'.

[4] See the statements by Indian Ambassador K. M. Chandrasekhar, Brazil's Ambassador Luis Felipe de Seixas Correa, and China's Ambassador Sun Zhenyu (TWN 2003).

[5] The US Farm Security and Rural Investment Act (FSRIA) of May 2002 has a value of about US$190bn over the next 10 years, about US$83bn more than under previous programs. It sets target prices which are lower than the pre-1996 levels, but the total effective support is larger because average world commodity prices have declined and the range of commodities included in FSIRA is larger than in the 1996 FAIR Act. That act was intended to phase out farm subsidies, but even before the passage of FSRIA, farmers had achieved additional support through emergency measures.

the link between subsidies and production decisions.[6] One year later, the EU's 2003 Luxembourg reform of the common agricultural policy (CAP) was also disappointing. The EU reform shifts support from production-limiting subsidies (the so-called Blue Box subsidies) to other, more acceptable forms of farm support (i.e. the Green Box subsidies, which are deemed to be less trade-distorting). However, the level of producer support will remain virtually constant—projected to fall only from 57 per cent to 56 per cent (OECD 2004). Moreover the reform has little impact on export subsidies or import barriers. Both of these initiatives fell far short of expectations and signaled the limited commitment of the US and EU to agricultural reform. Consequently both plans had a depressing effect on the mood of multilateral agricultural negotiations.

After the Uruguay Round, there was a clear understanding that there would be further liberalization of agriculture. There is now a strong sense that the United States has reneged on that commitment: whether the huge increase in agricultural subsidies is an explicit violation of earlier agreements is of less importance than that it represents a violation of the spirit of the agreement (or at least what was taken as the spirit of the agreement by the developing countries.)[7] Just as the agreement has to be viewed as a whole, so too, a Development Round agreement has to be viewed in the context of the unbalanced agreements that preceded it.

In addition to their disappointment on agriculture, developing countries are skeptical about the effects of the new items on the agenda. There is significant opposition from developing countries to the Singapore Issues.[8] In the space of a month from early June 2003, 77 developing countries, including over half the WTO membership,

---

[6] It provides counter-cyclical payments (CCPs) to US farmers which respond negatively to world prices. This type of measure has allowed the US to dump its farm surplus on world markets. For example, the US exports corn at prices 20% below the cost of production, and wheat at 46% below cost. See Cassel (2002).

[7] The recent preliminary WTO ruling against American cotton subsidies (based on a complaint from Brazil) has lent support to the critics. America claimed, remarkably, that their subsidies did not adversely affect other cotton-exporting countries. Such claims clearly undermine the credibility of the position of the developed countries.

[8] Ministers from WTO member countries decided at the 1996 Singapore Ministerial Conference to establish three new working groups: on trade and investment, on competition policy, and on transparency in government procurement. They also instructed the WTO Goods Council to look into ways of simplifying trade procedures, an issue sometimes known as 'trade facilitation'. Because these issues were introduced to the agenda at the Singapore Ministerial Meeting, they are often called the 'Singapore Issues'.

made public statements urging that the Singapore Issues not be included as part of the Doha Round.[9] Since these issues are not priorities for developing countries, their emerging centrality in the agenda prior to Cancún was an incongruous feature of the Development Round.

Several developing countries see the Singapore Issues as incursions into their national sovereignty that are not justified by the benefits they bring. Multilateral regulatory disciplines hold the specter of repeating the worst elements of Uruguay by restricting the options for individual governments to pursue development policies based on their own national priorities and problems.

In addition there are concerns that the initiatives based on the Singapore Issues may impose a large burden on the administrative capacity of developing countries. There are significant costs associated with both the creation and enforcement of new regimes in competition policy, investment regulations, and trade and customs procedures.[10] Many developing countries have been unable to meet their Uruguay Round obligations because of these high costs.[11]

Another area where achievements have lagged behind rhetoric is in the delivery of non-reciprocal trade preferences.[12] These preferences are special market-access rights provided by developed countries to the poorest developing countries, i.e. they normally involve a full or partial reduction of tariff rates on goods imported from very poor countries. Recently there have been a number of initiatives in OECD countries to discriminate further in favour of least developed countries (LDCs). Most notable among these are the EU's Everything but Arms (EBA) initiative and the US's African Growth and Opportunity Act (AGOA), both of which remove tariffs on a wide range of goods imported from the poorest nations. The EU has argued that the EBA will 'significantly enhance export opportunities and hence potential income and growth' for LDCs (CEC 2002). However,

---

[9] CAFOD (2003) 'Singapore Issues in the WTO: What do developing countries say?'.

[10] Finger (2000) estimated the implementation costs of three of the Uruguay Round's six agreements that required regulatory change (customs reform, intellectual property rights, and sanitary and phytosanitary (SPS) measures). His analysis suggests that the average cost of restructuring domestic regulations in the 12 developing countries considered could be as much as US$150m.

[11] By January 2000, up to 90 of the WTO's 109 developing country members were in violation of the SPS, customs valuation, and TRIPS agreements.   [12] These preferences are discussed in Ch. 9.

studies show that preferential schemes have only limited impact on LDC exports. Brenton (2003) concludes that trade in goods given preferences for the first time under the EBA in 2001 amounted to just two hundredths of one per cent of LDC exports to the EU in 2001.[13] Even earlier preferences were not focused on goods exported by LDCs: up to 50 per cent of the exports of non-ACP countries to the EU did not receive preferential access and paid the most-favoured nation (MFN) tariff (Brenton 2003). Overall, the impact of these schemes has not yet been very significant, with the exception of African apparel exports to the US under AGOA (World Bank 2003).[14]

The failure of the round to deliver on the expectations created at Doha had, by the middle of 2003, sapped the goodwill that had been created two years before. In particular, two issues had generated acrimonious debate and attracted considerable adverse public attention. Soon after the completion of the Uruguay Round, developing countries began seeking revisions of the TRIPS agreement. The agreement required all member states to guarantee strong protection to all intellectual property—rules which were widely thought to inhibit technology transfer and exacerbate the technology gap between rich and poor countries. In particular, the implications of the TRIPS Agreement for developing countries' access to life-saving drugs attracted considerable attention. TRIPS allowed developing countries to acquire licenses enabling them to produce drugs *domestically* at a fraction of the cost of the purchase price from patent-holding corporations. But the licensing provision was useless for developing countries with little or no manufacturing capability, since TRIPS restricted trade in generic drugs between developing countries.

[13] Part of the reason the EBA has had such a limited effect is that almost all EU imports from LDCs (more than 99% in 2001) were already eligible for preferences under other schemes (Brenton 2003). In 2001 the EBA initiative granted duty-free access to imports of all products from the least developed countries (except arms and munitions). Total exports from these LDCs to the EU increased by 9.6% in 2001. However, in practice, the EBA was only relevant to the remaining 919 products (of the EU's 10,200 tariff lines) which had not previously been granted duty-free status under either the GSP or Cotonou Agreement. Of these 919 products, imports from LDCs were recorded in just 80 products in 2001. Brenton (2003) notes that total exports of these products actually fell from 3.5m in 2000 to 2.9m in 2001. Moreover trade in these goods in 2001 amounted to just two hundredths of one per cent of the total value of LDC exports to the EU. Thus it appears that the direct impact of the EBA initiative has not been significant in the short term and, given the small size of trade in affected products, is not likely to be large in the medium term.

[14] Moreover, beginning in 2008, cotton textile producers will have to use American cotton, further limiting the benefits of AGOA.

Public support rallied around the plight of these countries, particularly those in Africa dealing with the AIDS pandemic. The WTO and the US (who had refused to consider revisions of the rules) attracted public criticism which soured the atmosphere of the negotiations. In August 2003, an agreement was finally reached when the US changed its position to allow least developed countries to import generic drugs from low-cost non-patent-holding producers in developing countries. But by 2003, the issue had done considerable damage to the reputation of the WTO among developing countries and their allies.

Just as public health concerns rallied opposition to the WTO's intellectual property rules, the plight of West African cotton farmers served to focus world attention on the injustice of the rich countries' agricultural policies. In 2001, cotton production in Benin, Burkina Faso, Chad, and Mali and accounted for 5 to 10 per cent of gross domestic product and an average of about 30–40 per cent of overall export revenues. More than ten million people in West and Central Africa directly depend on cotton production. These countries complained that their cotton industries were suffering from cotton subsidies in the US (and to a lesser extent in the EU). In 2001, rich countries provided subsidies to their farmers which amounted to six times the amount of their development aid, respectively US$311 billion and US$55 billion. President Blaise Compaore of Burkina Faso addressed the Trade Negotiations Committee of the WTO in Geneva on 10 June 2003. He claimed that these subsidies have caused economic and social crises in African cotton-producing countries: 'As a consequence of cotton subsidies, in 2001, Burkina lost 1 percent of its GDP and 12 percent of its export incomes, Mali 1.7 percent and 8 percent, and Benin 1.4 percent and 9 percent respectively. The massive subsidies awarded to cotton farmers in some WTO member states are among the most important and direct causes of the problems encountered on the international cotton market. These subsidies artificially inflate the offer and depress export prices.' The African countries' demands, including that the subsidies be reduced and compensation be paid to African farmers, were swiftly rejected by the US.

In this climate of quashed expectations, WTO members met for the Fifth WTO Ministerial Conference in Cancún, from 10 to

14 September 2003. The Doha Declaration had called for the Fifth Ministerial Meeting to 'take stock of progress in the negotiations, provide any necessary political guidance, and take decisions as necessary' with a view to completing the round by January 2005. But, after two years of missed deadlines and failed negotiations, there was little progress to take stock of. In response to their frustrations, developing countries united in several groups to strengthen their negotiating voice. A group of twenty developing countries, the G20,[15] formed an effective negotiating block on agricultural issues. Led by South Africa, Brazil, India, and China, the G20 pressed the US and EU for greater market access and subsidy reduction. However, the richest countries, as they had signaled on the cotton issue, were unwilling to offer serious concessions: the developing countries were frustrated again.

There was also disagreement in Cancún about the Singapore Issues. As we have seen, these new issues in the round were primarily of interest to developed countries. A diverse group of developing countries, the G90, consisting of the least developed countries as well as the other African, Caribbean, and Pacific countries, united in their opposition to the inclusion of these issues in the round. When negotiations began on the Singapore Issues on the morning of Sunday, 15 September, the symbolism could not have been worse. After several days of frustrating negotiations on the 'development' issues—during which the developing countries felt that the developed countries had not offered significant concessions—the agenda turned to a set of issues that the developing countries feared would restrict their policy freedom and impose large implementation costs on them. At 3.30 on Sunday afternoon George Odour Ong'wen from Kenya descended an escalator in Cancún's convention center and declared that Kenya had abandoned the negotiations. By 6 p.m. Dr Luis Ernesto Derbez, the Mexican Finance Minister and chair of the meeting, said that the positions of various countries were just too diverse to make further debate worthwhile. The proceedings were brought to a close and the meeting ended in failure.

---

[15] The G20 consisted of Argentina, Bolivia, Brazil, Chile, China, Colombia, Costa Rica, Cuba, Ecuador, El Salvador, Guatemala, India, Mexico, Pakistan, Paraguay, Peru, the Philippines, South Africa, Thailand, and Venezuela. Membership however has been fluid.

Cancún represented a striking turnaround: less than two years after the WTO's Fourth Ministerial Meeting had ended in success at Doha, the Fifth Ministerial Meeting had collapsed in bitterness. Many developing countries refused to proceed with the agenda because they came to the view that no agreement was better than a bad agreement. The EU and the US blamed the developing countries and asserted that they would be the main losers from the setback. The EU Commissioner for Agriculture Franz Fischler dismissively noted that if the G20 wanted 'to do business, they should come back to Mother Earth. If they choose to continue their space odyssey they will not get to the stars, they will not get the moon; they will end up with empty hands.'[16]

While some delegates berated the developing nations for their lack of cooperation, others have argued that the assertion of power by developing countries represented a victory for democracy. Developing countries united to form voting blocs from which they could oppose EU and US agricultural policies and make their case on new and emerging issues. In addition to the G20 and G90 described above, the G33 (the Alliance for Strategic Products and a Special Safeguard Mechanism),[17] led by the Philippines and Indonesia, wanted to maintain their ability to protect their own agricultural interests. Some governments were supportive of these new groupings. The UK's Secretary of State for International Development, Hilary Benn, said 'the better developing countries are able to articulate what they want, the better chance we have in the end of reaching agreements that will make a difference to poverty'.[18]

Little progress was made on any aspect of the negotiations in the aftermath of Cancún. But by the middle of 2004, the EU and US top trade negotiators (EU Trade Commissioner Pascal Lamy and US Trade Representative Robert Zoellick) came back to the negotiating

---

[16] Franz Fischler, 'Ten Ingredients to Make Cancun [a] Success', press conference, Brussels, 4 Sept. 2003.

[17] The G33 actually comprises 42 developing countries of the WTO. They are: Antigua and Barbuda, Barbados, Belize, Benin, Botswana, China, Côte d'Ivoire, Congo, Cuba, Dominican Republic, Grenada, Guyana, Haiti, Honduras, India, Indonesia, Jamaica, Kenya, Korea, Mauritius, Mongolia, Montserrat, Mozambique, Nicaragua, Nigeria, Pakistan, Panama, The Philippines, Peru, Saint Kitts, Saint Lucia, Saint Vincent and the Grenadines, Senegal, Sri Lanka, Suriname, Tanzania, Trinidad and Tobago, Turkey, Uganda, Venezuela, Zambia, and Zimbabwe.

[18] International Development Committee (IDC), *Trade and Development at the WTO: Issues for Cancun, Geneva*, Seventh Report of Session 2002–03, HC400-I.

table with an attempt to salvage the round by offering a simplified agenda and promises of compromise on some key issues.[19] By August 2004, the General Council adopted a new framework for progress in the round. The new agenda excluded all the Singapore Issues other than trade facilitation. The round would focus on core market-access issues in agriculture, services, and industrial goods. In particular the new text signals that the EU and US are willing to compromise on agriculture and recommit themselves to special treatment for developing countries.

In summary the agenda for the 'Development Round' has evolved disappointingly for developing countries since Doha. It has done little to address their concerns in agriculture and it has done little to address problems posed by non-tariff barriers. It has not given priority to a developing-country service sector agenda and there have been no reforms in basic procedures.

In addition, the proposed agenda's new issues could have made life worse for developing countries. The US wanted capital market liberalization as part of an investment agreement, even though the weight of evidence was that capital market liberalization did not promote growth but did lead to more instability. Under competition policy, rather than creating a true competitive environment—hindering the use of dumping duties as protectionist devices—there was fear of restricting development and socially oriented preferences.

---

[19] See the letter of 9 May 2004 by Pascal Lamy and Franz Fischler, and the letter of 11 Jan. 2004 to Trade Ministers from Robert Zoellick. Letter to all Trade Ministers, unpublished.

5

Founding Principles: The Basis of a Fair Agreement

One reason the Development Round is faltering is that the WTO (like its predecessor the GATT) has been, by process and structure, a mercantilist institution that has worked on a principle of self-interested bargaining. The concept of a Development Round implies a fundamental departure from the system of mercantilism towards collectively agreed principles. However, there has been almost no discussion, let alone agreement, on what such principles might be. The lack of commonly agreed values has deprived the WTO's members of any means of collectively choosing a set of policies from among competing proposals.

Progress in the Development Round needs to be accompanied by a debate about principles, how those principles apply to trade, and how they should be implemented in the current round of negotiations. In this chapter we make a contribution to this debate by considering several fundamental questions: 'What are the appropriate boundaries for the WTO's agenda?', 'What would constitute a 'fair' agreement?', 'What are the characteristics of a 'fair' negotiating process?' There are no universal answers to these questions, but there are answers that derive legitimacy from commonly agreed values implemented in a democratic process.

We begin with an analysis of the principles that should underlie a development round of trade negotiations. It seems self-evident that:

1. Any agreement should be assessed in terms of its impact on development; items with a negative effect on development should not be on the agenda.
2. Any agreement should be fair.
3. Any agreement should be arrived at fairly.
4. The agenda should be limited to trade-related and development-friendly issues.

These principles may be widely agreed to; however, there may be important differences in the way various terms such as 'fairness' are interpreted and understood and about the meaning of terms and about how to respond to conflicts among the principles.

Impact assessment

Any agreement should be carefully designed to promote, not hinder, development but there is surprisingly little economic analysis of the precise consequences of various potential trade agreements on participant countries. Where analytical studies have been done, they have not penetrated to the core of negotiations and do not seem to play a central role in setting the agenda. The absence of this type of analysis raises the question of what is driving the prioritization of trade issues on the WTO agenda, other than a mélange of prevailing orthodoxies and the momentum of special interest groups.

The WTO Secretariat should be responsible for producing a general equilibrium incidence analysis, analogous to what is conducted when taxes are imposed, attempting to assess how different countries are affected by different proposals. Publicly available analysis would benefit developing countries, many of which are at an information disadvantage relative to developed countries. Publicly available information would also be an important source for consumers, who are less equipped to lobby for favorable outcomes than producer groups.

Analysis based on general equilibrium models must be sensitive to the fact that different developing countries are likely to be affected differently, and different groups within developing countries are likely to be affected in different ways. For example, eliminating developed country agricultural subsidies is likely to raise the price of agricultural products, thereby benefiting countries that export these commodities and hurting those that import them. Within individual countries it is likely to benefit the producers of agricultural goods, and hurt consumers. Thus the elimination of subsidies presents a welfare trade-off for developing countries. But the net effect of the elimination of subsidies is likely to be pro-development. Even if net-importing countries experience aggregate losses, the reform has potentially positive distributional consequences within the poor countries since it is the producers (and those rural populations that survive on agricultural production) who are among the poorest communities in those countries. These communities are the most likely to benefit, even if the country as a whole loses because it is a net importer of subsidized commodities.

The results of general equilibrium models are sensitive to their assumptions. Much of the analysis of the impacts (including, for instance, judgments about whether particular types of agricultural subsidies are trade-distorting) relies on a particular model of the economy, the neo-classical model, which assumes full employment of resources, perfect competition, perfect information, and well-functioning markets, assumptions which are of questionable validity for any country, but which are particularly problematic for developing countries.

Most of the tools used to analyse general equilibrium effects of trade liberalization are static models. They describe the movement from one 'steady state' to another but do not incorporate the costs associated with transition or the consequences for economies which are initially out of steady state. For example the models typically assume that there is full employment. Trade liberalization measures are good for a country because they enable resources to be redirected from low-productivity protected sectors to more productive sectors as the economy specializes in their areas of comparative advantage. Under full employment, developing countries would unambiguously benefit from trade liberalization measures, were it not for terms-of-trade effects (changes in relative prices.) Most of the studies cited in Appendix 1 that assess the impact on developing countries thus focus principally on these terms-of-trade effects.

But with unemployment, trade liberalization is not needed to 'release' resources into more productive sectors and trade liberalization may simply move workers from low-productivity protected sectors into unemployment. This lowers the country's national income and increases poverty. There can be multiplier effects, so that the total impact is far greater than the direct effect. Much of the opposition to trade liberalization arises because of the perceived effects on employment. In more developed countries, monetary and fiscal policy should, in principle, enable the country to maintain nearly full employment. As the advocates of trade liberalization repeatedly emphasize, the objective of trade liberalization is not to create jobs, but to increase standards of living by allowing countries to specialize in areas of comparative advantage. But in many developing countries, with persistent unemployment—with unemployment rates sometimes in excess of 20 per cent[1]—it is evident that monetary and fiscal policies are unable to maintain the economy at full employment. While the standard neo-classical models typically deployed to assess trade impacts do not identify the impact of trade liberalization on the equilibrium level of unemployment[2] (by assumption there is none), even if trade liberalization had no impact on the *equilibrium* level of unemployment, it may take the economy considerable time to adjust, and the costs of adjustments—lost income and increased poverty—may be considerable.

Another important assumption made in most of the analyses is that there is no uncertainty, no risk. But *changes in trade regimes affect countries' exposure to risk.* In the absence of good insurance

---

[1] In 2001 average unemployment rates reached 14.4% in Africa; 12.6% in transition economies; and 10% in Latin America. Such statistics, however, often under-represent the true level of unemployment—for instance, the prevalent high levels of disguised unemployment.

[2] See for instance the papers cited in Appendix 1, especially the contributions by Hertel (1997) and Anderson, Dimaran, Francois *et al.* (2000).

markets, there can be first-order welfare effects arising from this increased exposure to risk.[3] For instance, with a quota, those who compete with imports know precisely how much will be imported, and therefore, if there is relatively little domestic volatility, they will face relatively little price uncertainty. But with the tariffication of quotas, countries are exposed to considerably greater volatility.[4]

It is important that any incidence analysis take into account other pre-existing distortions. For instance, tax policies (often advocated by international institutions), which effectively tax the informal sector less than the formal sector, already distort production in favor of the informal sector. In this context, trade regimes which lower the international price of agricultural goods, typically produced by the informal sector, have a larger adverse effect than would be the case if tax policy were more neutral.

It is also important that any incidence analysis be based on an assessment of the *global general equilibrium impacts*, which takes into account the effects of a change in a trade regime on global relative prices. For instance, if a single small country were to subsidize cotton, it would have a relatively small effect on the global price of cotton. But if a large producer—e.g. the United States—subsidizes cotton, it has an effect on the international price of cotton.

The fact that implementation and adjustment costs are likely to be larger in developing countries, unemployment rates are likely to be higher, safety nets weaker, and risk markets poorer are all features of developing countries that have to be taken into account in conducting a relative incidence analysis. If trade liberalization has a large effect on inequality, then governments may be required to strengthen their redistributive welfare system. Larger taxes generate increased deadweight loss, which reduces the efficiency gains from liberalization.

Large adjustment costs imply not only that the process of liberalization should be conducted gradually, but also that there should not be oscillations. Bilateral agreements *on the way to a multilateral*

---

[3] For instance, Dasgupta and Stiglitz (1977) show that the change from quotas to tariffs may expose countries to much greater risk. Newbery and Stiglitz (1984) show that the adverse effects from increased exposure to risk may be so great that everyone in both countries may be worse off.

[4] The incidence, in this case, depends on the extent to which there are disturbances in the domestic markets, and the extent to which the external disturbances are correlated with the domestic disturbance.

agreement may be particularly detrimental when there are important elements of trade diversion. The greater adjustment costs in developing countries may mean that the net benefit (net of the adjustment costs into and out of the sector having temporary preferential treatment) may be small and/or that there will, in fact, be relatively little benefit, as expansion into that sector may be limited as investors recognize its short-term nature.

Finally, it is of the first importance to distinguish between provisions which should, in principle, make a country better off on its own, almost regardless of the circumstances; provisions which might or might not make a country better off on its own; and provisions which essentially are *redistributive* in nature, with the gains to one side being largely offset by losses to the other. We have argued that many of the trade liberalization measures would, in a world of full employment, make a country better off on its own. In the real world, the question is often posed: 'Why is there any need for a trade agreement?' Trade agreements are used only as a bargaining weapon. The threat of not opening up one's own market (which has a cost) is used to force the opening up of the foreigner's markets.

Note that many of the arguments that are currently used in favor of certain provisions of proposed trade agreements contend that they are good for the developing countries.[5] To the extent that such arguments are correct, of course, it implies that there is no need for a trade agreement, other than the *political economy* argument that it is only by bringing to bear the pressure from the gainers from trade liberalization that one can overcome the resistance of the losers in a world in which compensations are typically not made. Moreover, to the extent that such arguments are correct, it implies that (apart from global terms-of-trade effects) the issue of fairness only pertains to the distribution of *relative* gains (relative costs and benefits) since *every country* benefits. It also means that any country could unilaterally increase its gains simply by lowering its trade barriers further, thereby expanding trade. To be sure, some of the opposition against

[5] This includes not only trade liberalization, but also investor protections. Investor protections will attract more investment. But if that is the case, then countries will have an incentive to undertake such actions on their own. There are some legitimate worries, spelled out below: excessive investor protection may compromise general welfare concerns, e.g. about safety or the environment.

trade liberalization comes from those who would be hurt by it, in particular special interests who benefit from protection; but some opposition may arise because particular countries may be adversely affected *as a whole.*

These cases need to be distinguished from intellectual property rights, where stronger intellectual property protections may increase the incomes of those in the more advanced industrial countries *at the expense of those in the less advanced industrial countries.* Here the issue is primarily redistributive, and is accordingly fundamentally different from those that arise in connection with trade liberalization.[6] Again, the developed countries make a self-serving argument that stronger intellectual property protections will (1) induce more research or (2) induce more investment in intellectual-property-intensive industries. But for most goods there is relatively little evidence that the incremental profits generated in developing countries have much impact on research. This is certainly the case for most drugs, where the overwhelming bulk of the profits are generated by sales in the North—the drug companies do little research related to illnesses whose primary incidence is in the South. In many areas, such as soft drinks, trade secrets, not patents, have been the basis of expansion into the South. In any case, again, if it were true that stronger intellectual property protections led to faster growth, countries interested in enhancing growth would provide such stronger protection on their own.

Any agreement should be fair

Article 2 of the Doha Ministerial Declaration contains an implicit principle of fairness: it focuses the Doha Round on the 'alleviation of poverty' in developing countries and recognizes 'the need for all our peoples to benefit from the increased opportunities and welfare gains that the multilateral trading system generates'.

---

[6] See e.g. Bhagwati (2002), which argues, accordingly, that intellectual property should never have been part of trade negotiations.

Similarly, the analysis in this book is based on a concern for social justice and a degree of equity between nations. There are those that would criticize this premise on the basis that notions of fairness which are fairly well defined in contexts involving individuals are not easily extended to bargaining among collectives such as nation states. That brings us to the crucial question—should international law, the rules and regulations that govern relations among countries and among individuals and firms in different countries, be based simply on realpolitik, or should considerations of social justice and fairness play a role? This is a long-debated subject, and we cannot pretend in this book even to touch on the merits of the alternative positions. We believe that the view that international trade regulations should be governed by *principles* rather than just economic power is at least a respectable one—and one to which the international community has seemingly subscribed. While we accept that the application of principles of fairness is much weaker in the international context than it is inside nations, it is an important exercise to explore the implications of principles of fairness between nations, and that is what we do in this book.

Indeed, as globalization has proceeded, and there has been increasing recognition of the need for global collective action, principles of fairness have increasingly come to play an important role. The fact that principles of equity underlying international relations are not precisely defined does not mean that they are not relevant. Just as arguments about equity hold sway in domestic debates, they are also relevant in the international arena. International agreements require the agreement not just of the rich countries, but also of the poor, and if the citizens of democratic poorer countries believe that they are being unfairly treated, they will refuse to agree or comply. Just as information about the distributional impacts of domestic programs has become an important force in shaping legislation in the democracies of the advanced industrial countries, so too can information about the development and distributional impacts of proposed international trade regimes become an important force in the outcome of international bargaining.

Opponents of the view that fairness should be a consideration in trade negotiations often argue that it is unnecessary because trade agreements are voluntary, and so developing countries do not have to sign up to any agreement which they think will make them worse off. And since countries can withdraw from the WTO, the fact that they do not do so shows that they must believe that they are net beneficiaries. Such views almost certainly misconstrue the nature of the power relationship between the developed and less developed countries. The advanced industrial countries are still able to get their way, particularly by withholding aid unless developing countries accept their demands. Moreover, countries may benefit from having the 'rule of law' that the WTO provides for trade between nations— the United States may, for instance, be restrained from the use of its brute economic power but that does not mean that the rules themselves are fair, in any sense of the term. Still, the benefits of trade liberalization may go disproportionately to the richer countries.

Moreover, those who put forth this argument fail to note the difference between individual and group actions. Given that other developing countries had agreed to sign, it might pay any country that is holding out to sign on; but it still may be true that the developing countries as a whole (or a subgroup of these countries) would have been better off if they, as a group, had not signed. (The prisoners' dilemma arises not only in the case of prisoners, but also in the case of poor countries engaged in bargaining with the rich.) Asymmetric trade agreements give rise to terms-of-trade effects— changes in relative prices—which any single country may ignore, but which become significant in a global agreement.[7]

However, although we believe that fairness is an important element of trade negotiations, we do not pretend that it is easy to state precisely its implications for the agreements. Underlying conflicts about perceptions of fairness is the fact that *because the circumstances of the different countries are different, any agreement that applies 'fairly' or 'uniformly' to all countries may still have large differential effects.* This is why we have emphasized the importance of an incidence analysis, an assessment of the differential effects on different countries. *Any agreement that differentially hurts developing*

---

[7] The poorest developing countries play such a small role in international trade that even though their tariffs may be high, their impact on global relative prices is small. This is not so for the advanced industrial countries.

countries more or benefits the developed countries more (say, as
measured by the net gains as a percentage of GDP) *should be presumptively viewed as unfair.* Indeed, it should be essential that any
reform be *progressive,* i.e. that a larger share of the benefits accrue to
the poorer countries. This was almost certainly not true of the
Uruguay Round.

There is one key difficulty in interpreting this requirement. Many
of the costs of, say, agricultural subsidies are borne by the developed
countries. Not only are there huge budgetary costs associated with
the subsidies, but the subsidies distort production, and thus there is
an efficiency loss associated with them. Were developed countries to
eliminate their subsidies, they would therefore be among the main
beneficiaries. Thus, a refinement of the above criterion would look
at the benefits granted others: in competitive markets, it would be
reflected in the general equilibrium terms-of-trade effects received
by producers or paid by consumers; in non-competitive markets (or
markets with quota restrictions) it would be the value of access
granted.

One particular aspect of this should be emphasized: in trade disputes, *both de jure and de facto,* the more developed countries are in
a better position to prevail. For instance, the costs to a developing
country of bringing a claim against a developed country or to defend
themselves against a claim from a developed country may be very
high; in practice the developing country is at a disadvantageous position in any process entailing resort to complicated and expensive
legal proceedings.[8]

There is a long history within developed countries of those in positions of power using the legal system to maintain their privileges.
More recently, many developed countries have tried to come to terms
with the resulting inequities by providing public legal assistance.
Typically, because of the relatively low pay of those employed to
provide such assistance, this can go only a little way in redressing the
imbalance. But at a minimum, the developed countries should

---

[8] More generally, as we discuss later, the WTO dispute system favors rich countries with the resources to
use it effectively for their own interests.

provide financial assistance to less developed countries involved in such legal disputes to create a more level playing field.

By the same token, even were a developing country to prevail in a WTO tribunal against the United States or Europe, the enforcement system is asymmetric, and consequently unfair. The sanction for violating a WTO agreement is the imposition of duties. If Ecuador, say, were to impose duties on goods that it imports from the United States, it would have a negligible effect on the American producer; while if the United States were to impose a duty on goods produced by Ecuador, the economic impact would more likely be devastating. In practice, the WTO system has no effective way of enforcing penalties against an unfair trade action whose main impact is on small developing countries. When, of course, a major industrial country takes a global action then there can be a global response (for example, when the US increased protection on their steel industry, the whole world responded and forced its removal).

But the other side of 'fairness' is *the initial condition*. Currently, developing countries have higher tariffs than do developed countries.[9] The United States might claim that it is only fair that developing countries cut their tariffs proportionately; this would entail a greater amount of tariff reduction by the developing countries—and accordingly the adjustment costs to the developing countries might be greater.[10] But the developing countries also point out that *at the very least* the principle of progressivity should rule out adverse discrimination against developing countries. Yet, currently, the developed countries impose higher tariffs against the developing countries than they do against the developed countries, even taking into account the so-called 'preferences'.

Balancing these concerns are those dealing with historical inequities. If a country's relative weakness in part is due to a colonial heritage, or more pertinently, to earlier unfair trade agreements (e.g. that resulting from the Opium War in the nineteenth century in China), to what extent does fairness and equity demand that current

---

[9] For manufactured goods average tariff rates are 1.5% for developed countries and 11.5% for developing countries. For agriculture, average tariff rates are 15.6% for developed countries and 20.1% for developing countries (Hertel and Martin 2000).   [10] See Ch. 8 for a discussion of adjustment costs.

agreements not reflect these past injustices? Trade negotiators from the North would like to pretend that such inequities never occurred. Those from the South might argue that one cannot separate events today from the historical context.

The nature of trade agreements is, of course, that not every provision in the agreement is viewed to be 'fair'. Some are intended to give more to one party, others to another party; it is the package as a whole which should be viewed as fair. But each trade agreement is forward-looking: there are implicit and explicit understandings about the direction of future agreements.

Fairness between foreign and domestic producers

While most of the discussion of this chapter concerns 'fairness' *among countries*, there is a related issue: fairness between domestic and foreign producers. One of the purposes of trade liberalization is to ensure that foreign producers are treated 'fairly'. But again there are questions: 'What does fairness mean in this context?' Foreign producers and domestic producers are often inherently in different situations. In the case of a developing country, the foreign producer may have greater access to capital. He almost surely has greater access to international technology. Much of the debate about protection concerns 'leveling the playing field', correcting these initial inequities.

Most of the economics literature eschews the 'fairness' vocabulary in favor of efficiency language. Protecting domestic firms is *inefficient*: the country would be better off if it did not. But for reasons hinted at in the previous section, these arguments are contentious. There may be important learning benefits from protection. And while economists have typically argued in favor of open subsidies and/or government loan programs rather than the hidden subsidies protection provides, direct subsidies may, for a variety of reasons, be difficult or impossible to implement. As we discussed in Chapter 2, in a second-best world, some protection may be efficient.[11]

---

[11] For a historical argument, see Chang (2002). More recent theoretical analysis includes that of Dasgupta and Stiglitz (1985).

Thus, there is contentiousness in both the efficiency and the fairness arguments. But what cannot be justified in terms of either are developed country non-tariff barriers, such as dumping, which treat developing country producers disadvantageously relative to their own, subjecting them, for instance, to a far higher standard for what amounts to predatory behavior than that to which they subject their own firms.[12]

By the same token, it is hard to justify demanding developing countries to provide *foreign* firms with *greater* protections than provided to domestic firms. While there is some debate about the validity, or abuse, of the infant industry argument, there is no argument for protection of the 'grown-up' industry'.

So too, America has found it desirable to impose lending requirements on its banks to ensure that they provide capital to underserved communities, through the Community Reinvestment Act. Such measures recognize that there is a role for government in encouraging particular sectors of the economy. It seems *unfair* (and inefficient) to preclude developing countries from undertaking similar measures.

Other problems in the interpretation of fairness

One of the most difficult issues is how to treat policy failures within each of the countries. Suppose that it is true (as asserted earlier) that the Uruguay Round in fact differentially benefited the United States. But suppose the imbalance could have been reduced if only the developing countries *reformed* their economies. They might, for instance, have been able to benefit more from the reduction in tariffs on manufacturing if only they had invested more in infrastructure, so that they could have attracted more manufacturing.

By the same token, to what extent should the international trading regime be *blamed* for inequities which arise, in part, because of how other parts of the international system operate? Suppose, for instance, that a 'fair' trade negotiation occurs within the WTO, but

---

[12] For instance, the US anti-trust laws impose a very high standard for predatory pricing, much higher than is employed in the US fair trade laws which pertain to the actions of foreign firms. Indeed, it has been argued that using the US domestic standard, few foreign firms would ever be found guilty of dumping, but using the dumping standard, most American firms could be found guilty.

that after the trade negotiations are over, the developing country has to turn to the IMF for assistance, and that the IMF imposes further trade liberalization as a condition for assistance. Viewing the two negotiations together, as a package, clearly the developing country may have given far more than it got *within the trade package*, but of course it got, in addition, some foreign assistance. (Admittedly, in the case of many of the bail-outs, the primary beneficiary of the bail-outs may be banks in the more advanced industrial countries.) But even apart from these demands that are put on developing countries, the United States makes demands on other countries (Section 301 and Super 301 actions[13]), to which they often feel compelled to accede.

Similarly, when international institutions encourage tax policies which have the effect of distorting production towards the informal sector, it implies, as noted above, that the West's subsidies of agriculture have a greater adverse effect on the developing countries than they otherwise would have had. In talking about the inequities of the trade regime, should we assess its fairness coming on top of distortions imposed or encouraged by the North, or in terms of what the incidence would have been had a more neutral tax system been imposed? Should we view the two actions together, assessing the incidence of the two policies in conjunction, or should we only assess the fairness of the trading regime itself?

By the same token, when countervailing duties are imposed against a developing country which has 'subsidized' interest payments, by bringing them down from the usurious levels insisted upon by the IMF to levels still slightly higher than in international capital markets, is this unfair? Should the government only be viewed as undoing a distortion? The problems are exacerbated by demands (included in the recent bilateral trade agreements between the United States and Chile and the US and Singapore) for capital market liberalization. Capital market liberalization increases economic volatility,[14] and the increased economic volatility increases the risk premium that investors demand,[15] effectively

---

[13] Super 301 authority—which expired in 1997 but was reinstituted in January 1999—enables the US Trade Representative to identify the most significant unfair trade practices facing US exports and to focus US resources on eliminating those practices.

[14] See, for instance, Prasad, Rogoff, Wei *et al.* (2003) and Stiglitz (1999a, 2001, 2004).

[15] See Stiglitz (2003).

increasing the interest rate charged. It seems unfair to force upon the developing countries provisions which effectively increase the interest rate they have to pay, and then, when the government tries to undo the consequences, to slap a countervailing duty upon them.

In the South, there is a propensity to see such actions as coordinated, pushed by special interests in the North. While they may see more coordination than actually occurs, the impacts are often closely akin to what they would be if they were coordinated. The high interest rates, tax policies, and trade liberalization policies demanded by the IMF do exacerbate the adverse effects on developing countries of whatever trade liberalization measures they agree to within the WTO. The two cannot be seen in isolation. This provides the basis of one of the important recommendations that we make below.

With such disparate views of fairness, it is no wonder that the South may feel that a trade agreement proposal is grossly unfair, and yet the North might feel no pangs of conscience. Some might conclude that, as a result, we should simply drop the criterion of equity as a desideratum of a Development Round agreement. That would be a mistake. In a democracy, any trade agreement must be freely entered into, and the citizens of the country must be persuaded that the agreement is essentially *fair*. Moreover, there are several widely accepted philosophical frameworks—in particular that of John Rawls[16]—which at least provide some guidance for thinking about whether any agreement is fair.

Any agreement should be fairly arrived at

Procedural fairness becomes an important complement to the kind of fairness discussed in the preceding section (where fairness is judged in terms of the outcomes) when there is some ambiguity

---

[16] See Rawls (1971). Rawls's method generates basic principles of justice that provide some guidance in evaluating the fairness of particular trade agreement proposals—in particular, his 'Difference Principle', that 'Social and economic equalities are to be arranged so that they are . . . to the greatest benefit of the least advantaged' (Rawls 1971: 83). For alternative frameworks (which in the current context would arrive at quite similar views) see Sen (1999).

about what should be meant by 'outcome fairness'. Procedural fairness focuses on the openness and transparency of the negotiation process, and the manner in which the discussions are conducted. It is hoped that the outcomes that are achieved through fair procedures are more likely to be fair, though, of course, even an open and transparent bargaining process is likely to result in 'unfair' outcomes when the parties to the bargaining are of markedly different strengths. But it should be clear: a fair agreement is unlikely to result from an unfair process.[17]

Transparency is essential because it enables more voices to be heard in the negotiating process and limits abuses by the powerful. This is particularly important for developing countries, because of the limited size of their negotiating teams. Of particular concern is the lack of transparency of the negotiations. In the Uruguay Round the developed countries negotiated via the infamous 'green room' methods, in which only a few chosen countries from the developing world engaged directly in negotiations with the United States and Europe. The 'Green Room' process has now been formally abandoned but the ongoing negotiating practice continues to place the developing countries in a disadvantageous position because of the complexity of the negotiations and their limited staffs.[18] Procedural fairness needs to deal with the asymmetry of power and the asymmetry of information among WTO members. While the effects of power disparities are difficult to reduce, informational disadvantage can be remedied.[19]

The WTO's Dispute Settlement System also lacks procedural fairness in some important ways. In trade disputes, the system favors developed countries both *de jure* and *de facto*. For example, the costs

---

[17] There is now a large literature which establishes that setting the agenda may have a large effect on the outcome; hence having a voice in the setting of the agenda is essential. The agenda in previous trade negotiations has been unbalanced. This is evidenced by the fact that issues of benefit to the developed countries have been at the center of the discussion. Issues like liberalization of unskilled labor-intensive services have been off the agenda, while liberalization of skilled labor-intensive services have been on it. Since the bargaining process affects the outcome of the bargain, the WTO needs to ensure that the process has clear rules that ensure the effective participation of the weakest players.

[18] See for example the open letter, dated 6 Nov. 1999, sent by 11 developing countries to the WTO chairman Ambassador Ali Mchumo of Tanzania, expressing their concern over the lack of transparency in the WTO green room process.

[19] Both increased transparency and the provision of (impact assessment) information, discussed in Ch. 5, reduce information asymmetries.

to a developing country to attack a claim of intellectual property by a Western company in a case involving bio-piracy may be very high. In practice the developing country is at a disadvantageous position in any process entailing resort to complicated and expensive legal proceedings. Thus the WTO dispute system favors rich countries with the resources to use it effectively for their own interests. The EC, Japan and the US were complainants in almost half (143 of 305) of all bilateral disputes in the WTO Dispute Settlement system between 1995 and 2002. By contrast the 49 members classified by the UN as Less Developed Countries did not bring a single challenge in that period.[20]

To be sure, current arrangements were introduced because of dissatisfaction with the previous GATT regime. The dispute settlement system operated under the GATT was rarely used by developing country members, and thus the new system has been reformed in an attempt to increase participation from all members. In some areas there has been significant progress. The DSU has reduced the length of proceedings, leading to more timely 'trials', introduced automatic adoption of reports to remove the potential for a recalcitrant defendant to block a ruling, and increased the consistency of rulings through review by the appellate body. Taken together, it has been predicted that these reforms would create a system in which, unlike in the GATT years, 'right perseveres over might' (Lacarte-Muro and Gappah 2000), and which would therefore entice developing countries to bring more cases to the WTO than they did to the GATT.

However, the increasingly legalistic process has raised the transaction costs of settling disputes (Busch and Reinhardt 2003)[21]—one factor that has contributed to the ongoing under-representation of LDCs in the process. With the exception of Nigeria, which participated as a third party in the United States–Shrimp dispute, and the Afro-Caribbean Pacific (ACP) countries, which participated as third

---

[20] See Horn and Mavroidis (2003).

[21] Welcome reforms have been implemented to prevent powerful defendants from delaying cases. In particular, procedures and terms of reference have been standardized. One unforeseen consequence of this is that it has increased the importance of the quality of the legal preparation before the case is heard and, in some cases, increased the cost of initiating a case.

parties in the European Communities–Bananas dispute, no African country and no other least developed country has participated in proceedings before the appellate body to date. This imbalance in participation is also reflected in the outcomes of disputes. Whereas developing country complainants have increased their success rate under the WTO rules (the proportion of times defendants fully liberalize disputed measures)—up from 36 per cent of cases under the GATT to 50 per cent under the WTO—developed countries have been even more successful—their success rate rose by 40 per cent under the GATT to 74 per cent under the new regime (Busch and Reinhardt 2003).[22]

The low participation rates of developing countries and the imbalanced outcomes are partly a consequence of the asymmetry of the final punishment mechanism. The final punishment mechanism is triggered if the defending country continues to fail to comply with a ruling after a 'reasonable period of time' for implementation.[23] In this event the complaining country may initiate action to seek authorization to 'suspend concessions or other obligations'. In practice this has involved complainant governments imposing 100 per cent *ad valorem* tariffs on a list of products from the target country. However, in the seven episodes where action was, authorized, the complaining government actually performed the act in only three instances and in each case the imposing government included a large country.[24] This

---

[22] Moreover 17 of the 24 WTO-era *developing* country complaints yielding full concessions came from the wealthiest and most dominant developing countries (Argentina, Brazil, Chile, India, South Korea, Mexico, Singapore, and Thailand). See Busch and Reinhardt (2003).   [23] DSU, art. 21.3.

[24] This happened in Bananas, when the United States raised tariffs against the EC, and in Hormones, when the United States and Canada raised tariffs on EC goods. For example, in Bananas, the United States imposed 100% tariffs on the European Communities on a list of products that included, among others, handbags and electrothermic coffee-and tea-makers. The Hormones case concerned an EC ban on imports of beef from cows treated with hormones for growth-promotion purposes (oestradiol 17ß, progesterone and testosterone, trenbolone acetate (TBA), zeranol, and melengestrol acetate). The EC claimed the ban was necessary for food safety; the US and Canada claimed there was no evidence of harm to human health. The WTO Panel found that the EC measure violated art. 3 of the Agreement on the Application of Sanitary and Phytosanitary Measures: the EC measure was not based on these standards; it reflected a higher level of protection and was not justified by a risk assessment, as required by art. 3.3. When the EC was unable to implement the panel's findings by the 13 May 1999 deadline, the US and Canada sought the right to retaliate to the amount of US$202m per year and CDN$75m per year. The arbitrators found the appropriate level to be US$116m and CDN$11.3m per year, respectively. The United States raised tariffs against the EC on a list of goods including Roquefort cheese and *foie gras* among others, and Canada's list included cucumbers and gherkins, among others. The four episodes so far where action has been granted but not used are Bananas (Ecuador v. EC), Export Financing for Aircraft (Canada v. Brazil), Foreign Sales Corporations (EC v. US), and Export Credits for Aircraft (Brazil v. Canada).

enforcement mechanism is a powerful weapon for large countries, but a weak one for poor countries.

The policy space should be interpreted conservatively

Defining the policy space appropriate for attention within the WTO is a difficult task. There has been a tendency to expand the WTO's agenda to include all manner of international problems from intellectual property rights to protection for foreign investors. The international community has found that bringing formerly intractable international issues within the ambit of trade provides both a convenient negotiating forum and a ready mechanism for enforcement of agreements. If the only test of inclusion in the agenda is that a policy must affect trade flows, then the boundaries of WTO activity are very hard to define because almost all international problems can be linked to trade flows in some way. In this regard, policy-makers have liberally employed the prefix 'trade-related aspects of' to expand pragmatically the WTO's mandate into a growing number of issues.

However the growth of the WTO's policy space comes at a price. First, developing countries have limited capacity to analyse and negotiate over a large range of issues. Second, the experience of the Singapore Issues suggests that larger agendas burden the negotiations. Third, the expansion creates room for developed countries to use their superior bargaining power in trade negotiations to exploit developing countries over a larger range of issues. For instance, when the agenda was extended to competition policy, the issues relevant to the foreign business interests of developed countries became the main focus of negotiations while insufficient attention was given to key areas of concern for developing countries, such as rules against predation and the development of global anti-trust enforcement. Similarly the focus of intellectual property negotiations has been determined by the pharmaceutical industry in the industrialized world. Almost inevitably, the determination of these issues will reflect the consequences of the exercise of power.

For these reasons a 'principle of conservatism' needs to be introduced to guide the growth of the WTO's mandate. Further issues should only be included in the agenda of a Development Round if they score highly on three criteria: (1) the relevance of the issue to trade flows, (2) its development-friendliness, and (3) the existence of a rationale for collective action.

This third element reflects a general presumption in favor of national sovereignty. There is no reason to force nations to undertake certain actions unless their actions have effects on the trade of others which require collective action to resolve. There are areas in which a trade agreement is absolutely essential. These include an international rule of law (procedures) for dealing with trade disputes and/or agreements to prevent beggar-thy-neighbor trade policies. There are areas in which international agreements would be beneficial in managing cross-border externalities or global public goods.[25] But modern trade agreements have been extended into areas which intrude into national sovereignty with no justification based on the need for collective action and without clearly identified and fairly distributed global benefits.[26] The presumption of consumer sovereignty is based on the premise that society should only interfere with individual choices when those choices have consequences for others, when there is a need for collective action, and the same is true in trade.

---

[25] For a discussion of the concept of global public goods, see Kaul *et al.* (2003). See also Stiglitz (1994, 1995).

[26] Trade agreements might also be useful as a mechanism for governments to overcome domestic political opposition to trade reform.

6

Special Treatment for Developing Countries

There is considerable dissatisfaction with the treatment given by the World Trade Organization to its poorest members. The development of an appropriate framework which maintains the 'rules-based' trading system but differentiates between rich and poor countries is one of the most important issues facing the Doha Round.

WTO members include 32 of the 50 least developed countries (LDCs) recognized by the UN.[1] The economic and social development of these countries, in particular the eradication of extreme poverty, is a major challenge for LDCs themselves, as well as for the international community. Least developed countries are characterized by their exposure to a series of vulnerabilities and constraints, such as limited human capital and productive capacity; weak institutions; geographical handicaps including poor soils, vulnerability to natural disasters, and communicable diseases; poorly diversified industries and underdeveloped markets for many goods and services; limited access to education, health, and other social services; poor infrastructure; and lack of access to information and communication technologies.

---

[1] These are Angola, Bangladesh, Benin, Burkina Faso, Burundi, Cambodia, Central African Republic, Chad, Democratic Republic of the Congo, Djibouti, Gambia, Guinea, Guinea Bissau, Haiti, Lesotho, Madagascar, Malawi, Maldives, Mali, Mauritania, Mozambique, Myanmar, Nepal, Niger, Rwanda, Senegal, Sierra Leone, Solomon Islands, Tanzania, Togo, Uganda, and Zambia. Eight additional LDCs are in the process of accession to the WTO: Bhutan, Cape Verde, Ethiopia, Laos, Samoa, Sudan, Vanuatu, and Yemen. Furthermore, Equatorial Guinea and Sao Tome and Principe are WTO Observers.

The WTO recognizes that the trade policies which maximize welfare in the rich industrialized countries may not be the same as those which do the most to promote development in the poorest countries. The WTO recognizes the particular needs of developing countries[2] via 'special and differential treatment' (SDT)—special provisions which give developing countries special rights and which allow developed countries to treat developing countries more favorably than other WTO members. Common SDT provisions include support to help developing countries pay the costs of effectively participating in the WTO, as well as aid to increase their capacity to take advantage of new trading opportunities; exemptions from agreements, which allow developing countries to choose whether or not to implement agreements requiring regulatory or administrative reform; and provisions allowing developed countries to give preferential market access to developing country members. In market access, SDT gives developing countries greater freedom to use industrial policies, including subsidies, and more latitude in tariff reduction (either higher bound tariffs or longer transition periods).

SDT is controversial. Proponents argue that the special circumstances of developing countries demand that they be given the freedom to pursue industrial development through trade policies, even if these policies involve some negative externalities for other countries. Opponents express hostility to SDT because they see it as an abrogation of the principle of reciprocity, and others believe that SDT leads to protectionist trade policies which are inefficient tools for industrial development and are likely to create vested interests and misallocate resources. They argue that by granting exemptions to WTO disciplines, members are doing developing countries a disservice by encouraging protection, prolonging their exclusion from the global economy, and denying access to the benefits of openness.[3] The neo-liberal view, embodied in the

---

[2] There are no WTO definitions of 'developed' or 'developing' countries. Developing countries in the WTO are designated on the basis of self-selection, although this is not necessarily automatically accepted in all WTO bodies.

[3] It should be noted that the benefits of openness are controversial. In particular, the relationship between openness and growth is contentious. Rodriguez and Rodrik (2000) analyse the seminal paper by Sachs and Warner (1995) which linked openness and growth. Rodriguez and Rodrik disaggregate the Sachs–Warner openness measure and find that only the component relating to the black-market premium is significant in growth regressions. They conclude that this indicates that macroeconomic stability, rather

Washington Consensus, is that most WTO rules, which commit members to liberalize their trade policies, are good rules and should be followed by poor countries as well as rich ones, i.e. the best strategy for all countries and in all situations is to liberalize. The neo-liberal approach relies on strong theoretical assumptions about the efficiency and completeness of markets which, as we discussed in Chapter 2, are unlikely to hold in developed countries, let alone developing countries.

The alternative view places less confidence in markets and recognizes a stronger role for government in economic development. Markets are certainly powerful forces but where they are imperfect, especially in developing countries, government intervention may be required to correct their failures and make them work efficiently. This view has been greatly influenced by the success of the East Asian Tiger economies,[4] whose reliance on market forces did not preclude an active role for the government, including interventionist policies in trade, FDI, technology transfer, and domestic resource allocation (Lall 1992).

As noted earlier, neo-liberals responded to the East Asian success by arguing that it was due to free trade and other non-interventionist policies. To the extent that East Asian governments had been interventionist, they argued that this was a redundant and unnecessary policy approach that coincided with the liberalization policies which were in fact the true cause of their success (see World Bank 1993a and Noland and Pack 2003). Given that the issue remains undecided, developing countries themselves should decide whether they wish to use industrial policies which, it should be pointed out, almost all of the successful industrialized countries used at similar stages of development (Chang 2002).

At the same time, it is increasingly recognized that laissez-faire policies may not be optimal in developing countries which suffer from various types of market failures (see Chapter 2). Many developed countries currently have comparative advantage in agricultural commodities and natural resources. However, reliance on production

than trade protection, matters for growth. Further analysis (e.g. Warner 2002) has revisited the issue, and the relationship remains controversial.

[4] See e.g. Stiglitz (1996).

of these goods can be problematic because historically, their prices have been extremely volatile. In addition the production of these goods may not embody the management and organizational skills necessary to build an industrial economy. If this is true, then by concentrating production in the goods in which they have static comparative advantage, developing countries may be preventing themselves from establishing the foundations of an industrial economy.

However, the existence of justifications for government action does not necessarily suggest that trade policy is the appropriate instrument for intervention. Hoekman, Michalopoulos, and Winters (2003) argue that the use of traditional trade policy instruments are likely to impose more costs than benefits on developing countries. These authors are right to claim that the case for various trade instruments of industrial policy is controversial, but it is wrong to conclude that there is a strong case for restricting the policy options of developing countries on these grounds. It requires us to believe that developed countries in the WTO are better informed (and persistently so) than developing countries. In reality SDT provides developing countries with additional freedom to use a range of industrial policies, which are in some cases used efficiently, and in some cases are not. However, the *ex post* identification of failed industrial policy experiments is not necessarily evidence of bad policies. Rodrik (2004) points out that in the case of subsidies for entrepreneurship, even under the optimal incentive program, some of the investments will turn out to be failures. Failed industrial policy experiments are examples of the 'self-discovery' of comparative advantage. The costs associated with these failures may be more than offset by the gains from the successes. All that is required to justify industrial policies is that their expected value be positive. Indeed if there are too few failures, this might be a sign that the industrial policy is not aggressive enough.

In addition there is a difference between openness and liberalization. Developing countries with large populations working in protected industries must be mindful of the costs of adjustment. Trade liberalization creates adjustment costs as resources are moved from one sector to another in the process of reform. When tariffs are reduced, import-competing firms may reduce their production in the face of new competition, causing some of their workers and capital to lie idle for a period. The firm's laid-off workers will incur costs while searching for new jobs and may need to invest in retraining. Governments will be called upon to provide assistance to the unemployed while also incurring costs associated with implementing the new systems to manage reform. In developing countries which are already characterized by high unemployment, weak insurance markets, and low levels of social protection, adjustment costs may have a particularly severe effect.

Discomfort with the consequences of the neo-liberal view of special and differential treatment led the Zedillo Commission, in its 'Report of the High-Level Panel on Financing for Development' to the Monterrey Conference on Financing for Development in 2002, to assert the following on infant industry protection: 'However misguided the old model of blanket protection intended to nurture import substitute industries, it would be a mistake to go to the other extreme and deny developing countries the opportunity of actively nurturing the development of an industrial sector' (Zedillo 2001).

Similar support for SDT was expressed in article 44 of the Doha Declaration, which affirmed 'that provisions for special and differential treatment are an integral part of the WTO Agreements'. The article provides that special and differential treatment provisions shall be reviewed in the Doha Round 'with a view to strengthening them and making them more precise, effective and operational'.

SDT in the Doha Round: Exemption, not exclusion

At the WTO's Fifth Ministerial Conference in Cancún, in September 2003, the negotiations collapsed and the meeting ended in failure. One reason for the deadlock was that developing countries were worried about being forced into accepting obligations which would hurt their industries or impose large implementation costs on them. Many developing countries had felt disadvantaged by the last round, the Uruguay Round, and they came to the view that no agreement was better than another bad agreement. After Cancún, developing countries stepped up their demands for special and differential treatment as a prerequisite for progress in the round. For wary developing countries, SDT was an insurance policy—it would give them the flexibility to opt out of any agreement which proved to be too onerous for them. A group of developing countries, the G33,[5] united behind the issue of SDT. As the round began to regain momentum in 2004, they renewed their calls for SDT to be given a higher degree of clarity and specificity. In particular they wanted the right to identify special products of interest to developing countries on which there would be no tariff reduction commitment and no new tariff-rate quota commitments.[6]

In May of 2004, EU Trade Commissioner Pascal Lamy attempted to placate the developing countries and salvage the round by offering a significant compromise on SDT. In a letter to trade ministers he wrote: 'on agriculture and [industrial goods], we propose that the least developed countries and other weak or vulnerable developing countries ... should not have to open their markets beyond their existing commitments, and should be able to benefit from increased market access offered by both developed and advanced developing countries. So in effect these countries should have the "Round for Free".'[7]

The danger of the blanket approach to SDT embodied in the 'Round for Free' approach is that it may act as a disincentive to the participation of developing countries in the Round. If the least developed countries are required to do nothing, they may be pushed to the periphery of the negotiations. It would be unfortunate if the 'Round for Free' rhetoric came to imply an agreement between developed

---

[5] For a list of the membership of the G33, see the Glossary.

[6] See the statement issued by Indonesia on behalf of the G33 member countries in Geneva, 28 July 2004.

[7] See the letter of 9 May 2004 by Pascal Lamy and EU Agriculture Commissioner Franz Fischler. After attracting criticism from other developed countries for his 'capitulation', Lamy quickly backed away from this grandiose offer. In June he noted that the 'Round for Free' slogan was perhaps a misnomer since developing countries would be required to make commitments on binding their tariffs in some areas, and participating in negotiations in trade facilitation. He coined the somewhat less catchy slogan 'Round at a Modest Price'. See his speech 'Where Next for EU Trade Policy?' to the Deutsche Gesellschaft für Auswärtige Politik, Berlin, 11 June 2004.

countries with only a peripheral role for developing countries. Then the Development Round would bear a striking resemblance to the early rounds of trade negotiations, in which the GATT operated as a club for the advancement of rich-country interests. In those early rounds, developing countries were burdened with few obligations, but they had only a weak voice in the negotiations and little power with which to assert their interests. Developing countries benefited from industrial country liberalization, thanks to the Most Favored Nation (MFN) principle,[8] but their peripheral role meant that they could exert little pressure on the *way* that industrialized countries liberalized. Thus liberalization of goods of interest to developed countries proceeded swiftly, but goods of interest to developing countries, especially labor-intensive goods, lagged behind and developing countries ultimately suffered. Some developed countries were happy with this system because the small poor countries did not have sufficiently attractive markets to bother with: the benefits of market access were smaller than the costs of liberalizing their own labor-intensive import-competing sectors. The 'Round for Free' approach smacks of the same two-tiered system which exempted developing countries from commitments but excluded them from the negotiations. However, as Keck and Low (2004) argue, 'where new policy areas or new rules are under negotiation, or consideration for negotiation, the best interests of developing countries would be served through engagement with respect to the substance of core proposals'. Another problem with the 'Round for Free' approach which concerns many negotiators from developed countries, is that it allows the poorest countries to retain a veto over a Round in which they are contributing very little. This creates a 'hold-up' problem which does not benefit their interests in the system—it merely encourages the OECD nations to liberalize further outside of the WTO system, which takes us back to the problems of previous rounds.

Moreover the 'Round for Free' approach may result in forgone opportunity costs on developing countries by robbing them of the

---

[8] MFN is enshrined in the first article of the GATT, which governs trade in goods. MFN is also a priority in the GATS (art. 2) and the TRIPS Agreement (art. 4), although in each agreement the principle is handled slightly differently.

benefits of liberalization of South–South trade. If developing countries suffer from barriers in other developing countries, then proposals in the Doha Round to allow minimal liberalization by poor countries could backfire. Developing countries now account for around one-third of global trade. Intra-developing country, or South–South, merchandise trade has grown at twice the pace of world trade over the past decade. Yet barriers to South–South trade are high. For example, Latin American exporters of manufactures face average tariffs in the rest of Latin America that are seven times as high as tariffs in industrialized countries (ESCWA 2004). East Asian exporters face tariffs in other East Asian countries that are 60 per cent higher than in rich nations. Indeed, developing countries stand to benefit a great deal from improved market access to other developing countries. The World Bank (2002b) estimates that developing countries stand to realize welfare gains of more than US$30 billion per year if other developing countries eliminate tariffs on industrial goods and a further US$30 billion if they remove their barriers to agricultural trade.

A Doha Round Market Access Proposal

In this section we describe a framework—the Doha Market Access Proposal (MAP)—which maintains the 'rules-based' trading system, but differentiates between rich and poor countries.[9]

The challenge is to design special and differential treatment which gives developing countries flexibility to deal with their development problems and minimizes adjustment and implementation costs, without marginalizing their participation in the global trading system or forgoing the gains from South–South liberalization. To achieve this, all WTO members could commit themselves to providing free market access in all goods to all developing countries poorer and smaller than themselves. Thus all developing countries could expect free access to all markets with (1) a larger GDP and

[9] This proposal is based on Charlton (2005).

(2) a larger GDP per capita. This special and differential treatment provision would bind developing and developed countries alike. For example, a middle-income country like Egypt, with GDP per capita of US\$1,390 and total GDP of US\$82 billion, would receive free market access to countries like the United States, but would be required to give free market access to a country like Uganda (GDP per capita of US\$240 and GDP of US\$6.2 billion).

The principle underlying this proposal is that all countries should participate in an enforceable system of preferential market access in which rights and obligations are distributed progressively according to objective criteria. The proposal presented in this section represents one straightforward means of implementing this principle. Additional provisions for specific sectors, alternative dimensions to differentiate between countries, implementation periods, and various other complexities that would undoubtedly be part of any applied version of this proposal are left out of the exposition in this section.

Advantages

This proposal has several advantages over alternative schemes:

1. *It involves significant liberalization.* Figure 6.1 plots the GDP and GDP per capita of WTO members. The dotted lines illustrate the implications of the proposal for Egypt, a country in the middle of the distribution in both size and wealth. MAP would require Egypt, after a negotiated implementation period, to provide free market access to more than fifty developing countries to its south-west in Figure 6.1 (with total market size of US\$500 billion). In return it would receive free market access to more than twenty developed and upper-middle-income countries to its north-east in the figure (with a total market size of US\$28 trillion).[10]

As with existing preferential schemes, the effect of MAP would to some extent be limited by rules of origin. It is beyond the scope of

---

[10] In this calculation the EC is treated as one member; this makes little difference to the market size numbers.

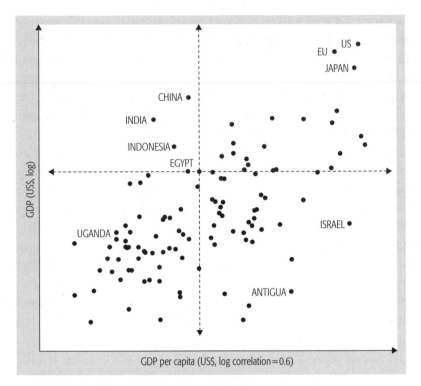

Figure 6.1. **WTO members' GDP and GDP per capita**

this discussion to describe options for rules of origin that might be required to implement MAP, but it is worth noting that MAP would significantly reduce the distortionary effect of rules of origin on LDCs' trade compared to current SDT approaches, since many of the middle-income countries from which LDCs might import intermediate inputs would also receive preferential access under MAP to some of the rich countries to which the final goods are exported. Thus, while not eliminating the problem of rules of origin in SDT, MAP would reduce its effect in practice compared to the status quo.

2. *In particular, it involves significant South–South liberalization.* Another advantage of MAP is that it takes South–South liberalization seriously. Many existing types of SDT (and several proposed changes) do little to promote South–South trade, the liberalization of which, we have noted, could bring large gains to developing

countries. Indeed most Doha Round estimates indicate that the scope for welfare gains for developing countries is larger from the liberalisation by other developing countries than from liberalisation by developed countries (Francois, van Meijl, and van Tongeren 2004).

South–South liberalization has progressed slowly. Attempts at preferential market access agreements have been made outside the WTO under the auspices of the Global System of Trade Preferences among Developing Countries (GSTP).[11] Unfortunately, the GSTP is based on reciprocity—one reason for the low participation of least developed countries among its members—and it has struggled to make significant progress.[12] Bilateral and regional free trade agreements (FTAs) between developing countries are increasing in number, but it should not be assumed that South–South FTAs are unequivocally good for development, since they discriminate against third-party developing countries and the margin of discrimination is higher than is the case in North–North FTAs because developing country MFN tariffs tend to be higher. Thus, there may be a strong case for introducing a development dimension into South–South agreements. There are schemes being considered by some larger developing countries including India, China, and Brazil which would give special access to the least developed countries. While additional market access would be welcome, these schemes, like the existing GSTP schemes operated by the advanced industrial countries, would be a patchwork of discretionary and conditional promises rather than clear legal rights enforceable within the WTO.

Within the WTO, developing countries have often been urged to reduce their MFN tariffs on the grounds that this would lead to an increase in South–South trade. MAP recognizes that, for this purpose, liberalization need not occur on an MFN basis.

3. *Obligations are distributed progressively*. MAP is progressive in the sense that it requires significant South–South liberalization from middle-income countries and very little from the poorest and most vulnerable countries. It requires the most liberalization from

---

[11] The GSTP, established in 1988 and promoted by UNCTAD, provides trade preferences to developing countries without extending them to developed countries.

[12] The two previous GSTP rounds, in the past two decades, were not as successful as expected, due to the economic situation of the poorest developing countries and the poor negotiating capacity of member states.

the countries in the north-east of Figure 6.1 (in particular the Quad countries—Canada, the EU, Japan, the US) and less of those in the south-west of the figure (mostly African LDCs). Under this scheme, all but the very poorest countries do *not* get the 'Round for Free', since all countries accept the obligation to provide market access to other WTO members smaller and poorer than themselves. In return the developing countries receive considerably more market access, under well-defined commitments, than under existing preferential schemes, which are discretionary schemes operated by industrialized countries that are not subject to detailed WTO regulation governing their implementation.

All developing country WTO members benefit from the scheme.[13] Even the largest and richest developing countries receive free access to markets, whose total size is more than seven times the size of the markets to which they must give free access. The median ratio of market access rights to obligations under MAP is 303 : 1, i.e. the median developing country receives access to markets 303 times the size of the markets to which it must *give* free access. Alternatively, measured by imports, the median developing country receives free market access to countries whose total imports are 113 times the size of the imports of the countries to which it is required to give access.

4. *Countries can manage major import threats.* The proposal imposes no extra obligation on developing countries to open their markets to larger or more developed economies. This gives developing countries the *option* to provide their key industries with some protection from imports from economies with cost advantages derived from either the scale of their economies (e.g. larger countries, particularly China) or technological advantages (more developed countries). The prevalence of import barriers in some sectors indicates that developing countries wish to protect particular industries from import competition. This protection may form part of an industrial strategy based on 'infant industry' protection,[14] but is more likely to originate in a desire to avoid adjustment costs, which

---

[13] For purposes here, developing countries are defined as those that had a GDP per capita below US$10,000 in 2003.

[14] See the discussion of chapter 2 for the controversy over the impact of such protection.

could be particularly severe in developing countries characterized by high unemployment, weak risk markets, and low levels of social insurance.

As Hoekman *et al.* (2003) point out, protectionism can be self-defeating for developing countries in a world where multinational corporations have made production increasingly fragmented internationally. For many developing countries, 'the only option to reach the minimum scale required for sustained growth in output is integration with the rest of the world' (Keck and Low 2004).

This proposal facilitates integration by providing all developing countries with significantly increased market access to larger and richer markets, while providing the option of protection from imports from countries which are at later stages of development or have scale advantages.

5. *It is consistent with other MFN liberalization schemes*. It is important to point out that this proposal is not opposed to openness. It does not involve any increases in existing MFN rates. Each country would continue to apply MFN rates uniformly to larger and more developed countries.

In addition, this proposal is squarely in the realm of SDT. There is still a role for the WTO to negotiate MFN tariffs, i.e. it complements other proposed modalities for MFN tariff reduction, rather than replacing them.

One concern with the proposal is that it may affect the bargaining positions of developing countries in future rounds. One of the unfortunate side-effects of existing preferential schemes is that they create an inbuilt incentive for developing countries to block MFN liberalization which would erode their preference margins. But this problem is much less severe for MAP than for existing preference schemes because MAP is far less distortionary: large rich countries do not give LDCs preferences that they do not also give to middle-income countries. Thus MFN liberalization by developed countries does not cause LDCs to lose out relative to middle-income countries.

6. *It transforms discretionary preferential schemes into well-defined obligations within the WTO*. One of the main advantages of

this proposal over existing types of SDT is that it delivers clearly defined and legally binding rights to developing countries in a way that existing preferences do not. Many of these existing preference schemes were originally spawned by part IV of the GATT, which includes provisions on preferential treatment for developing countries. This exception was further expanded in 1979 in the decision which has come to be known as 'the Enabling Clause'. This consolidated the concept of 'differential and more favourable treatment' for developing countries as well as the principle of non-reciprocity in trade negotiations.[15]

However, the problem with this (potentially) wide-ranging clause is that it has never placed any formal obligations on developed countries. Instead, piecemeal preferential deals have been established which cover a limited range of goods from a limited group of countries. These preferences, the most important of which are offered by the Quad countries, often divert trade from other poor countries.

Another problem with preferential schemes is their uncertainty. Keck and Low (2004) argue that SDT should enshrine 'legal rights and obligations', whereas existing preferences have become merely 'legally unenforceable statements of intent or best-endeavour undertakings'. Preferences are not binding on the countries which grant them, and can be altered to exclude certain products or withdrawn entirely at the discretion of the preference provider. For example, in 1992 the US withdrew US$60 million worth of pharmaceutical imports from their preference scheme because the US Trade Representative determined that India had weak patent protection which adversely affected US companies.

Without binding obligations, preference providers have faced pressure from their own import-competing domestic lobbies to minimize the scope of their preferential schemes. As the Sutherland report notes, it is 'grantor, rather than grantee, country interests [which] have determined the product coverage and the preference margins in GSP schemes' (Sutherland 2005).

---

[15] The most significant provision of the Enabling Clause is that which enables members to accord differential and more favorable treatment to developing countries as a departure from the MFN Clause. It stipulates that 'contracting parties may accord differential and more favourable treatment to developing countries, without according such treatment to other contracting parties'.

7. *It balances simplicity against the need to differentiate.* The idea that SDT should be provided to countries based on objective access criteria has been previously addressed by Stevens (2002). Stevens's proposal suggests that a new SDT regime involve 'greater differentiation of treatment between WTO members which, in turn, implies the establishment of objective criteria on which to determine the differentiation'. For example, he suggests that access to some types of SDT in agriculture should be based on measurable criteria relating to food security, e.g. countries could qualify for special treatment if they have a per capita calorie intake of less than a certain level (indicating vulnerability to food insecurity) and a high share of agriculture in GDP (indicating the importance of agriculture in livelihoods) and a high share of food imports to GDP (indicating import dependency). Stevens's approach involves setting objective criteria on an agreement-by-agreement basis. Thus, special and differential treatment would be available to countries which met objective preconditions indicating their need for exception and/or assistance. The appeal of this approach is that it closely matches the needs of specific countries to special treatment in different provisions. In addition, it provides more certainty to developing countries since, once the conditions are predetermined, eligibility would be automatic rather than at the discretion of other WTO members.

The disadvantage of this approach is that it would add to the complexity of trade negotiations and greatly increase transactions costs. SDT measures are already overly complicated in many areas. Hudec (1987) refers to preferences as systems of 'refined complexity', determined by an 'orgy of fine-tuning'. The process of tailoring objective criteria for SDT in each agreement requires countries to agree on measurable criteria and on eligibility cut-offs. As Stevens (2002) himself notes, 'the whole process is likely to be fraught with political difficulty'. It is likely that neither the international consensus on these issues nor the necessary negotiating capacity currently exists to operate such an ambitious and resource-intensive SDT system.

By contrast, MAP is simple to negotiate. It would entirely do away with the whole 'spaghetti bowl' of GSP preferences (although not FTA preferences) and it would save the EU the bother of negotiating the market access part of the economic partnership agreements with African, Caribbean, and Pacific states.[16]

Moreover, it includes an inbuilt flexibility that removes the need for renegotiation over time. As countries develop and overtake others, they will, after an implementation period, lose some preference rights and accept obligations to poorer countries. Alternatively, the scheme could be designed to include a 'one-way' provision so that free trade would monotonically increase in a dynamic world where rankings change.

Concluding remarks

Developing countries have been understandably reluctant to commit themselves to large reductions in their tariff levels. They are concerned that open borders will lead to a flood of cheap imports from more efficient producers, which could destroy their fledgling industries before they have a chance to develop. Because they are already characterized by high unemployment and weak private and social insurance, many developing countries believe that the adjustment costs from significant MFN tariff reduction are too large to be seriously considered. Consequently developing countries have not offered large reductions in border protection in WTO negotiations. As a result, South–South trade has suffered, and developing countries have little bargaining power in their negotiations with developed countries.

The proposal in this chapter distributes new market access progressively, ensuring that the largest gains accrue to the smallest and poorest countries, and it distributes liberalization obligations progressively, requiring that the largest and richest countries liberalize most. There are many other issues associated with tariff reduction in poor countries, including adjustment costs and declining revenue to governments. These issues, and their implications for the need for

[16] The Cotonou Partnership Agreement between the African, Caribbean, and Pacific (ACP) countries and the European Union, signed in June 2000, mandates the negotiation by 2007 of a series of economic partnership agreements (EPAs) between regional groups of ACP states on the one hand and the EU on the other.

technical and development assistance to poor countries, are not discussed here. The advantage of MAP is that it provides significant liberalization, does not demand reciprocity from poor nations to richer ones, and places simple and well-defined obligations on both rich and poor countries alike.

Special and differential treatment in rules

In the previous chapter we suggested that the WTO's 'policy space' be limited to areas in which there are clear international spillovers or development gains to justify the prioritization of multilateral disciplines over national-policy autonomy. There is now a recognition that many WTO agreements which impose 'behind the border' rules may have gone too far in the direction of restricting the autonomy of developing countries to determine their own industrial policies. The WTO's Agreement on Subsidies prohibits export subsidies for all but least developed countries. The Trade Related Investment Measures (TRIMS) Agreement prohibits the use of a number of investment-performance-related measures that have an effect on trade, including local content and sourcing requirements. Both of these policies were widely used by East Asian economies during their rapid industrialization in the last century. Further restrictions have been imposed by the WTO's TRIPS Agreement, negotiated in the 1986–94 Uruguay Round, which introduced intellectual property rules into the multilateral trading system. The TRIPS Agreement has considerable implications for technological and industrial policy. By strengthening intellectual property rights in developing countries, it is likely to increase the royalty payments demanded by technology holders there, and also to create or reinforce monopolistic positions in small markets. It also restricts reverse engineering and other important methods of imitative innovation, thereby limiting the ability of firms in developing countries to reduce their technological disadvantage.

To prevent further incursions on their policy autonomy, developing countries should demand exemptions from restrictive multilateral rules. This includes proposals by developed countries in the Doha

Round to develop multilateral disciplines for national competition and investment policies. Proponents of an investment agreement would like binding global rules that allow foreign investors the rights to enter countries without any conditions and regulations which do not apply to domestic firms, i.e. to be granted 'national treatment'. This type of international investment agreement is designed to maximize foreign investors' rights while restricting the authority, rights, and policy space of governments. Similarly, the proposals in the Doha Round to introduce multilateral disciplines in competition policy would limit the ability of governments and local firms in developing countries to take actions which are to their advantage.

Certainly the WTO can serve as a device for commitment to good policies, but such commitments should be part of voluntary plurilateral agreements rather than compulsory elements of the WTO's 'single undertaking'. Compulsory commitments should not be made in areas where the purported gains are controversial and where implementation and opportunity costs are high. And where the gains are certain and the costs are low for developing countries (such as allegedly in efforts to liberalize some aspects of foreign direct investment regulations), there is no need for compulsion, because developing countries can be persuaded of the benefits of taking unilateral action. For example, in FDI policy, developing countries have been persuaded of the benefits of more open foreign investment regimes. In 1999 alone, there were 140 changes to FDI regulations worldwide; 131 of these liberalized conditions were for FDI (UNCTAD 2000). Developing countries have seemingly acted responsibly in their own interests, without the need for multilateral compulsion.

There is a growing recognition that the WTO needs to move away from agreements which enshrine compulsory rules under the 'single undertaking'. Hoekman (2004) suggests dividing the WTO's disciplines into 'core' and 'non-core' agreements. Core disciplines would be required to be unconditionally accepted by all countries. Developing countries could be permitted to pass over non-core WTO rules on development grounds.[17]

---

[17] Hoekman (2004) suggests a consultative multilateral mechanism within the WTO to authorize policies which deviate from 'non-core' commitments. This authorization would be based on an assessment of the effectiveness and impact of such policies.

Such differential treatment would facilitate the design of trade agreements which are more likely to promote economic development. A blanket proscription against government subsidies to technology (industrial policies) is likely to have an adverse effect on developing countries and, indeed, it is likely in practice to be unfair: the United States conducts its industrial policy largely through the military, which supports a wide variety of technological developments that eventually have important civilian applications. And it is hard to conceive of a trade agreement that would prohibit the development of such technologies through defense programs. (Even the EU has complained about America's use of defense expenditures as a hidden subsidy for its aerospace industry.)

Thus, each provision of a trade agreement should be assessed for its impact on development, and designed to ensure that development is enhanced, employing where necessary provisions for special and differential treatment. Moreover, the totality of the trade agreement should be assessed to ensure that a fair share of the benefits (the net incidence) accrues to developing countries.

7

Priorities for a Development Round

The natural question to be asked by each developing country as it enters trade negotiations is 'What agreement would make the most difference for us?' There is a corresponding question for the developed countries: 'What is it that we could *give*, which is of most benefit to the developing countries, and which has the least cost (or perhaps even benefit) to us at the same time?'. The developed countries' natural response may be to demand a *quid pro quo*. But such a demand would be to look at the current negotiation outside of its historical context. The developed countries have to date received the lion's share of the benefits from previous trade negotiations. Accordingly, they *ought* to be willing to do more for the developing countries in this round.[1]

With little progress on the issues of concern to developing countries—non-tariff barriers, intellectual property, migration, unskilled intensive services, and agriculture—and new demands in areas of dubious benefit to the developing countries, it has been hard to see how the developing countries can benefit significantly.[2] Actually,

[1] The problem, of course, is that political globalization has not kept pace with economic globalization: issues of international trade agreements are seldom looked at through which the same kind of lens through which we look at domestic legislation. In national economic debates, we do not demand that the poor give up an amount commensurate with what they get. Rather, we talk about social justice and equity.

[2] Anderson (2001) compares the benefits of developed country liberalization on developing countries with the benefits of developing country liberalization on developed countries. As a proportion of GDP in each group the benefits to developing countries of the former exceed the benefits to developed countries from the latter by a factor of 6. Given this imbalance in payoffs it is not surprising that developed countries are in such a strong bargaining position.

in several areas, there is significant scope for gains to the developing countries. In market access what matters is not just the *average* tariff rate,[3] but also the structure of tariffs. Escalating tariffs, where there are higher tariffs on more-processed goods than on those less-processed, inhibit the ability of developing countries to increase their manufacturing capacities, especially in areas which might represent a natural comparative advantage, such as food processing or textiles.

For some goods, particularly skilled labor-intensive industrial goods, the fact is that average developed country tariffs are already much lower than those in developing countries.[4] In these areas, the large reductions in tariffs by developing countries would have put large strains on these same countries. Were they at full employment, a strong argument could be made that they would nonetheless benefit, if they are given enough time and resources to adjust. But the speed of adjustment that is likely to be demanded, and the absence of adequate resources to facilitate the adjustment, mean that developing countries may be significantly worse off.

There is an important asymmetry of power in the negotiations: what developing countries do in opening up their markets to developed countries has a much smaller impact on the developed countries than the converse–what the developed countries do in opening up their markets to the developing world. In short, the developed countries themselves gain from liberalizing their own markets, because they are able to adjust, and the disturbances posed to them by the developing countries are small. The developing countries are in a far more disadvantageous position—they will need assistance in making the required adjustments, and they should be given a longer time within which to adjust.

Accordingly, in this book we propose that:

1. all WTO members commit themselves to providing free market access in all goods to all developing countries poorer and smaller

---

[3] Average tariff rates–when weighted by the amount of trade–may be particularly misleading, since high tariffs lead to little trade, and accordingly such high tariffs may be given little weight in the computation of the average, even though they have a very distortive effect.

[4] Average tariff rates on industrial goods imported into the OECD countries fell from around 40% in 1950 to 1.5% in 1998 (Hertel 2000). In spite of these low average rates, there are tariff peaks, many of which adversely hurt developing countries, so that, provided these are addressed, developing countries *do* have something to gain.

than themselves. Thus all developing countries could expect free access to all markets with (a) a larger GDP and (b) a larger GDP per capita;

2. developed countries commit themselves to the elimination of agricultural subsidies; and

3. the promise of market opening not be undermined by technical provisions like rules of origin.[5]

In short, reciprocity should *not* be the central feature of these negotiations, as they have been in the past.

There is one other aspect of the context in which trade negotiations are currently occurring. What distinguishes developed from less developed countries is not only the extent and nature of market imperfections, but also labor and physical resources. Developing countries are intensive in unskilled labor; their greatest shortage is probably in the ownership of physical capital. Developing countries are disproportionately in the tropics[6] and, currently, are more engaged in the export of *commodities*, including natural resources.[7] Thus, they differ from the developed countries in the products that they export and import, which is why decisions about which goods and services to liberalize, and which should be subject to restrictions on subsidies, can make a great deal of difference for the general equilibrium incidence.

Finally, we should note the dramatic transformation of the global economy. In the nineteenth century, the (now) advanced industrial economies transformed themselves from agriculture into manufacturing. Today only 14 per cent of employment and output in the United States is in manufacturing, and the proportion in Europe is not much higher.[8] Now, they are transforming themselves from manufacturing economies into service and knowledge economies. Meanwhile, the developing world itself is divided into several groups: subsistence agriculture (much of Africa); export agriculture (Brazil and Argentina); and those breaking out of agriculture and becoming increasingly

[5] In the discussion in future chapters we address the concerns that preferential liberalization is inhibited by strict or complicated rules.   [6] See Gallup, Sachs, and Mellinger (1998).

[7] See FAO (2003).

[8] Developed countries' share of world trade in manufactures has fallen from 90% in 1970 to 72% in 2000 (World Bank 2002a).

centered on manufacturing. For the agricultural exporters, of course, the failure to liberalize trade in agriculture and to remove subsidies has been particularly costly.[9]

There is, as a result, a fundamental tension in current trade negotiations. The developed countries want to protect their declining industries and to gain market access for their expanding industries. But their declining industries are declining largely because of competitive pressures from the developing countries. Hence, the sectors that they are most interested in protecting are precisely the sectors that are of the greatest concern to the developing world. It is not as if America is mostly concerned with protecting itself against Europe, or vice versa (though there is some element of that). And the sectors that are declining are, by the same token, those with the lowest-wage workers. Hence protection elicits concerns about equity and social justice *within* the developed countries—but the failure to extend these concerns to developing countries shows a particularly narrow vision which is out of step with economic globalization.

At the same time, by demanding market access for the sectors which are growing, the developed countries hope to catapult the advantage that they already have—the first-mover advantage—into a longer-term advantage. For that very reason, were such a strategy accepted, it would inhibit the development transformation of the poorer countries, making it all the more difficult for them to move from traditional products to become effective competitors with the more developed countries.

The chapters which follow present pro-development priorities that should form the core of the Doha Round agreements. Much of the recent discussion has focused on agriculture, but there is much more to a true Development Round. Primary attention should be given to market access for goods produced by developing countries. There is an urgent need to reduce protection on labor-intensive

---

[9] But note that most of the progress in trade negotiations during the past half century has focused around liberalization of manufacturing (other than textiles)—the goods that are of diminishing importance to the advanced industrial countries but of increasing importance to middle-income developing countries. There is a certain irony: while the United States and Europe may have thought that they were negotiating trade agreements that were of most benefit to themselves, in fact they negotiated a global trading regime that, if it is fairly implemented (and setting the non-tariff barriers aside), is likely in the future to be of most benefit to China and other middle-income developing countries.

manufactures (textiles and food processing), and on unskilled services (maritime and construction services). Priority should also be given to the development of schemes to increase labor mobility—particularly the facilitation of temporary migration for unskilled workers. As tariff barriers have come down, developed countries have increasingly resorted to non-tariff barriers as one remaining protectionist instrument. These need to be circumscribed. The proposals are motivated by empirical analysis of the gains and costs of liberalization. For ease of exposition the analysis of this evidence is presented separately in Appendices 1 and 2 and a summary of some of our conclusions is briefly set forth in Table 7.1.

Table 7.1. Development issues in the Doha Round

Issues	Context for developing Countries	Doha: commitments made and subsequent progress	Agenda for a true Development Round
Labor migration and unskilled labor-intensive services	More important than capital flows, especially for developing countries. Liberalization of services has hitherto focused on skilled intensive services. Migration discussion has focused on the movement of high-skill rather than low-skill workers.	Largely ignored at Doha and little progress since. WTO members are currently submitting proposals regarding both the structure and the contents of the new negotiations—the vast majority of proposals concern the liberalization of skilled labor-intensive services.	Development of provisions for temporary movement of unskilled workers and the facilitation of remittance flows. Priority to the liberalization of unskilled labor-intensive services.
Agriculture	Huge developed-country subsidies and protection. Since Uruguay Round, subsidies increased rather than reduced. Uruguay Round created a distinction between trade-distorting and non-trade-distorting subsidies; allegedly non-trade-distorting subsidies still hurt developing countries.	Clear expectation at Doha that protection would be reduced. Since Doha, EU and US have offered to reduce export subsidies, but little progress in eliminating production subsidies. Preliminary ruling against US cotton subsidies weakens US bargaining position.	Eliminate production as well as export subsidies, focusing first on commodities whose benefits to producers far exceed costs to consumers. Provide assistance to consuming nations. In interim allow countervailing duties.
Industrial goods	Existing tariff structures (including tariff peaks) discriminate against the goods of interest to developing countries. Tariff escalation (higher tariffs on processed and semi-processed goods) restricts industrial diversification in developing countries.	Doha committed nations to reducing tariffs 'in particular on products of export interest to developing countries'. Recommitment to same principles in 2004, but little concrete progress on modalities.	Eliminate all tariffs against least developed countries. Eliminate tariff peaks and tariff escalation. Reduce tariffs on industries where developing countries have natural comparative advantage: labor-intensive goods and agricultural processing.
Non-tariff barriers	As tariffs have been reduced, developed countries have put increasing reliance on non-tariff protectionist measures; implementation	Doha referred to competition issues of interest to developed countries, but made little reference to concerns of developing countries.	Eliminate dumping duties—establish a single fair competition regime for domestic and foreign producers.

	discriminates especially against developing countries. Increasing use by both developed and less developed countries represents threat to liberalized trade regime.	US has used safeguard measures on steel, but rejected by adverse WTO ruling.	Ensure that developing countries can subsidize infant industries and offset high interest rates without countervailing duties.
Development box	Developing countries' attempts to use domestic policies to promote development should not be circumscribed by the WTO.	The Doha Declaration recognized the need for 'Special and Differential' treatment (STD) of developing countries. However, STD as currently envisaged amounts to little more than longer implementation periods and some broader exemptions for the poorest nations.	Developing countries to use measures that are in their development interests even if proscribed for developed countries—particularly actions to protect poor farmers. Ensure food security.
Intellectual property	Access to advanced technology important for development. Lack of access to life-saving drugs, jeopardizing lives. Biopiracy—western companies patenting traditional foods and medicines.	Doha promised a more balanced intellectual property regime, with special attention to health issues. Some progress on compulsory licensing, but problems remain. Little progress on biodiversity and other issues. Bilateral agreements restrict access to generic drugs, showing lack of concern for welfare of developing countries.	Pro-generic-drug policy. Compulsory licensing for any life-saving medicine. Higher novelty standards and more restrictions on scope, especially in relationship to threatened bio-piracy.
Restrictions on tax concessions	Developing countries compete with tax concessions to attract foreign businesses; net beneficiary is international businesses.	Not addressed.	Increased transparency of subsidies to foreign firms. Restriction of tax concessions.
Arms sales and corruption	Have major deleterious effect on development.	Not addressed.	Prohibition of arms sales. Criminalization of bribery; allowing tax deduction only for royalty payments that are 'published'.

Table 7.1. *continued*

Issues	Context for developing Countries	Doha: commitments made and subsequent progress	Agenda for a true Development Round
Dispute resolution and fairer mechanisms for enforcement	Dispute system favors rich countries and is under-utilized by developing countries. Asymmetries in enforcement: trade sanctions by small developing country unlikely to have major effect.	Not on agenda.	Elimination of secret bank accounts. Commitment to repatriate corrupt funds. Multilateral enforcement. Monetization of sanctions (auctioning off right to sanction). Expansion of technical assistance to ensure that developing countries have access to equal protection under the WTO's dispute settlement system.
Extension of unilateral disarmament	Cost to developed countries of opening markets would be small; benefits to developing countries would be large.	Doha recognized principle of special and differential treatment recognized. Europe has already adopted Everything but Arms initiative, although rules of origin limit benefit. US has adopted AGOA for poorest African countries.	Extend to more countries and eliminate restrictions which limit its impact.
Institutional reforms	Bargaining process lacks fairness, disadvantages the poor, and is undemocratic. Impacts on developing countries are never assessed before adoption.	Doha hinted at reforms to processes. Since then there has been slight progress in transparency.	Replacement of 'green room' procedures by 'principle of representativeness'. More openness and transparency. Creation of evaluation/research unit to assess impacts of proposals, as well as bilateral and regional agreements to determine whether they 'create' or 'divert' trade.

8

How to Open up Markets

ᛘ

The general argument in favor of trade liberalization is that it allows the expansion of the size of markets, allowing the global economy to take further advantage of the economies of scale (the argument Adam Smith put forward more than two-hundred years ago), and it enhances global efficiency in production and exchange. Thus trade liberalization must be managed carefully to ensure that developing countries benefit from it and are not left worse off. In this chapter, we discuss the most important market access issues in the Doha Round and we show what must be done to promote development. As noted earlier, the standard argument that trade liberalization necessarily makes all countries better off (though not necessarily all individuals within each country) is predicated on a set of assumptions that is not satisfied in most developing countries: full employment, perfect competition, and perfect capital and risk markets.

Labor mobility and unskilled labor-intensive services

The General Agreement on Trade in Services (GATS) recognizes four modes of service delivery. The temporary movement of natural persons (so called Mode 4 service delivery) has received by far the smallest attention in terms of the volume of scheduled concessions. Yet differences in factor payments across countries provide evidence that factor movements would substantially increase global productivity. If factor payments equal marginal products,[1] then the largest discrepancies are associated with the payments to unskilled labor, then to skilled labor, and lastly to capital. Accordingly, agreements that provide for the mobility of unskilled labor would do most to increase global efficiency.

Yet despite the tremendous development potential of this reform, the limited progress that has been made in this area has been largely associated with the intra-corporate movement of skilled personnel—an issue of interest to developed countries. Thus far Mode 4 has not progressed in a way that allows developing countries to use their comparative advantage in low- and medium-skill labor-intensive services. Nor has enough attention been given to proposals to facilitate remittances—the payments from migrant workers back to their families in developing countries. Governments have a role to play in maximizing both the value of remittances and their impact on development. Efforts to formalize the structure of remittance flow (much of which currently moves through informal channels) could make it easier, safer, and cheaper to transfer funds. For example, governments could ensure that migrants have access to secure and low-cost financial services and could regulate remittance-handling intermediaries to prevent malpractices. As well as increasing the flow of remittances, remittance policies can improve the development impact of remittances at the receiving end. For example, microfinance and micro-enterprise support initiatives have encouraged remittance-receiving clients (especially small businesses) to access credit and savings accounts.[2] Finally, the further development of remittance-backed bonds could help liquidity-constrained

---

[1] They may not, and the disparity between factor payments and the value of marginal products may differ across countries, if the degree of market imperfections differs.

[2] For an example of an initiative in this area see the case of the financial institution PRODEM in Bolivia, which focuses on the promotion of savings and the offer of new financial services to remittance receivers. See UNDP (2003b). A number of best-practice scenarios from Latin America and Asia were presented and documented in the November 2000 ILO conference in Geneva on 'Making the Best of Globalization: Migrant Worker Remittances and Micro-Finance'.

developing countries to use future flows of remittances to raise external finance relatively cheaply.[3]

As well as facilitating the movement of natural persons (Mode 4), there is scope for liberalization of other service industries of importance to developing countries. Services account for, on average, 50 per cent of developing countries' GDP, but developing countries account for only 25 per cent of the world's services exports. While the last decade has seen considerable liberalization of high-skill services, there has been less progress in those unskilled-labor-intensive services of interest to developing countries.

The liberalization of services could yield significant welfare gains to developing countries—indeed a large number of empirical studies suggest that service sector liberalization has the potential to deliver larger gains than agricultural or manufactured goods.[4] The estimates are large because protection levels are high in the service sector, and services make up a large (and growing) share of world trade. Additionally, services are key inputs into the production of almost all goods.

However, the large predicted gains from service sector liberalization have to be weighed against the relative complexity of service sector reform, where the identification and elimination of trade barriers is significantly more difficult than in merchandise trade. In particular, three concerns commonly arise. First, there is a view that only a small fraction of service sector reform is actionable through WTO negotiations. Second, several important elements of the reform agenda (particularly liberalization of restrictions on foreign direct investment within Mode 3 service delivery[5]) are successfully progressing through unilateral policy changes outside the WTO. Third, multilateral commitments within the WTO are seen by several developing countries as a particularly blunt instrument of

---

[3] In 2001, Banco do Brasil issued US$300m worth of bonds through Merrill Lynch using the future yen remittances from Brazilian workers in Japan as collateral. The terms of these bonds were more favorable than those available on sovereign issues (with a BBB+ Standard and Poors rating compared to BB− on Brazil's sovereign foreign currency rating). For a review of securitization of remittance flows see Ketkar and Ratha (2000).

[4] See, for example, Hertel *et al.* (2000), Dee and Hanslow (2000), Brown, Deardorff, and Stern (2001), Francois, van Meijl, and van Tongeren (2003), Verikios and Zhang (2004).

[5] Mode 3 refers to trade in services delivered through foreign commercial presence, particularly foreign subsidiaries of multinational firms.

reform, lacking the flexibility to deal with the country-specific implementation challenges thrown up by liberalization in the service sector. Together these concerns contribute to the continued low priority given to GATS commitments within the overall agenda. This is unfortunate because it undervalues the significant and growing service export interests of developing countries and also because it has drawn attention away from those policy proposals (scattered throughout the agenda) which could facilitate and improve the effectiveness of unilateral reform in developing countries.

Many developing countries have large and growing export interests which could be pursued in the Doha Round. The substantial growth in offshore outsourcing (Modes 1 and 2)[6] has led to high growth rates of exports from developing countries in particular business services[7] and ICT, but also in health, education, and audiovisual services. Barriers to trade in these areas include national authorization, local authentication requirements, and regulatory standards. There is significant scope for liberalization in Mode 1, which lags behind Mode 3 in terms of both the number and scope of commitments. The Uruguay Round left many areas of Mode 1 trade without bound commitments. A large proportion of commitments provided only partial market access (60 per cent in legal services; 78 per cent in voice telephone services; 41 per cent in accounting; see Matoo and Wunsch 2004). In several areas where developing countries have a comparative advantage there is a case for broad formulaic rules in favor of national treatment and increased market access.

At the same time there are other non-market access reforms which could complement service sector reform and increase the benefits available to developing countries. The tourism sector (Mode 2) is one of the most important sources of foreign exchange for many developing countries. While the sector is generally quite liberal in terms of government restrictions,[8] developing countries suffer from rampant anti-competitive activities with the industry (centered in

---

[6] Service delivery through Modes 1 and 2 refers to cross-border supply and consumption abroad respectively.

[7] In India exports of business services grew by 43% between 1995 and 2000 (Matoo and Wunsch 2004).

[8] There has been a high number of commitments in major tourism sectors, in particular hotels and restaurants (123 members). See WTO (1999).

the North) which minimize spillover and multiplier effects. In this and other areas (for example maritime transport), an effective multilateral anti-trust framework could deliver large gains to developing countries and support further unilateral liberalization.

The same is true in Mode 3 liberalization, where the enthusiasm for FDI in the cross-country empirical literature is tempered by negative experiences at the national level. While it is true that the unilateral liberalization of restrictions on foreign investment continues apace without multilateral action, there are nonetheless several opportunities for WTO action which could increase the benefits that developing countries derive from the liberalization of FDI. For example, developing countries' experiences with FDI could be improved by agreements to limit the adverse consequences of competition for investment through fiscal and financial incentives[9] and also by agreements to facilitate anti-trust enforcement actions.

Another problem is that in many cases, the ramifications of service sector reform extend beyond the impacts on trade. Inevitably, then, debates about service sector liberalization devolve into fundamental debates about national economic and social policy. Is it right that the media, for instance, be controlled by a few rich foreign firms, who are able to use their wealth to control the flow of information to the citizenry? A further concern is that many service sector liberalizations might have social consequences for the poor, for example by increasing prices of essential services or by reducing access. Opening up markets has been accompanied at times by a reduction in competition, and an increase in prices;[10] in the case of financial services, there are even allegations that the supply of credit to medium and small domestic enterprises has been reduced. Private firms may be less willing to engage in cross-subsidization of market segments in poor and rural areas. Even if liberalization leads to lower average costs through increased competitiveness and efficiency, prices for some end-users may rise. The WTO could promote service

---

[9] For a discussion of harmful tax practices see OECD (1998). For welfare losses from international tax competition see Charlton (2003). See also discussion in chapter 9.

[10] For example, privatization of utilities—such as South Africa's experience of granting its newly privatized telecommunications utility Telekom a 5-year monopoly—can lead to inefficient services. Similarly the poor regulation of financial sectors across South-East Asia contributed to instability prior to the crises of the late 1990s. Poor electricity deregulation has led to problems in many countries.

sector liberalization by acting to mitigate (or at least not exacerbating) these concerns through other parts of the agenda. For example, regulatory agreements which constrain the ability of governments to avail themselves of appropriate industrial, social, and redistributive policies might reduce the incentive for governments to engage in liberalization programs which entail adjustment costs.

Service sector reform thus offers large benefits to developing countries but is not receiving commensurate attention in the Doha Round. There is much to be done within the WTO to unlock welfare gains from service sector reform, including pursuing the developing countries' market access agenda in labor-intensive and outsourced services and promoting reform in other parts of the agenda to amplify the benefits of service sector liberalization and limit its costs.

Agriculture

Chapter 3 highlighted the persistently high levels of agricultural protection in the OECD.[11] Yet agriculture is crucial to developing countries. It represents almost 40 per cent of their GDP, 35 per cent of exports, and 70 per cent of employment.

Because agriculture is such an important part of both national economic development and daily livelihoods in developing countries, agricultural reform must proceed carefully. Agricultural liberalization presents developing countries with the benefits of increased market access, but also the (potential) costs of higher prices for domestic consumers. The fundamental point is that consumers benefit from lower prices that result from large agricultural subsidies, and producers lose.[12] The producers are typically poor farmers, often far worse off than the urban net consumers. Given the limited capacity of

---

[11] Total OECD spending on agricultural subsidies is more than US$300bn per year. This is almost six times the total aid from OECD countries to all developing countries (US$50–60bn per year).

[12] There is another reason to be wary of an *excessive* focus on agriculture. Development requires less developing countries to move into sectors with higher rates of potential productivity improvements, to develop their *dynamic* comparative advantage, not just their static comparative advantage.

developing countries to effect redistributions, there can be a significant welfare loss from such adverse distributional impacts. The net effect of wide-ranging agricultural reform varies across developing countries depending on the composition of their exports and imports of different commodities, and the price sensitivity of those commodities to liberalization. The potential for losses highlights the need for a more fine-grained approach which would differentiate among crops and countries, and emphasizes the importance of adjustment assistance, which would need to vary among developing countries, depending on the magnitude of the adverse impact.[13]

The WTO should focus on liberalizing those commodities which have the largest positive effect on producers and the smallest adverse consumption effects. One determinant of the net effect of this kind of reform is the level of protection for each commodity and the consequent impact of liberalization on prices.[14] Another important determinant of the welfare effects of liberalization is the agricultural trade balance across countries. There is a division between temperate products (some types of crops and livestock), where developing countries are largely net importers and developed countries are largely net exporters, and tropical products, for which developing countries are largely net exporters. Most developing countries are net importers of program crops,[15] which are precisely the commodities that have the highest domestic support and stand to experience the largest price increases. It is therefore not surprising that most studies predict that most developing countries are worse off as a

[13] In addition, countries which are importers of subsidized commodities as well as producers should be allowed to impose countervailing duties. Such duties would simultaneously enable producers to receive prices that would correspond more closely to what they would have received in the absence of the distortionary subsidies in the advanced industrial countries and provide the revenues with which these countries could protect consumers from the adverse consequences of the price increase. Moreover, since those in the advanced industrial countries would receive less benefit from their distortionary subsidies, such a reform might reduce political pressures for the subsidies.

[14] There are large differences in the extent to which different agricultural crops are subsidized. Tariffs are particularly high in the feed grains, dairy, and food grains sectors, while dairy products, meat, and livestock are the world's most subsidized exports. Producer payments are highest for grains and oilseed sectors and lowest for meat, livestock, and dairy (Hertel et al. 2000).

[15] This includes Mexico, 'Rest of South America' (a regional average which excludes Argentina and Brazil), China, Indonesia, South Korea, 'Rest of South Asia' (a regional average which excludes India), Tanzania, Zambia, 'Rest of Sub-Saharan Africa' (a regional average which excludes Tanzania and Zambia), and the average of the Middle East and North African Countries. Brazil, India, Argentina, and Vietnam are net exporters (Dimaranan, Hertel, and Keeney 2003).

result of the terms-of-trade effects following this kind of reform. Indeed Dimaranan, Hertel, and Keeney (2003) find that gains accrue primarily to developed countries in the Cairns Group as well as the two largest developing country exporters, Argentina and Brazil. These countries are the strongest advocates for the existing agricultural reform agenda. Still, it is possible that, as producer prices increase, some developing countries will switch from being net importers to net exporters.

The existence of net losses for developing countries in some areas of reform should not imply that no reform is required—rather it suggests that a selective and gradual approach is needed and that considerable adjustment assistance may be required. The most important subsidies to eliminate would be those where the consumption benefits of the current subsidies are small relative to the cost to producers. Attention should be focused on the elimination of tariffs and quotas on tropical products, processed foods, and other commodities which developed countries export or for which they have high export elasticities with respect to price. Elimination of cotton subsidies would raise producer prices for cotton, but have a small effect on standards of living in developing countries as a result of the small increase in the price of cloth. Similarly, subsidies for crops which are disproportionately consumed by the wealthy will have the least adverse distributional effects.

Furthermore, the potential adverse effects of agricultural liberalization on large segments of society suggest the importance of a gradual approach, allowing urban workers time to adjust. It would also be desirable for developed countries to give some of the money they previously expended on subsidies to assist the developing countries in the transition.

Appendix 1 reviews the empirical evidence on the effect of agricultural liberalization in OECD countries on various regions of the world. Clearly more research needs to be done to identify the precise effects of liberalization on individual poor countries. The studies surveyed in Appendix 1 indicate that uniform elimination of all agricultural protection could result in negative terms-of-trade shocks for some of the poorest developing countries and sharp declines in farm incomes in Europe and North America. The latter are in a position to bear the costs, especially given the large savings from the elimination of subsidies: the former may not be. A reform agenda must carefully discriminate between liberalization instruments and targets. Such an agenda would have three key components.

First, there should be a significant reduction in border protection in developed countries (particularly the EU), including tariff cuts and the elimination of export subsidies. Tariffs on the goods produced primarily by developing countries as well as those consumed primarily in developed countries should be reduced most rapidly. For example, the elimination of US and EU quotas and tariffs on sugar and tropical products would increase the price received by developing world producers but only have a small effect on consumer prices in developing countries. Similarly, the elimination of cotton subsidies would have only a small effect on consumer prices in developing countries.

Second, domestic production support for price-sensitive necessities that are widely consumed in developing countries should be reduced gradually, with some of the savings in developed country subsidy budgets being directed at ameliorating the adjustment costs of those in the developing world. Many developing countries in North Africa, Sub-Saharan Africa and Latin America (though not Brazil, Argentina, or Mexico) rely on imports of subsidized grains and oilseeds from OECD producers. The empirical evidence reviewed in Appendix 1 suggests that these countries are particularly exposed to agricultural reforms which might increase the price of some commodities.

Third, domestic support should be shifted from market price support to alternative payment systems. Reinstrumentation of protection in OECD countries towards the least trade-distorting instruments (such as land-based payments) is one possible means of compensating OECD farmers while minimizing the impact on developing world consumers. But many of the so-called non-trade-distorting subsidies do in fact lead to increased production, and too much has been made of the distinction between export subsidies and production subsidies. The WTO makes a distinction between explicit export subsidies and other forms of domestic subsidies, yet both types of payment can increase production and exports and depress world prices.[16] Since domestic subsidies are treated more permissively in the WTO, several OECD countries have reduced their export subsidies and increased their direct domestic support payments to comply with their WTO commitments. In the US and EU, the annual values of export subsidies for cereals and beef declined by US$4.1 billion between 1990 and 1998–9. In the same period, domestic support in the form of exempt direct payments for those commodities rose by an estimated US$18.9 billion a year in the European Union alone (ABARE 2001). However, the trade effects of various types of domestic subsidies are often understated. While the impact of export support on developing countries per dollar of subsidy is greater than production-based support, the difference is small if the elasticity of demand is small, which is the case for many agricultural commodities. Even non-production-based support ('decoupled' payments primarily in the 'Green Box') have an impact on output and prices. These payments favor OECD producers by providing them with cheap (or free) credit to use potentially for investment and expansion of production. The distinction between trade-distorting subsidies and non-trade-distorting subsidies is based on a particular economic model, in which capital markets are perfect. Trade-distorting subsidies are then subsidies which change the marginal return to production or which reduce the marginal cost of production. Thus generalized income supports in this view are not production-distorting, nor are payments to keep land fallow. But both of these may, in fact, be production-distorting if, for instance, farmers face credit constraints. Then, in effect, the subsidies provide additional finance which allows farmers to expand production.

Liberalization of industrial goods

While average developed country tariff rates are low, developed countries maintain high barriers to many of the goods exported most

[16] The WTO classifies domestic subsidies according to their distortionary effect on trade: amber (directly trade-distorting); blue (indirectly trade-distorting production payments); green (non-trade-distorting).

intensively by developing countries (US$31 billion). When weighted by import volumes, developing countries face average manufacturing tariffs of 3.4 per cent on their exports to developed countries, more than four times as high as the average rate faced by goods from developed countries, 0.8 per cent (Hertel and Martin 2000).[17]

Moreover, aggregate data hide the existence of tariff peaks (discussed in Chapter 3). OECD tariffs are particularly high for goods of importance to poor countries, such as low-skill manufactures (especially textiles) and processed foods. For example, in 2001, clothes and shoes accounted for only 6.5 per cent of US imports in value terms but they brought in nearly half of the US$20 billion of US tariff revenue. More tariff revenue was collected by the US government on the import of shoes than on the import of automobiles, even though the value of shoe imports is around one tenth of the value of automobiles.

Comparisons of nominal tariffs do not fully represent the distortion caused by escalating tariff structures, and do not provide information about the impact of tariffs on the value-added of processed products. Thus nominal tariff levels tell us little about the real trade impact of the tariff escalation, and to look more closely at the trade effect we need to examine the 'effective tariff rate'. The effective tariff rate is a function of the tariffs assessed on the component parts and the final product, the technological process involved, and the relative prices of all inputs into the final product. Analysis of tariff escalation using effective tariff rates demonstrates the effect of the existing tariff structures in many developed countries on the industrial development of poorer countries. By imposing higher tariffs on the output of manufactured goods than on primary products, developed countries are in effect imposing significantly higher trade taxes on manufacturing value added in developing countries. Such tariff 'escalation' serves to discourage the development of, for example, food processing in less developed countries since the *effective* tariff rate on value added in food processing is very high. Such tariff peaks and tariff escalation are manifestly unfair and have a particularly pernicious effect on development by restricting industrial diversification in the poorest countries.

[17] The distortion is even larger if one recognizes that the quantities imported are reduced as a result of the high tariff barriers. (In the measure cited, a prohibitive tariff would have no weight in the measure, since there would be no imports.)

A second reason why developing countries should be pushing to have industrial tariffs given high priority in the Doha Agenda is that barriers to South–South trade are quite high. The average import-weighted tariff on the exports of manufactured goods from developing countries to developing countries is 12.8 per cent (Hertel and Martin 2000). Anderson *et al.* (2000) estimate that the welfare gains to developing countries derived from the liberalization of trade in manufactures by other developing countries is US$31 billion.

Non-tariff barriers

It is not surprising that as tariffs have come down, non-tariff barriers have assumed increasing importance. Trade agreements may do little to alter protectionist sentiment—and the politics of special interests. They do, however, change the form that such protection can take. Just as developed countries have discriminated against developing countries in the structure of their tariffs, so too many of their non-tariff barriers have particularly adverse effects on developing countries.

Developing countries have repeatedly found that as they make inroads into a market in the United States or Europe, they are slapped with dumping duties or face some other form of non-tariff barrier. Though ostensibly the Uruguay Round marked the end of the so-called voluntary export restraint, the United States has talked about reinstating such restraints against China. The effect of these non-tariff barriers is far greater than indicated by the actual duties imposed. The fear that they will be imposed has a chilling effect on development: it increases the risk associated with investing in an export-oriented industry, which is particularly important in economies already facing high interest rates. Often initially high duties are imposed only to be revised down substantially but the initially high duties suffice to drive the exporting firm out of business. Some solution to the problems posed by non-tariff barriers should be high on the agenda of any development round.

There are four important categories of non-tariff barriers: (1) dumping duties, which are imposed when a country (allegedly) sells products below cost; (2) countervailing duties, which can be imposed when a country subsidizes a commodity; (3) safeguards, which can be imposed temporarily when a county faces a surge of imports; (4) and restrictions to maintain food safety or avoid, say, an infestation of fruit flies. The advanced industrial countries have used all of these at times to restrict imports from developing countries when the latter have achieved a degree of competitiveness which allows them to enter the markets of the developed countries. Many of these measures are described as ensuring 'fair trade', but from the perspective of developing countries, they ensure 'unfair trade'. They are evidence of the hypocrisy of the North. Increasingly, however, developing countries are using such measures against each other and against the advanced industrial countries, and in that sense they represent a hidden threat to a trade liberalization regime.

There has been a large increase in the number of anti-dumping claims. Between 1995 and 2002, 2,063 dumping cases were initiated. The US (279) and the EU (255) were two of the largest initiators. It does not seem sensible that the countries with the largest capacity to absorb shocks and compensate import-competing interests should be the most common users of anti-dumping laws.

The problem is that dumping has been used as a safeguard measure when there is a separate safeguard measure for this purpose. There is a reason for this: safeguard measures provide for only temporary protection, to assist in adjustment, while dumping can provide longer-term protection.

Part of the problem with the schemes is how they have been implemented. Consider, for example, America's use of dumping duties. The accused must respond in a short period of time to a long demand for information (in English), and when the accused is unable to do so, the US government acts on the 'best information available' (BIA), usually the information which has been provided by the American company trying to keep out its rivals. High initial duties are imposed, which regularly get revised downward when better information becomes available. But meanwhile, long-term damage has been done, as American buyers will not purchase the commodity given the uncertainty about the level of tariffs they may have to pay.[18] America's provisions for dumping duties (and in some cases countervailing duties) for China and some of the former communist countries have been particularly egregious. In the 'surrogate country methodology' which is used to assess the cost of production (the benchmark against which charges of dumping are assessed) costs of production are compared with those of a 'similar' country. In one instance, the United States used Canada as the country most similar to Poland. Not surprisingly it was found that the costs of production were high, justifying a high dumping duty.

Safeguards are another form of non-tariff barrier. A WTO member may take a 'safeguard' action (i.e. temporarily restrict imports of a product) to protect a specific domestic industry from an increase in imports of any product which is threatening to cause serious injury to the industry. Recent years have seen a dramatic increase in the use of safeguards around the world: the incidence of safeguards has risen from 2 in 1995 to 132 in 2002. The increase is a cause for concern because many of the safeguard measures implemented by WTO members are not consistent with WTO rules. Indeed, all safeguard measures examined by WTO panels and the Appellate Body have so far been found to be inconsistent with those rules.

Safeguard measures have been available under the GATT (Article XIX). However, they were infrequently used. The Agreement on Safeguards clarifies and reinforces Article XIX. It sets forth criteria for the application of safeguard measures: (1) the product is being imported in increased quantities, absolutely or relative to domestic production; (2) the product causes or threatens to cause serious injury to domestic industry; and (3) the safeguard measure shall only be applied to the extent necessary to prevent or remedy serious injury and to facilitate adjustment.

The safeguard measure has probably been underused by developing countries and has certainly been overused by the United States. American safeguard legislation, for instance, makes insufficient distinction between industries which are declining *because* of trade

---

[18] For a more complete description of these abuses, see, for instance, Stiglitz (1997).

and those which would be in decline even in the absence of trade liberalization.

The US Presidential Proclamation of 5 March 2002 imposed safeguard measures on ten steel product groupings in the form of additional tariffs up to 30 per cent. Almost immediately, several countries, including the EC, Japan, South Korea, China, Switzerland, Norway, New Zealand, and Brazil, engaged WTO dispute settlement procedures against these measures. These countries argued that none of the US measures had been taken as a result of unforeseen developments, as required under the WTO rules. For most products, imports had not increased; for all products but one the US had not properly established the necessary causal link to the alleged serious injury suffered by the US steel industry; the US had exempted imports from Canada, Mexico, Israel, and Jordan from the measures in a manner inconsistent with the WTO rules. The WTO's panel substantially agreed and concluded that each of the US measures was in violation of the WTO rules. President Bush's action in imposing steel tariffs exemplifies the misuse of safeguards.

While the argument for safeguard measures is persuasive, they have been widely abused, especially by the developed countries. If the richest country in the world, the United States, with a strong safety net, relatively high employment level, etc. has to resort to safeguard measures to protect itself against a surge of imports, how much more justified are developing countries in imposing such measures. Indeed, it is hard to conceive of many important liberalization measures against which safeguard protections could not justifiably be invoked by developing countries. This highlights again the need to set clearer standards *at the international level*. For instance, for a safeguard measure to be imposed, the country should have to show that there is injury but that it is substantial, entailing a loss, say, of at least 1 per cent of the jobs in the country, and that the burden on the country's social safety net is such that it would be hard pressed to absorb it. The threshold standard should be lower in developing countries. Such a reform would ensure that the safeguard measures would only be used in cases where trade disturbances imposed significant adjustment burdens.

There are three reforms that would make a great deal of difference. The first is to recognize the principle of *national treatment*: in addressing problems of unfair trade, the legal framework should be the same for domestic firms as it is for foreign firms. In the case of dumping, for instance, firms are charged with selling below cost. To an economist, the natural question is, 'Why would a firm ever sell below *marginal cost* (and what is the relevant economic concept)?' The answer is to try to drive out rivals, to establish a monopoly or dominant position in a market that would enable it later on to sell at a high price, well above costs. Thus American anti-trust law, in assessing whether predatory pricing (the equivalent of dumping in a domestic context) has occurred, attempts to assess whether price is below the *relevant* cost, and whether there is evidence that it is likely that the accused will recoup his loses. As a result of this high standard, few cases of predatory pricing have been successfully prosecuted. Subjecting foreign firms to the same standard would ensure that dumping charges were being used to preserve competition, not to reduce the threat of foreign competition. (The double standard is highlighted by the fact that if American firms were subject to the standard used in a dumping case, a large proportion of American firms would be found guilty of dumping.)

The second is to create a new international tribunal as the first 'court'. Today when, for instance, the United States accuses firms of a foreign country of dumping, it acts as prosecutor, judge, and jury. Though the process is governed by a 'rule of law', in the sense that there are well-defined procedures, the process often operates in a highly unfair way. There is a costly and lengthy WTO process which can be, and has been, used to rectify gross abuses, as in the case of the US-imposed steel tariffs. But it would be far better if the original decision was taken out of the hands of the country and put into those of a specialized international tribunal.

The third is that the implementation legislation and practices of countries should be reviewed to ascertain whether they are is fair and non-discriminatory, both *de jure* and *de facto*, and are in conformity with widely accepted economic principles. An example already referred to is the use of BIA. As another example, almost all economists agree that the relevant cost concept for judging dumping is *marginal* not average costs, yet legislation in many countries uses average costs. This means that dumping charges are often sustained in cyclical industries, in downturns, where marginal costs are considerably below average costs.[19]

The determination of whether subsidies have been provided is another example which has been highly contentious. A Development Round should clarify this, in ways which ensure that governments may undertake industrial policies to promote nascent industries. This is particularly important because the *form* of subsidy in countries like the United States—e.g. research in the defense industry, the benefits of which spill over to civilian uses—is markedly different from that in the developing world. Allowing one, but not the other, creates an uneven playing field. Similarly, the IMF often forces developing countries to have high interest rates, well above the global 'market rate'. Lending money at more reasonable rates should not be viewed as a subsidy.

A third example concerns the sale of privatized assets, particularly in the former communist economies. Assume that the original investment was subsidized, but the government privatizes the industry through a competitive auction. Such an auction should extinguish the subsidy: the new investor pays, in effect, fair market value for the asset. In a way one can look at the privatization as a bankruptcy/restructuring proceeding. When a firm goes bankrupt, its assets are sold in an auction. The acquiring firm is not viewed as having received a subsidy. The communist economies can be viewed as a large bankrupt enterprise, the assets of which are now being disposed of. On the other hand, when the government effectively gives away the asset, then the subsidy is clearly not extinguished. (A side-benefit of a rule that distinguishes between the two kinds of privatizations is that it would encourage more honest privatizations.)

Summary

Trade negotiations have traditionally focused on expanding market access. But in the past, the agenda for expanding market access has been set by the developed countries. More recently, attention has

---

[19] Moreover, dumping is sometimes found in competitive industries, in which no rational firm would ever engage in predatory pricing, since there is no way it could establish the monopoly power required for it to recoup the losses it makes when it sells below marginal cost.

focused on the failure to expand market access to agriculture. This chapter has shown, however, that a *true development round* market access agenda goes beyond agriculture, and is markedly different from the Doha round. It includes unskilled services, migration, industrial tariff structure, and of increasing importance, the non-tariff barriers that are of increasing importance as tariffs are brought down.

But a true development round should go beyond market access. There are new issues where international agreements could help developing countries. We turn to these in the next chapter.

9

Priorities Behind the Border

⚓

Restrictions on tax and incentive competition to attract investors

One arena in which an international agreement might be of immense benefit to developing countries concerns their competition for investment through concessionary tax rates and financial subsidies. The main beneficiary of that competition is international business, and often countries suffer large fiscal losses without commensurate gains to either their domestic economy or to the efficiency of the location of international production.[1] If authorities were to embark on cross-country (or cross-jurisdiction) policy action, to reduce the harm from such competition to attract business. There are essentially three options, representing three levels of ambition with regards to the objectives being pursued. In ascending order these are: (1) transparency-enhancing obligations on firms and countries;[2] (2) co-operation between jurisdictions;[3] and (3) the putting in place of enforceable international rules.[4]

[1] For a discussion of harmful tax practices see OECD (1998). For welfare losses from international tax competition see Charlton (2003).   [2] See Oman (2000).

[3] OECD countries adopted a similar approach in their efforts to identify and reduce 'harmful tax competition' (OECD 1998). While the OECD's mandate here covers mainly general tax rates rather than specific incentives, the criteria used to determine 'harmful' tax policies is instructive for investment incentives. Two of the criteria cover transparency and discrimination between foreign and domestic firms. The European Commission's 1999 'Code of Conduct (Business Taxation)' has taken a similar approach.

[4] Three alternative frameworks could regulate incentives with reference to (1) size (capping the total financial benefit available); (2) use (e.g. specifying geographical areas or sectors in which they are allowed/prohibited); or (3) instrument (proscribing instruments perceived to be particularly harmful).

Just as international agreements circumscribe subsidies in general, there should be a strong proscription on firm-specific competition. The spirit of the WTO's Agreement on Subsidies and Countervailing Measures (SCM) could be extended to new rules limiting investment competition. Under the SCM, subsidies are actionable if they can be shown to cause adverse trade effects. One of the adverse effects triggering actionability under Part III is 'serious prejudice to the interests of another member'—a principle which could be analogously applied to the incentive instruments used in investment competition.

The European Union (which has been operating state aid guidelines now for several decades) provides an example of how rules might be developed. Although grants and subsidies to foreign direct investors are not explicitly targeted by Commission policy, in practice they are one of the main forms of state aid regulated by it. The definition of state aid clearly encompasses traditional instruments of investment attraction. Indeed the European Commission classifies state aid as including (1) grants to firms; (2) loans and guarantees; (3) tax exemptions; and (4) infrastructure projects benefiting identifiable end-users. These payments are regulated by the European Commission, which claims some success in reducing subsidies in the EU.[5]

Anti-corruption policies

While trade in general may benefit developing countries, some kinds of cross-border transactions clearly harm them. One particularly insidious interaction between foreign firms and developing countries is rampant corruption: it is often less expensive to bribe government officials to obtain, say, a concession than to pay the full market price. International non-bribery legislation (such as America's

---

[5] See Charlton (2003) for a discussion of the EU's state aid regulations as applied to foreign investment incentives.

Foreign Corrupt Practices Act) should be made part of an international agreement. There should be full disclosure of all payments made to foreign companies (publish what you pay). There should be an agreement that only disclosed payments will be tax-deductible; but even stronger enforcement measures should be undertaken. There should also be a commitment to repatriate funds stolen or otherwise illegally obtained (e.g. through corrupt transactions) from developing countries. And transactions giving rise to other sources of illicit revenues, particularly those which support armed insurrection, such as 'conflict diamonds', should be proscribed.

Secret bank accounts facilitate corruption, by providing a safe haven for funds stolen from a country. This adversely affects developing countries to a significant degree. There should be an international agreement proscribing bank secrecy (the importance of which has recently been recognized in the case of terrorism). This too can easily be enforced. No bank should be allowed to deal with any bank in a country which does not conform to agreed transparency standards. It should be possible to sue any country that does not enforce such a sanction (e.g. under provisions similar to those discussed above under fair competition).

Finally, as we have noted, arms sales have had a devastating effect on many of the poorest of the developing countries. The developed countries are the major source of these arms. Developed countries must make a commitment to restrict these sales.

Anti-civil-strife policies and pro-environment policies

Trade agreements have largely been designed to *expand* the scope of trade, on the premise that trade is beneficial. Trade policy has become controversial because there are some notable instances where that does not seem to be the case. The most obvious are trading in arms, especially small arms, trafficking in diamonds and other minerals which help finance the purchase of arms, and the narcotics trade.

It has become well accepted that countries that export drugs have a responsibility for containing the sale of those drugs. This perspective has been pushed by the advanced industrial countries; as they have come to recognize their inability to control consumption and the demand side, they have put increasing responsibility on the supply side. The same principle should hold for arms trade—it may be far easier to control the sale of arms than the purchase.

The recent trade dispute known as the Shrimp–Turtle case[6] raised concerns about the WTO's role in sustainable development issues. This dispute arose over US restrictions on imports of shrimps from countries that did not have conservation programs for migratory turtles. Each year, thousands of sea turtles are killed in shrimp trawl nets. To protect these endangered animals, the US passed a law to prohibit the import of shrimp from nations which do not require shrimp boats to be equipped with 'turtle-excluder devices' (TEDs)—attachments that enable turtles to exit unharmed from nets. The US measure was challenged at the WTO by India, Malaysia, Pakistan, and Thailand. These countries argued that the law was an illegal restriction on their shrimp exports and thus contravened WTO obligations. In response, the United States argued that their measure was covered by Article XX of the GATT, exempting WTO members from their trade obligations in order to protect human, animal, and plant life (Article XX(b)) or conserve natural resources (Art. XX(g)) when deemed necessary. In its adjudication, the WTO's Appellate Body made clear that the WTO gives countries the right to take trade action to protect the environment, in particular relating to human health, endangered species, and exhaustible resources. It argued that the preamble to the WTO recognized the goal of sustainable development as an objective of the organization and this made environmental protection a legitimate and important goal of policy, ranking with protection of international trade as a WTO objective. The Appellate Body also said that measures to protect sea turtles would be legitimate under GATT Article XX,[7] which

---

[6] Appellate Body Report WT/DS58/AB/R, adopted 6 Nov. 1998; original panel report WT/DS58/R and Corr. 1, as modified by the Appellate Body Report WT/DS58/AB/R.

[7] Article XX provides specific instances in which countries may be excepted from WTO rules. These include two sets of circumstances for environmental protection.

provides exceptions to the WTO's trade rules so long as certain basic criteria such as non-discrimination are met. The US lost the case, not because it sought to protect the environment but because it discriminated between WTO members. (The United States was discriminating by giving Asian countries only four months to comply with its law, but allowing Caribbean Basin nations three years.) But the significance of the Shrimp–Turtle rulings is that they endorse the use of trade policy to enforce environmental standards. There is, of course, a danger here that the economically powerful nations, principally the US and the EU, but soon probably China, will be able to impose their political will upon countries which are economically dependent on uninterrupted access to these huge markets. But the WTO's law is evolving in a responsible way which defers to multilateral attempts to deal with global environmental problems.

Several environmental treaties already enshrine the right to use trade policy to enforce the agreement.[8] Where two countries are party to an environmental agreement the WTO should enable countries to use trade policy to enforce it, consistent with the agreement. Where there is a multilateral environmental agreement and a signatory country attempts to take action affecting the trade of a country that has not signed and is not in compliance, the WTO should also enable this if the treaty is genuinely multilateral (as in the case of the Kyoto Protocol). Countries that have signed multilateral agreements to deal cooperatively with global problems should be able to apply the agreement even to goods and services from countries that have not. Certainly restrictions on environmentally unsound techniques of production can have adverse effects on particular developing countries. The discussion above suggests that nonetheless there may be a compelling case for such restrictions. This is especially true for global warming, which may itself have a particularly adverse effect on some

---

[8] There are more than 200 multilateral environmental agreements. About 20 of these include provisions that can affect trade: for example they ban trade in certain products, or allow countries to restrict trade in certain circumstances. Among them are the Montreal Protocol for the protection of the ozone layer, the Basel Convention on the trade or transportation of hazardous waste across international borders, and the Convention on International Trade in Endangered Species (CITES).

developing countries, like Bangladesh and many of the countries in the tropics.

Responding to crises: from beggar-my-neighbor to help-my-neighbor

In the event of a crisis afflicting one member the WTO should encourage *other* countries to take special measures to assist it. Crises can restrict the availability of short-term trade finance and hence dramatically reduce trade. Trade finance is particularly important in developing countries where exporters may have limited access to working capital and will often require financing to undertake production before receiving payment. At its Fifth Ministerial Meeting in Cancún the General Council of the WTO presented a report to Ministers stating that, 'Based mainly on experience gained in Asia and elsewhere, there is a need to improve the stability and security of sources of trade finance, especially to help deal with periods of financial crisis' (WTO Document WT/WGTDF/2).

Already public institutions, including regional development banks, have had some success in making trade financing and guarantees available to emerging economies. Trade finance facilities provided by regional banks to importers and exporters can include the provision of working capital loans or overdrafts, issuing-performance, bid, and advance payment bonds, and extending letters of credit (see Stephens 1998). For example, in 2000 the Asian Development Bank made available a US$150 million Political Risk Guarantee Facility to international banks confirming Pakistani letters of credit. The facility provided open access to any international bank, covering only political risks, while leaving commercial risks to the banks. In 1998 the Export–Import Bank of the United States provided short-term insurance for more than US$1 billion of US export sales to South Korea (see Auboin and Meier-Ewert 2003).

Many types of export assistance, including export credit insurance schemes, are subject to binding rules under the WTO's rules on subsidies and countervailing measures (SCM). The SCM prohibits subsidies that are contingent upon export performance—and export credits, guarantees, and insurance may under certain circumstances fall within the scope of that prohibition. Under Article 1 of the SCM, a subsidy is defined as (a) a financial contribution (b) by a government or public body within the territory of a member (c) which confers a benefit. The principles of the SCM might contradict trade finance assistance because export credits, guarantees, and insurance schemes involve 'financial contributions', and central banks, export credit agencies, and other government-owned or controlled entities that provide such schemes likely constitute 'governments'. Thus as well as working to develop multilateral mechanisms to improve trade finance during periods of crisis, the WTO must ensure that the SCM does not restrict this kind of assistance (at appropriate interest rates) during periods of crisis by governments or regional development banks.

Since trade will ultimately be the route through which countries in crisis achieve a balance-of-payments recovery, the WTO should encourage members to assist countries in crisis by undertaking special measures to open up their markets. For instance, in the Argentine crisis, if countries had provided special access to Argentinian beef or wine, it might have modulated the downturn and facilitated a quicker restoration of the economy. An international panel within the WTO should assess whether a crisis which might benefit from special trade-opening measures exists, and how those 'help-thy-neighbor' policies might be implemented.

One of the original motivations for international trade agreements was the fear of the kinds of beggar-thy-neighbor policies which marked the Great Depression. Nonetheless, even within the WTO, there are provisions (almost never invoked) that allow countries to take emergency measures. The issue is important because given the unstable global financial and economic system, country after country has faced a crisis in recent years. By one reckoning there have been a hundred crises in the last three decades. Rather than resorting to beggar-thy-neighbor policies, encouraging countries to return to protectionist measures in the event of a crisis, it would be far better to encourage *other* countries to take special measures to open up their markets.

Trade implementation and environment facility

The developing countries are at a marked disadvantage, not only in negotiating fair trade agreements, but also in implementation. We noted one aspect of this earlier: their difficulty in mounting challenges to bio-piracy actions under the TRIPS Agreement.

Some developed and many less developed countries give substantial subsidies to energy consumption, which has adverse effects on the global environment. The costs of global warming are likely to be particularly severe for some developing countries, such as Bangladesh.[9] The international community has recognized the need to assist developing countries in facing the incremental costs associated with implementing environmentally sound technologies, which should include adjustment assistance to help developing countries bear the costs of eliminating subsidies to (fossil fuel) energy.

Assitance for implementation

Chapter 13 lays out the broader case for why adjustment costs to a new trade regime are likely to be greater for developing countries, and why the international community needs to increase it assistance to developing countries for these purposes.

---

[9] More broadly, because on average developing countries lie in warmer climates, and they are more heavily dependent on agriculture (which itself is more sensitive to climate) the adverse effects on them will be larger. There are also likely to be further adverse effects on health.

10

What should not be on the Agenda?

The preceding is a partial list of the items that should have a high priority in any round of trade negotiations that pretends to call itself a *development* round. Many of the items listed have received little or no attention. Equally remarkable are several of the items (especially within the so-called Singapore Issues) that were put on the table. Some of these would almost surely impede development. The fact that the United States and Europe put such items on the agenda and continued to push them for so long within the so-called Development Round is of concern: were they merely bargaining chips? Was there no real comprehension about what should be meant by a Development Round?

Intellectual property rights

Recent debates about intellectual property need to be put into context. Intellectual property provides innovators with temporary monopoly power. Monopoly power always results in an economic inefficiency. There is accordingly a high cost of granting even temporary monopoly power, but the benefit is that by doing so, greater motivation is provided for inventive activity. The dynamic gains, it is hoped, exceed the static losses.

Much of the most important innovative activity is outside the realm of intellectual property. Behind the inventions associated with atomic energy or lasers were basic discoveries in physics. Behind the computer were basic discoveries in mathematics. The basic research which underlies practical innovation in almost all arenas occurs in universities and government research laboratories, and few of these discoveries are protected by intellectual property.

In many cases, it is neither desirable nor practical for this to happen. Often the applications which give market value to the discovery occur years after the original discovery (beyond the normal patent life). Ideas give rise to other ideas, and there is no way to ascertain which ideas proved instrumental in the creation of follow-on ideas.

Most important, it should be recognized that material reward provides little of the motivation for much of this intellectual activity. To be sure, it could not occur without financial support. The salaries of the researchers have to be paid, and if the financial support is woefully inadequate, many would-be researchers will divert their attention to other areas. Yet there is little evidence that stronger intellectual property protection would generate a greater flow of basic ideas.

Knowledge is a public good, and this is especially true for the fruits of basic research, which is why governments have an important responsibility for its support. Intellectual property protection thus constitutes only a part—and not the most important part—of what may be called our knowledge and research system. Providing greater support to this one part of the system may actually harm other parts of the system and impede the progress of science. Note that the system under which basic research is conducted is a very open one in which ideas freely move around, and in which, in fact, scientists put considerable effort into disseminating their ideas and encouraging others to use them. In many ways, this is the opposite of the premises underlying intellectual property, which seeks to circumscribe the use of knowledge, limiting it only to those who are willing and able to pay.

Thus, whether within the WTO or through an alternative forum,[1] a new intellectual property regime needs to be created which

---

[1] For example the World Intellectual Property Organisation (WIPO) might be an appropriate forum. As we noted earlier, it is not clear that the WTO is the best forum for the establishment and arbitration of intellectual property rights.

balances more carefully the interests of the users and the producers of knowledge[2] and goes some way toward closing the North–South 'knowledge gap'.

In some areas weaker patent laws are actually necessary to safeguard public health and promote development. The use of compulsory licensing and government use of patents could be extended for these purposes. Indeed many governments in developed countries already have strong national laws for public use of patents. Under 28 USC Sec 1498, the US government can use patents or authorize third parties to use patents for virtually any public use, without negotiation.[3] Patent owners have no rights to seek injunctions and may not seek compensation through tort litigation. Other developed countries have similarly permissive laws. Before NAFTA, Canada routinely granted compulsory licenses on pharmaceutical products for the purpose of reducing health costs through widely available generic drugs. Canada assigned royalties to the patent holders, usually of 4 per cent of the generic competitor's sales price. In sharp contrast, and despite the HIV/AIDS public health crisis, no African country has issued a compulsory license for any medicine.[4]

This situation is curious because, unlike the spirit of many areas of the WTO's intellectual property regime, the TRIPS accord provides quite liberal powers to governments to authorize third parties to use patents without the permission of the patent owners. For example, Article 31(b) allows countries to use or authorize a third party to use a patent without negotiation or without a license if the use is for public non-commercial purposes, although the provision does require that 'adequate' compensation be made to the patent holder (Art. 31(h)).

Love (2001) points out that the existing TRIPS accord permits countries to create very simple and easily administered systems for permitting production or import of generic products from the competitive sector. In this particular area the key action required to promote development is not significant reform of the current WTO rules, but rather it is providing developing countries with the resources

[2] Knowledge is a global public good, and thus it is particularly appropriate that the funding for such global public goods be provided by those that are most able to pay, i.e. those in the advanced industrial countries.
[3] For a discussion see Love (2001).   [4] See Love (2001).

to develop national systems which take advantage of the current rules. In particular developing countries should be encouraged to develop compulsory licensing systems which are simple and not costly to administer. The median cost of US patent litigation in 1998 was US$1.2 million for each party (Love 2001). As a result of the high cost of disputes, large patent-holding corporations can use litigation to tie up any system which enables them to do so. Fortunately, TRIPS permits countries to administer most aspects of compulsory licensing through administrative processes (see Art. 31(c), (i)–(k)) and in several cases does not require governments to grant injunctive relief to patent holders (Art. 44.2), including when related to public health.

In other areas, the TRIPS Agreement does require further revision. In particular, compulsory licensing should be extended beyond national emergencies to broader 'refusal to deal' scenarios in which developing countries are unable to access products patented by corporations which choose not to serve their market, for example, because it is too small. The revenues lost to the patent-holders as a result of such compulsory licensing are likely to be small relative to the revenues generated by the exercise of monopoly power in the more advanced industrial countries and therefore are likely to have a negligible effect on the development of new technologies. By contrast, the cost to the developing countries of failure to provide technologies at affordable prices, particularly drugs, is enormous.[5]

In addition, Article 40 should extend the right of WTO members to provide in their national legislation for the prevention of anti-competitive licensing practices with respect to intellectual property rights. And pursuant to Article 66.2, new and additional measures need to be developed to ensure the transfer of technology from developed countries to least developed countries. The Doha Declaration recognized the potential for trade agreements to promote the transfer

---

[5] The *right* of a government to demand compulsory licensing has been recognized even by the United States, the staunchest defender of intellectual property rights. When it was worried about anthrax, it forced the compulsory licensing of Ciprio. The only issue is under what conditions such compulsory licensing should be allowed. A *Development Round* would have provided answers that more directly address the concerns of the developing countries.

of technology (para. 37) and proposed the establishment of a working group to develop recommendations on how progress might be made in this area. Suggested measures in this area include the establishment, by developed countries, of specific incentives to encourage their firms to transfer technology to developing countries.[6] However, little progress has been made in this area, and developing countries have been slow to demand effective measures.

The disparity between price and marginal cost of production can be viewed as a tax used to finance research. Basic principles of equity question the levying of this tax on some of the poorest people in the world. If the international community believes that there is a need to provide greater incentives for research for the development of medicines, then they should do so directly, through funding of research within either the public or private sector, not by levying a tax on the poor. One proposal has it that each country should make a contribution to research whose magnitude would be based on their income and whose form would be of their own choosing. This contribution, for instance, could be in the form of direct expenditures on research, licensing fees, or implicit taxes paid to holders of patents.

There are other issues which affect developing countries' access to life-saving medicines at affordable prices. One concern is the ease with which generic drugs are able to get established, and how quickly they can enter a market at the expiration of a patent. In some of its bilateral trade agreements, the United States has been working to make it more difficult. If there is to be an intellectual property agreement within a Development Round, it should enshrine principles facilitating the rapid entry of generics.

The problems posed by bio-piracy are equally serious. While, as noted earlier, some of the claims of Western firms may not be sustained when contested in court, it is costly for developing countries to mount the legal challenge. Article 27.1 (the requirement of universal novelty as a condition for patentability) should be strengthened to protect traditional knowledge. This could be done in part by amending the TRIPS Agreement to comply with the United Nations

[6] See 'Non-Paper Submitted to the Council for Trade-Related Aspects of Intellectual Property Rights' by South Africa (WTO Ref: Job(02)/15).

Convention on Biodiversity (CBD), which was signed by 170 countries in 1993. The CBD recognizes the collective rights of village communities over those of individuals or companies and decrees that a rich country's demand for patent rights should not come at the expense of providing incentives for the conservation of plant diversity. One proposal is that there be a change in the *presumptions* associated with patenting, say, traditional medicines, with the applying party having to show that there has been no previous recognition of its medicinal properties, with the adjudication occurring in an international tribunal, and with the legal expenses of the developing country being divided between the applicant and the developing country in proportion to the ratio of the income per capita.

The argument of Bhagwati and others that intellectual property should not be included in a trade agreement is sufficiently compelling that in fact there should be a complete rollback of the TRIPS Agreement. The issues should be switched to another international forum (e.g., WIPO). Whether within the WTO or this alternative forum, a new intellectual property regime needs to be created which balances more carefully the interests of users in both developed and less developed countries (including researchers, for whom knowledge is one of the most important inputs) and producers of knowledge. This should be reflected in all the provisions, including the tests of novelty,[7] as well as the breadth and scope of the patent. There should be a stronger presumption in the case of narrowly defined patents, and the issue of patents for business practices as well as other recent extensions of patent coverage should be examined *and agreed to* within an international process that is centered in the scientific community, not the trade ministers. There should also be sensitivity to the disadvantageous positions of developing countries in pursuing legal recourse.[8]

---

[7] Patents could not, for instance, be granted for traditional medicines or goods, or slight variants of those traditional medicines, when the usefulness of those commodities has already been recognized within the developing country.

[8] There is already in motion a backlash among the more technologically advanced of the less developed countries. Brazil is pushing for open source software, and China may adopt its own telecommunications standards which will enable it to avoid paying high royalties for the use of technology based on other standards. An unbalanced intellectual property regime can contribute to overall global inefficiency in the use and production of knowledge.

Competition Issues

Competition was supposed to be one of the Singapore Issues, but the discussions on competition have devolved more toward ensuring fair competitive access of developed countries to developing country markets than into ensuring that markets are really competitive, and that developing countries have fair access to developed country markets.

Ensuring competition

Today, many companies operate across boundaries. Competition policy in one country can affect others. The United States and Europe have increasingly come to recognize this. The United States instituted an action against Japan, claiming that anti-competitive practices in Japan (which the Japanese government had not stopped) had unfairly discriminated against Kodak. Europe took actions against Honeywell on anti-trust grounds, and the American government complained that its standards were too high. The EU is considering taking actions against Microsoft; even though American courts have found Microsoft guilty of violations of anti-trust laws, there is widespread concern that the remedies were insufficient.

The concerns are two-sided: there is a worry that anti-trust laws will be applied in a discriminatory way, to hurt foreign companies, and that anti-trust actions will fail to take account of anti-competitive effects in developing countries. Ideally, there should be harmonization of anti-trust laws *at the highest standard*. Advocates of strong competition worry, however, that harmonization will occur at the standard of the least common denominator, and an international agreement will legitimate such lower standards.

Given these difficulties, initial steps would include insisting on national (non-discriminatory) treatment. This would entail either eliminating dumping duties or revising anti-trust legislation, to apply the same standards to foreign and domestic firms.

A second reform would require that national authorities look carefully at anti-competitive effects outside their own jurisdiction.[9] Not only should domestic anti-trust regulators look at competitive effects abroad, but foreign consumers should have the right to take actions in foreign courts against corporations that abuse their market power. Cross-border class-action suits should be sanctioned, allowing consumers in multiple jurisdictions to band together to impose, for instance, treble damages, with judgments enforceable in the jurisdiction of the home country.

Third, consumers and governments in all countries should be able to take actions (including class-action suits) against international cartels, including those cartels in which governments are a party or which they have sanctioned. (While some developing countries may lose from such an action, the benefits received by others would almost surely outweigh the losses. For instance, oil producers may be worse off, but oil consumers would be better off.)

Ensuring fair access

With respect to fair access, the concern of developed countries is that restrictions imposed by developing countries (such as affirmative action or preferences for small and medium-sized enterprises) have a differential effect on multinationals. But a Development Round should recognize the legitimate role of such restrictions as social and developmental policy tools, and there should be a high burden of proof imposed on any challenge to such restrictions in order to establish that the restriction has no legitimate social or developmental objective or that those objectives could not be practicably achieved[10] in a significantly less trade-distorting way. At the same time, developed country regulations and practices which have an adverse effect on firms from developing countries (e.g. high licensing fees) should be held to a much higher standard.

[9] Fink, Matoo, and Rathindran (2001) suggest that the GATS should require domestic competition law to consider the effect of collusive agreements on foreign markets. (The relevance of this point, of course, goes well beyond the service sector.)
[10] For example, without significant adverse effects on other groups. The alternative should be 'Pareto-superior'.

Investor agreement

There are two separate issues that need to be considered; one is the desirability of an investment agreement and the terms which a pro-development agreement should embrace, and the other is whether such an agreement should be part of a trade agreement.

On the second issue, we have our doubts, for several reasons. First, the principle of *conservatism* articulated in Chapter 5 says that trade agreements should focus on trade. The Uruguay Round tried to expand the remit by including both intellectual property and investment, lightly clothed under the pretense that only trade-related measures were being considered (thus, we have the TRIPS Agreement, for trade-related intellectual property, and the TRIMS Agreement, for trade-related investment measures). But especially under the TRIPS Agreement, there is little in intellectual property law that is *nŏt* trade-related, in the superficial sense that almost all intellectual property is in some way embodied in tradeable goods.

Second, taking a broader perspective, why were labor and environmental issues not also included? After all, environmental and labor regulations also affect trade. The refusal of the US to restrict carbon emissions gives American producers an advantage over European producers in energy-intensive products. Firms that employ workers on terms that do not comply with core labor standards may have a competitive advantage over those who do.

More generally, we have our doubts about the importance to developing countries of an investment agreement, at least along the lines conventionally discussed. The absence of a multilateral agreement has not prevented substantial unilateral liberalization of investment regimes. UNCTAD (2002) reports that between 1991 and 2001, a total of 1,393 changes were made to national investment regulations and more than 90 per cent of these were liberalizing. In 2001, over 200 regulatory changes were made in 71 countries, only 6 per cent of which were restrictive. In this environment there does not seem to be a compelling rationale to force national governments to adopt a uniform multilateral agreement. Idiosyncratic national regimes are often more sensitive to national development priorities than one-size-fits-all multilateral disciplines.

Moreover, if, as the advocates of these investment measures claim, they are good for developing countries because they will help attract investment, countries will have an incentive to introduce them. Indeed, individually, their incentives to do so may exceed their collective incentives, because those that do adopt these provisions (according to this theory) would be viewed as more attractive sites for investment than those that do not.

In fact, the historical experience provides little evidence that investment treaties generate significantly increased investment flows. Bilateral investment treaties (BITs) surged in the 1990s to more than 2,000 in 2001. There was significant activity between developing countries, which accounted for 42 per cent of new BITs in 2001 (UNCTAD 2002). BITs often proscribe a range of investment protections that go further than many of the realistic proposals before the WTO. Yet there is not much evidence that the signing of bilateral investment treaties increased the flow of investment. UNCTAD (1998) found no relationship between the level of FDI and the number of BITs signed by host countries. A more comprehensive study by Hallward-Driemeier (2002) looked at the bilateral flows of OECD countries to 31 developing countries over twenty years. After accounting for trends, they found little evidence that BITs increased investment to developing countries. More research needs to be done on the effects of investment treaties on investment volume, but the existing evidence suggests that the benefits of additional treaties may be small.

If there is to be an investment agreement (either within the WTO or not) then the major subject of concern for developing countries is the *race to the bottom*—competition for investment that will erode taxes, environmental standards, or labor conditions. The kinds of investment agreements that have been pushed within the Development Round have focused on quite different issues, of benefit to the developed, not the developing, world.

Developed countries have put considerable efforts into expanding investor rights. As we noted earlier, facilitating the free mobility of capital is far less important for global economic efficiency or for the developing countries themselves than facilitating the movement of labor, particularly that of unskilled workers. Indeed, there is a strong case that capital market liberalization may actually lower global economic efficiency.[11]

Moreover, as we have also noted, to the extent that there is validity to the argument that improved investor protections will attract more capital, each country can do that on its own. A developing country does not have to rely on an international agreement. But it is only through international negotiations that free labor mobility can be achieved.[12] There is, accordingly, a far stronger argument for focusing on the 'rights of labor' than on the 'rights of capital'.

Equally troublesome is that arguably, some of the items that are on the agenda would actually have an adverse effect on the well-being of developing countries. The United States put the issue of capital market liberalization on the table, and has in fact insisted on such provisions in bilateral agreements (e.g. with Chile and Singapore). There is mounting evidence that full mobility of short-term speculative capital ('hot money') would actually increase economic instability, in turn increasing poverty. There is little evidence that it enhances economic growth. Indeed, the instability which it generates may well impede investment and growth. The problems of Latin America in recent years, and of East Asia at the end of the last decade, can be directly traced to capital market liberalization.

The problem with many investor protections is that other rights have been compromised in the attempt to enhance the rights of investors. Such investor rights are not costless. But those whose rights are being compromised do not have a seat at the table (see the discussion of institutional reforms in Chapter 9). For instance, Chapter 11 of NAFTA granted investor rights which compromised the rights of government to provide for the general welfare through health, safety, and environmental regulations. Recent decisions suggest that the right of a community to protect itself against toxic wastes may be compromised.

---

[11] See e.g. Stiglitz (2000).

[12] The distinction is perhaps not quite as strong as it has sometimes been put. Allowing immigration of labor will benefit both the recipient and donor country; but there are likely to be groups that are directly adversely affected in the recipient country and who will be vocal, and often politically effective, in their opposition. On the other hand, investors seldom oppose capital market liberalization, as they focus on the consequences of the lowering of the cost of capital. Of course, entrenched industry may resist the entry of competitors in their line of business.

There are already mechanisms for the protection of investors against expropriation, both internationally (e.g. MIGA, the Multilateral Investment Guarantee Agency) and on the part of many of the investing countries (e.g. the Overseas Private Investment Corporation, OPIC, in the United States). A convincing case has not been made that these are inadequate, or, if they are, that they cannot be strengthened. The new investor protections go beyond the concern for expropriation, to the granting of additional rights to investors.

Other services

In our list of priorities, we emphasized earlier the opening up of markets to unskilled labor-intensive services and the movement of unskilled labor (sometimes in support of such services). Earlier rounds of trade liberalization focused on, for instance, financial services, the benefits of which are arguable. The standard argument is that more efficient financial service intermediation lowers the cost of doing business and thus promotes economic growth. It is pro-development. But a closer look at the record reveals a more mixed picture. In at least some developing countries there are concerns that the purchase of local banks by foreign banks has reduced the flow of credit to small and medium-sized domestic enterprises, and thus impeded economic growth. (There is a long history of such concerns, evidenced in the United States for instance by restrictions on interstate banking, intended to prevent New York and other money-center banks from buying up other banks, thereby impeding regional, and especially rural, development.) Agreements on financial services should be re-examined to ascertain whether there is sufficient protection for developing countries. In particular, the right of developing countries to impose lending requirements to force more lending to underserved populations (analogous to those in the United States in the Community Reinvestment Act) should be explicitly recognized.

Other regulatory interventions

Developing countries worry that new trade agreements will create new barriers to the entry of their goods into developed country markets (impeding their development). They worry about blue tariffs (impediments based on labor standards) and green tariffs (impediments based on environmental standards).

Standard economic theory suggests that, with a couple of exceptions noted below, weak standards do not necessarily improve a country's competitiveness, and therefore the issue of standards should not, in general, be embraced within a trade agreement. In standard theory, in a competitive market, any costly provision (such as improved working conditions) simply gets reflected in the wage paid. Such restrictions affect the *form* of compensation, but not the overall level of compensation. In general, there is no reason for the international community to intrude into the forms of compensation.

There are three basic exceptions to these principles. The first is when the global community is affected (a principle which has already been recognized in the appellate decision in the Shrimp–Turtle case, in the area of environment and endangered species[13]). The international community has a right to take actions to address global public goods and externalities, and among the most important of these is the global environment. Trade policy should recognize, as we have noted earlier, that not forcing firms to pay the true social costs of their environmental damage is a form of subsidy which countries should have the right to take action against. Since developing countries as a whole are more likely to be adversely affected by global warming than, say, the United States,[14] using trade policy to force compliance by the advanced industrial countries with the Kyoto Protocol could well be considered an important part of a pro-development trade agenda.

The second is related to the first—matters of human rights. Clearly, when individuals are *forced* to provide labor services

---

[13] As noted earlier, the United States requires domestic shrimpers to use protective technology called turtle-excluder devices, which are a kind of trap door by which turtles can escape from shrimp nets. In 1989, Congress essentially banned importation of shrimp caught by foreign shrimpers who do not use turtle-excluder devices.

[14] This is because the developing countries, on average, are already in warmer climates.

(e.g. when they are prisoners) or *allowed* to use child labor, costs of production may be lowered. As a global community, we do not want to provide economic incentives for such behavior. On the contrary, we want to discourage it. By the same token, when governments have seized land of indigenous peoples, and provided the fruits of that land to others at discounted prices (even if those prices are above its cost of acquisition), then that should be viewed as an unfair subsidy. Countervailing duties against minerals and lumber produced in many countries would be justified by such a provision.

The third, which may also be related to the first, concerns circumstances in which countries can take actions which unfairly affect costs of production. The most notable example of this is restrictions on collective bargaining and the right to take collective action. Then, bargaining relationship between workers and firms is one-sided, and firms can use their economic power to drive down wages and labor costs, making their products more competitive than they otherwise would be.

In all of these cases, some argue that since these are not matters of trade (though the first clearly constitutes a trade-distorting subsidy) it is preferable to address these problems through other channels. Without prejudging the validity of this argument, the fact of the matter is that there are few other channels. Today, in the absence of alternatives, trade sanctions are one of the few ways that the international community can enforce its will, and though resort to such measures should be carefully circumscribed, the instances enumerated are among those in which sanctions may arguably be justified.[15]

On the other hand, there are a host of other regulatory interventions which may adversely affect foreign businesses, sometimes differentially so, but whose primary motivation is to enhance economic development. We referred to one earlier—restrictions on banks that require that they lend certain minimal amounts to small and medium-sized domestic enterprises and to other under-served communities. It is a legitimate role for government to undertake such actions. The United States, Japan, and many other countries did

---

[15] It is important that the decision about whether a trade sanction is to be imposed be taken by the international community; otherwise special interests within a country may well try to disguise protectionism behind a cloak of environmentalism or labor rights.

so in their earlier stages of development—and continue to do so. Because foreign banks may not be in a position to screen such loan applicants as well as domestic banks can, such regulations may have a differentially adverse effect on foreign banks.

By the same token, governments may decide that affirmative action programs are desirable for social purposes, and require that all employers hire workers from certain disadvantaged groups. These restrictions might, conceivably, impose greater costs on foreign firms, who are used to hiring Western-educated individuals, but they reflect a legitimate aspiration of governments to create a more equal society.

Exchange rate manipulation

The United States has recently leveled charges of exchange rate manipulation against China. Global financial markets have exhibited enormous instability. Volatility of exchange rates presents a particular problem for developing countries. Markets are thin, and thus subject to both more volatility and manipulability. Government intervention is, accordingly, often viewed to be desirable. There are a variety of mechanisms by which the government can affect the exchange rate, and there are a variety of government policies which affect the exchange rate indirectly. Bad economic policies (for instance, large deficits) may lead to a devaluation of the currency, whether that is the intent of the policy or not. Given the sizeable adverse consequences of trade deficits, there should be a presumption that countries which have only a moderate trade surplus are not engaged in exchange rate manipulation. The complexities involved suggest that there should be a high threshold test for taking action in the event of an accusation of exchange rate manipulation, and that, at the very least, only multilateral trade surpluses, not bilateral trade deficits, should be presented as evidence of such manipulation.

11

Joining the Trading System

Accession

Twenty countries have been added to the WTO since its creation in 1995.[1] Another 24 countries are negotiating membership,[2] of which eight are least developed countries (LDCs). Most of this book has been concerned with ensuring that the rules and procedures of the WTO deliver benefits to the developing countries within the WTO system. For the (equally needy) developing countries who are not yet members, the benefits of multilateral trade reform in the Doha Round are dependent on the speed and ease with which they are able to join the WTO, and the terms of their accession. The recent experiences of several acceding developing countries are reviewed below.[3] It shows that the WTO's accession process requires reform in several respects. In particular, there are no good arguments for maintaining the double standard which treats countries differently depending on whether they are existing members of the WTO or not. There is a need for transparent and objective rules and procedures for accession negotiations which ensure that the accession process is not unduly

[1] For analysis of the experience of accession see Kennett, Evenett, and Gage (2004). The 20 countries are: Albania, Armenia, Bulgaria, Cambodia, China, Croatia, Ecuador, Estonia, Georgia, Jordan, Kyrgyz Republic, Latvia, Lithuania, Macedonia, Moldova, Mongolia, Nepal, Oman, Panama, and Chinese Taipei.
[2] In order from oldest to most recent application: Algeria, Russian Federation, Saudi Arabia, Belarus, Ukraine, Sudan, Uzbekistan, Vietnam, Seychelles, Tonga, Kazakhstan, Azerbaijan, Andorra, Laos, Samoa, Lebanese Republic, Bosnia and Herzegovina, Bhutan, Cape Verde, Yemen, Serbia and Montenegro, Bahamas, Tajikistan, Ethiopia, and Libya.
[3] For reviews of the experience of individual countries see Grynberg and Joy (2000): Vanuatu; Oxfam (2003a): Cambodia; and Oxfam (2004): Vietnam.

costly for developing countries and that accession terms reflect the level of development of each new member.

The WTO's accession process is lengthy and arduous. At the Fifth Ministerial Conference, held in Cancún in September 2003, Cambodia and Nepal became the first two least developed countries to gain membership through the accession process. The times between their initial application and approval were nine years and fourteen years respectively. Vanuatu, Sudan, Samoa, and Laos are all currently in protracted accession negotiations which began more than six years ago.

Indeed, the time taken to complete the WTO's accession process appears to be growing. Figure 11.1 plots in sequential order the length of time taken to complete the first twenty accessions. Even without the longest accession (China, the fifteenth nation to join the WTO, in 1995), the trend is rising (Kennett, Evenett, and Gage 2004).

Part of the problem lies in the absence of clear and transparent accession criteria and negotiation guidelines. The formal rules of accession are set by Article XII of the Marrakesh Agreement establishing the World Trade Organization. It simply states that new members may accede on 'terms to be agreed between it and the WTO' (Art. XII.1) and that the Ministerial Conference shall approve the

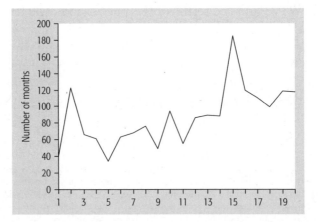

Figure 11.1. **Length of accession process for the first 20 countries to join the WTO**

Source: Kennett, Evenett, and Gage (2004).

agreement on the terms of accession by a two-thirds majority of the members of the WTO (Art. XII.2). Unfortunately, Article XII does not give any guidance on how those terms should be formulated, nor does it provide any membership criteria, or any elements in an accession process. Indeed for an organization which prides itself on being 'rules-based', the accession process is remarkably vague. This lacuna has left the accession process in the hands of member countries who have interpreted the 'terms to be agreed' as an opportunity to go beyond the existing WTO agreements and impose extra conditions (often referred to as 'WTO-plus conditions') on acceding countries. The US has been particularly successful in seeking WTO-plus provisions from its partners in bilateral trade agreements, and then using these as leverage in WTO negotiations. For example, Vietnam agreed to TRIPS-plus commitments in its bilateral trade agreement with the US. Now that Vietnam is seeking accession to the WTO, which operates under the Most Favoured Nation (MFN) principle, these concessions have become the effective starting point for accession negotiations.

In practice the accession process occurs in three stages. In the first stage the WTO establishes a working party, and the acceding country submits a memorandum explaining the detail of its trade regime. In the second stage the working-party members focus on identifying where the applicant's trade policies differ from the rules of the WTO. In the third stage the applicant undertakes a series of bilateral negotiations with working-party members which culminates in an accession agreement for approval by the Ministerial Conference. Since developed countries are always represented on the working party and since all members of the working party must agree to the terms of accession in order for it to be approved, the developed countries have an effective veto over the accession of any country that does not accept their terms. Samoa's senior trade consultant complained about the brinkmanship practiced by developed countries: 'They can ask for all sorts of commitments which Samoa isn't in a position to offer. If they insist, there are two options: we will never become a member or we have to give in to that request.'[4]

---

[4] In an interview with Tuala Falani Chan Tung published in *Sunline*, Apr. 2004.

Recognizing the weaknesses of the current arrangement, the WTO's members committed themselves in the Doha Declaration 'to accelerating the accession of least-developed countries' (para. 9). Following this decision, at the General Council in December 2002, the WTO membership adopted guidelines for LDCs accession. According to the guidelines, negotiations for the accession of LDCs will be facilitated and accelerated through simplified and stream-lined accession procedures. In addition the guidelines suggested that members should ensure that acceding LDCs are not subjected to obligations or commitments that go beyond what is applicable to the existing LDC members.[5] Yet, in several areas, the WTO's actions fall short of this rhetoric. The guidelines are not specific—there are still no objective membership criteria—and evidence from countries in the accession process indicates that they continue to be treated more harshly than existing members.

Recent-accession countries have been subjected to a glaring double standard in that they have been required to accept a higher level of market access commitments than existing members in many areas of the agenda. For example, Cambodia, Nepal and Vanuatu have had to commit themselves to more comprehensive tariff bindings and lower levels of tariff peaks. By way of comparison, while Cambodia, Nepal, and Vanuatu have agreed to bind 100 per cent of their tariff lines, other countries that are already members of the WTO have often bound a much smaller share of their tariff lines.[6] Furthermore, while Cambodia's bound rates are as high as 60 per cent for sensitive agri-cultural products, many least developed (and even developed) WTO members have much higher bound rates on agricultural goods.[7] In industrial goods, Cambodia was required to bind its tariff rates at a

---

[5] A decision of the General Council on Streamlining Accession of the LDCs, dated 10 Dec. 2002 states: 'WTO Members shall exercise restraint in seeking concessions and commitments on trade in goods and ser-vices from acceding LDCs, taking into account the levels of concessions and commitments undertaken by existing WTO LDC Members'; and 'Acceding LDCs shall offer access through reasonable concessions and commitments on trade in goods and services commensurate with their individual development, financial and trade needs, in line with Article XXXVI.8 of GATT 1994, Article 15 of the Agreement on Agriculture, and Articles IV and XIX of the General Agreement on Trade in Services'.

[6] See UNCTAD (2004). For example, both Tanzania and Cameroon have bound 13.3%, and one devel-oped WTO member, Australia, has bound 97%.

[7] For example, bound rates are as high as 550% in Myanmar, and other developing WTO member countries have bound tariff rates on agricultural goods as high as 3,000% (Egypt), while developed WTO members have bound tariff rates on some agricultural goods as high as 350% (United States). See UNCTAD (2004).

maximum level of 50 per cent, much lower than other least developed countries.[8] Similarly, in its accession negotiations, China had to agree to large tariff reductions in agriculture which went far beyond the obligations of existing members. It also agreed to a special safeguard clause allowing individual WTO members to take measures to limit imports of Chinese products in case of a surge. This extraordinary measure, which is in breach of the MFN principle and goes far beyond the GATT safeguard provisions (Art. XIX), could open the floodgate for the application of discriminatory measures against China. In services, Nepal was required to open up seventy service sub-sectors—far more than similar developing countries. Similarly Cambodia was asked to undertake a commitment on audio-visual and distribution services— an area on which no existing LDC member has made a commitment (Oxfam 2003*a*). It seems strange that the WTO's developed country members should force acceding countries, particularly small and poor countries like Cambodia and Nepal, into such strong concessions. Grynberg and Joy (2000) suggest that the motivation lies in the developed countries' desire to create a precedent that can be applied to future negotiations.

Moreover there is clear evidence that the price of accession is growing over time (Kennett, Evenett, and Gage 2004). Figure 11.2

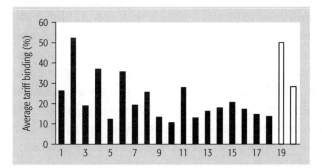

Figure 11.2. **Average tariff binding on agricultural products permitted to the first 20 countries to join the WTO**

Source: Kennett, Evenett, and Gage (2004).

---

[8] Other least developed countries also have relatively high tariff bindings in the non-agricultural goods sector. Bangladesh, Djibouti, Lesotho, and Niger all have peaks in tariff bindings at levels as high as 200%. See UNCTAD (2004). Nepal has bound tariff rates on non-agricultural goods at a maximum level of 130%.

shows that the average tariff binding on agricultural goods allowed to acceding countries is falling over time, with the exception of the last two countries, which are in a different category because they are the only two LDCs that have joined the WTO. The figure demonstrates that acceding countries are making larger commitments on their agricultural tariffs.

The terms of accession agreements should reflect the level of development of the new member, yet much recent experience suggests that acceding countries have been forced to offer concessions that have not been made even by developed countries. For example, Cambodia and Vanuatu made a commitment to bind export subsidies in agriculture at zero and not to apply such subsidies in the future. This means that these two developing countries have effectively forgone the right to use export subsidies for agricultural goods, a right that is granted to all other least developed member countries by the Agreement on Agriculture. This commitment goes further than most developed countries have been willing to go in restricting their own export subsidies.

As well as making more commitments than existing members, acceding developing countries have been denied access to different types of special and differential treatment. Cambodia, Nepal, and Vanuatu accepted a significant reduction of their rights to special and differential treatment—rights that are granted automatically to other least developed countries that are already members of the WTO. New members have been granted much shorter transition periods than existing members. Cambodia obtained the longest transition period—five years for customs valuation, three years for technical barriers to trade (TBT), four years for sanitary and phytosanitary measures (SPS), and three years for TRIPS. Nepal negotiated a three-year period for customs valuation, TBT and SPS, and TRIPS. Vanuatu received only a one-year transition period for customs valuation and a two-year period for TRIPS (UNCTAD 2004).

Insensitivity to the development needs of new members has been particularly manifest in the area of intellectual property rights. Developing countries have been reluctant to commit themselves rapidly to protecting the intellectual property of firms from the industrialized countries because that might hinder technology transfer, enable those firms to extract monopoly rents, and limit access to crucial technologies such as medicines to combat disease. For these reasons developing countries have sought long implementation periods for intellectual property commitments. The original TRIPS Agreement, which came into effect on 1 January 1995, gave developing countries an eleven-year transitional period to bring their national legislation in line with the agreements. Additionally, the Doha Declaration on the TRIPS Agreement and Public Health increased the transitional period for pharmaceutical products to 2016.[9] In their accession negotiations both Cambodia and Nepal were asked to commit themselves to elements of the TRIPS Agreement earlier than other least developed countries. Cambodia and Nepal obtained a three-year transition period, while Vanuatu obtained two years. Cambodia made explicit commitments to comply with all obligations concerning patents and protection of undisclosed information (Part II, sects 5 and 7 of the TRIPS Agreement), although the Doha Declaration on the TRIPS Agreement and Public Health provided an exemption until 2016 from these commitments. In other words, Cambodia has been required to eliminate immediately the use of affordable new generic drugs even though existing LDC members of the WTO need not do so until 2016.

There is an urgent need for the Doha Round to reform its accession procedures in accord with the General Council decision of December 2002, described above. To make these principles operational, there is a need to establish clear and objective rules and disciplines for accession negotiations. Members should ensure that the accession process is not excessively costly for the LDCs and that technical assistance is provided to assist them. It is also necessary that the terms of accession agreements are tailored to LDCs' levels of development and do not force commitments on acceding countries that are not required of existing members.

[9] The Declaration on the TRIPS Agreement and Public Health, WT/MIN(01)/DEC/W/2, 14 Nov. 2001.

Regional and Bilateral trade agreements and South–South trade

With the collapse of the Doha Round, the United States threatened to pursue a set of bilateral and regional trade agreements. Such agreements are against the spirit of the multilateral trading system, which has been based on most-favored-nation principles. Moreover, developing countries may be even more disadvantaged in one-on-one bargaining with the United States; a series of such agreements may leave many developing countries worse off than they would be even with another unfair multilateral agreement. While in principle, such agreements are only consistent with WTO rules if there is limited trade diversion, in practice, little attention has been paid to this requirement. The argument that these regional agreements are useful as a step towards improved multilateral agreements is also suspect. The kind of multilateral agreement to which they may lead may be more unbalanced than one which would be directly entered into, without the more circuitous route. More to the point, there is a high cost to the roundabout approach. For to the extent that there is *temporary* trade diversion, some industries are being *temporarily encouraged*, only to be later discouraged. Adjustment costs are typically high in developing countries; there may be significant costs of entry and exit, and with a scarcity of capital, the burden on developing countries may be particularly large.

In the next chapter, we propose institutional reforms that address these issues. But there is another arena in which trade agreements which fall short of full multinational agreements may be desirable, and those entail reducing the restrictions on South–South trade. South–South trade makes up some 40 per cent of developing country trade. And, as we noted earlier, developing countries have much higher tariff levels than developed countries. This suggests that considerable gains are available from liberalization of South–South trade.

How then should WTO agreements manage the trade-off between the need to protect domestic markets from competition from developed countries, while not hindering trade between developing countries? One solution might be to allow developing countries to offer preferential market access deals to each other in the same way that the EU's Everything but Arms initiative offers free access to developing countries only. Such a provision would have one further advantage: preferential treatment by some developed countries (most notably the US) is based on *political conditionality*—it is a 'gift' that is constantly in danger of being taken away, and this induced risk limits the value of the gift. Moreover, the granting of such preferences becomes a lever with which developed countries can extract other concessions from developing countries. A South–South agreement would likely focus more exclusively on trade issues, and would not suffer from these abuses.

12
Institutional Reforms

Procedures

There is widespread dissatisfaction with the way that trade agreements are made, partly stemming from a belief that current procedures put developing countries at a marked disadvantage. This is particularly important, given the increasing role that such trade agreements play in our societies. They define a broad set of rights and obligations, yet they are arrived at in a manner that is distinctly different from the way that other kinds of legislation are adopted. The terms are often negotiated behind closed doors, with little public debate about specific provisions. The legislative process is often truncated. The result is agreements, like Chapter 11 of the NAFTA agreement or the TRIPS Agreement, which contain provisions that would probably never have been accepted by a democratic parliament with open discussion in a deliberative process.

The hallmark of earlier trade agreements is that they were conducted in secret, with many of the terms not fully disclosed until the end of the negotiations, and then governments faced an 'all or nothing' choice. Because parliamentarians could have no effect on the outcome, they had little incentive to understand the intricacies. Given the extent to which trade issues overlap with other issues, including those touching on the environment, it is important that the procedural reforms make deliberations about trade issues more like other deliberative processes—including more open deliberation.

Trade has become too important to be left to trade ministers alone. Part of the deliberative process must entail the active involvement of others (meeting together, not just through the trade ministers). Thus when intellectual property matters are being discussed (if they are to be discussed at all), the science ministers must be involved. When trade policy affects the environment, there must be some mechanisms for the environmental ministers' voices to be heard. They would insist, for instance, that provisions be inserted that prevent a race to the bottom, that low environmental standards (e.g. those associated with allowing the pollution of the world's atmosphere) be viewed as a form of subsidy to be prohibited.

We emphasized in Chapter 5 that the fairness of the international regime is to be judged not only in terms of the outcomes, but also in terms of the processes. There is now a large literature documenting the deficiencies in the procedures,[1] and for reasons already noted, these procedural deficiencies disadvantage developing countries. That is why procedural reforms—particularly those relating to transparency and representation—should have a high priority. Civil society should be given a greater role in the negotiations.

The developed countries should continue the kind of support they have provided to help the developing countries participate more effectively in these deliberations. Trade negotiations involve complex issues, including economic issues on which even the experts are not in agreement. Meaningful participation in these discussions requires understanding these complexities, knowing the full import of each of the provisions, and how they might affect countries differently in quite different situations.

Structures and representation

As the number of WTO members has grown, and the demands for a more inclusive bargaining process have increased, the current system appears to be increasingly unwieldy. It is not the intent of this

[1] On participation see Blackhurst, Lyakurwa, and Oyejide (2000); on transparency see Francois (2001); on representation see Winters (2001).

chapter to provide a detailed analysis of alternative proposals for institutional reform, but rather to highlight its importance and to emphasize why such reforms should in fact be viewed as a priority in current discussions.

It is apparent that the opening up of the WTO to so many members has made negotiations cumbersome and difficult. This has been used as an excuse for secretive processes in which, somehow, a selected group of countries are chosen to negotiate with the United States, the EU, and Japan in the 'Green Room'. The Green Room process has been formally abolished, but small negotiating groups continue to set the agenda behind closed doors with inadequate openness and transparency. In other areas of democratic decision-making, especially those based on consensual processes, as trade negotiations are *in principle* supposed to be, the principle of *representativeness* is well accepted: a small group of countries is chosen to reflect the various interests and constituencies—say the largest trading countries, the United States, EU, Japan, China; a representative or two of the middle-income countries, say Brazil and one other country; a couple of representatives of the least developed countries; a representative of the Cairns Group, etc. Each would then consult with those they are representing on a regular basis. An open and transparent process would ensure that the views and voices of all are heard.

Trade negotiations entail a myriad of proposals for changing the rules of the game, and developing countries are often at a disadvantage in assessing the impact of each of these proposals on themselves, let alone the general equilibrium impact on the global trading system. Another requirement for a fair trade regime would be a new body within the WTO responsible for assessing the impacts of proposed trade provisions on development and developing countries. Its mandate would be to look objectively at the consequences of alternative proposals for all the countries of the world, recognizing that economic science is not at a stage where there is agreement about the 'right' model. Thus, such a body might attempt to assess the impact of the allegedly non-trade-distorting agricultural subsidies in a world in which there are capital constraints.

Such a body might help too in the enforcement of current agreements, providing guidance, for instance, on whether a particular proposed bilateral or regional trade agreement is consistent with the principle that 'trade diversion' should be limited, and should be less than the amount of trade creation.

Other functions of an expanded WTO secretariat might include an independent body to assess countries in crisis, to adjudicate and approve the imposition of trade restrictions ('safeguard measures'), and to investigate dumping charges, countervailing duties, and phytosanitary conditions.

There is a need to address the scope of technical assistance and the capacity of the WTO to provide this adequately within existing structures. Helping low-income countries strengthen their institutional capacity to permit them to meet WTO agreements will require not only technical assistance but also significant financial assistance. The costs of implementation of WTO commitments are very substantial.[2]

While a limited assistance program may assist developing countries to implement reform, technical assistance is not sufficient to deal with the economy-wide adjustment costs associated with structural change. These costs, which generate domestic opposition to trade liberalization, are no less important barriers to progress than the lack of institutional capacity.

In addition, lack of institutional capacity has the effect of limiting the access of developing countries to justice within the dispute system. Developing countries are disadvantaged in complex and expensive legal proceedings. An expansion of existing legal assistance schemes will be an important prerequisite for institutional fairness.

Responsibility for the bulk of technical assistance has fallen on international organizations. Both the World Bank and the WTO have increased their technical cooperation activities. However, as much as 90 per cent of financing for these activities is provided by trust funds provided by two or three bilateral donors, while the WTO itself has typically allocated less than one per cent of its total annual budget for technical cooperation activities—less than half a million US dollars (Michalopoulos 2000).

---

[2] Finger and Schuler (1999) 'The implementation of Uruguay Round Commitments: The development challenge', Policy Research Working Paper no. 2000, World Bank, Washington, DC.

13

Trade Liberalization and the Costs of Adjustment

Introduction

Trade liberalization creates adjustment costs as resources are moved from one sector to another in the process of reform. When tariffs are reduced, import-competing firms may reduce their production in the face of new competition, causing some of their workers and capital to lie idle for a period. The firm's laid-off workers will incur costs while searching for new jobs and may need to invest in retraining. Governments will be called upon to provide assistance to the unemployed, while also incurring costs associated with implementing the new systems for managing reform.

To take advantage of the opportunities offered by improved access to foreign markets, developing countries will be required to make investments—in infrastructure by government and in new facilities or technologies by exporters—before they can capitalize on the opportunities offered by improved access to foreign markets.

Significant trade liberalization will also affect the distribution of income among factors of production: the relative price of the factor which is in relative scarcity will decline, while that of the abundant factor will increase.[1] Agricultural subsidies get capitalized in the

---

[1] This is the implication of the renowned Stolper and Samuelson (1941) theorem; but even if the restrictive conditions under which it holds are not satisfied, there is a presumption that relative rewards to different factors will change in the way indicated.

price of land, and landowners will lose substantial amounts when such subsidies are eliminated.[2] Because there are large distortionary costs associated with taxation, there are large societal costs associated with the compensations designed to mitigate these effects.[3] Given the severe constraints on raising taxes in developing countries, the opportunity cost of funds diverted for even partial compensation may be very high.

Trade liberalization also reduces tariff revenues; as alternative sources of revenue are limited the costs of the revenue loss is high. Thus, either public expenditures get reduced or other taxes are increased, and either of these may have significant adverse effects on growth.[4]

Trade liberalization may impose further costs: the movement from quotas to tariffs, whatever its merits, may expose countries to additional risks.[5] Developing countries with weak social safety nets will have to devote more resources to strengthening these safety nets and will have to mitigate the cost of risks. This too needs to be viewed as part of the costs of trade liberalization.

In one sense, these adjustment costs can be thought of as the 'price' to be paid for the benefits of multilateral tariff reduction. Together these adjustment costs and trade benefits determine the net effect of trade reform for each country. The Doha Round has placed renewed emphasis on the importance of sharing the benefits of trade reform fairly among developed and developing countries. However, less attention has been paid to the distribution of adjustment costs among countries.

An understanding of the costs of trade reform is important for at least two reasons. First, if the 'development focus' of the Doha

[2] The numbers can be large. A US$4bn annual cotton subsidy, if fully captalized in land values, translates at a 5% interest rate into US$80bn.

[3] Thus, even if the dollar value of the gains to the winners from liberalization are greater than the dollar value of the losses to the losers, trade liberalization may *not* be welfare-enhancing when the costs of compensation are taken into account.

[4] Many countries have shifted to greater reliance on the value-added tax, but as Stiglitz (2003) has argued, this switch may have adverse effects on development.

[5] That is, countries now are more subject to the vagaries of international prices. See Dasgupta and Stiglitz (1977). More generally, trade liberalization may make countries more vulnerable to external shocks, and for countries in which trade looms large in GDP, the result may be greater macro-economic volatility. See Easterly, Islam, and Stiglitz (2001), and especially the fuller text of the Michael Bruno Memorial Lecture, 'Is there a Workable Macroeconomic Paradigm for LDCs?', presented by J. E. Stiglitz at the 12th World Congress of the IEA, Buenos Aires, 27 Aug. 1999.

Round is to have any meaning, then WTO members must be mindful of the fact that the cost of adjusting to their agreements will have serious consequences for development. Not only do adjustment costs fall particularly harshly on the poorest people in the world because they are least able to afford them, but also the costs consume resources that would otherwise be spent on alternative development priorities. For many people, the impact of trade reform will overwhelm the effects of other economic development programs.

The second motivation for understanding adjustment costs is the pragmatic need to win political support for reform. High adjustment costs give some groups a vested interest in the status quo. Identifying and compensating those groups may be an effective way of removing impediments to welfare-improving policy changes.

This chapter examines the effect of several sources of adjustment costs. A theme that runs through the empirical evidence is that the adjustment process resulting from the proposals emerging from the Doha Round will have a particularly harsh impact on the people and governments of developing countries—especially small developing countries. There are several reasons for this asymmetry. First, developing countries are most vulnerable to policy shocks because their export industries are the least diversified—many are dependent on the export and hence world price of just one or two commodities. Second, developing countries are likely to have to make the largest changes to comply with international regulations such as those embodied in the Singapore Issues. Third, the structure of world trade is most distorted in the industries of importance to developing countries. World markets for agriculture, processed foods, textiles, and other critical goods are those most distorted by developed countries' tariff policies. Consequently these industries will be highly affected by liberalization—even where reform has long-run net positive effects for developing countries, they will have to cope with adjustment costs, investment costs, and redistributive effects. Fourth, and most importantly, developing countries are home to the world's poorest people and the weakest credit markets. These people are particularly vulnerable to adjustment costs.

For these reasons, the adjustment to new trading rules is a radically different experience for developed and developing countries.

This chapter studies the process of adjustment and the costs it implies for developing countries. It notes that there are several policy measures that should accompany trade reform to minimize the costs of adjustment and the disproportionate welfare losses to particular social groups. Policies to assist developing countries to benefit from reforms are also surveyed briefly. Many of these policies will require assistance from developing countries and international institutions.

Costs of adjustment

Empirical studies have attempted to define and quantify adjustment costs in developed countries.[6] These studies suggest that labor bears the brunt of the costs, but that (ignoring the distributional consequences) for developed countries, the costs are small relative to the gains. Baldwin, Mutti, and Richardson (1980) analyse the adjustment costs for the US resulting from a 50 per cent cut in domestic tariffs. They focus on adjustment of the capital stock and the costs borne by laid-off workers. They find that labor bears almost 90 per cent of the adjustment costs. In total they conclude that adjustment costs account for 4 per cent of the gains from liberalization. De Melo and Tarr (1990) use a computable general equilibrium approach to analyse the welfare effects and adjustment costs resulting from the elimination of quotas in textiles, steel, and autos. In their model adjustment costs are measured as the lost earnings suffered by dislocated workers. They estimate that the adjustment costs are just 1.5 per cent of the gains from liberalization. Winters and Takacs (1991) found that the British footwear industry suffered just over 1,000 lost jobs as a result of the removal of quotas in the late 1970s and most of these workers remained unemployed for between 5 and 21 weeks. The study concludes that the lost income in the first year after the quotas were eliminated amounted only to between 0.5 and 1.5 per cent of the consumer gains from lower footwear prices.

---

[6] Several studies are reviewed in WTO (2003).

There is significantly less evidence on the size of adjustment costs in developing countries, but there are many reasons to expect that the costs identified in the studies above would be much larger in poorer countries. First, most of the industrial base of developing economies is concentrated in a few key industries. In 'one-industry towns' the costs of adjustment may be larger if the laid-off workers from the primary industry cannot be absorbed into alternative employment.[7] For example, liberalization of the cashew market in Mozambique in the late 1990s led to the loss of 85 per cent of the workforce employed in the local processed-cashew industry. Recent evidence suggests that whole towns have shut down as a result of the factory closures (WTO 2002).

Adjustment costs may also be exacerbated in poor areas because of limited access to credit. If capital markets are weak, viable firms may not be able to finance the short-term costs associated with new trade regimes, and laid-off workers may not be able to find funds to retrain themselves for alternative jobs.

In many developing countries unemployment rates are high, and accordingly, the length of time that individuals will spend unemployed will be larger.[8] Studies in the United States show that the costs of adjustment for dislocated workers is lower for more-educated workers—evidently their higher education makes them more adaptable, and hence more mobile.[9] With education levels typically low in developing countries, one might expect the transition costs to be correspondingly greater.

There are other reasons why developing countries might suffer larger adjustment costs than developed countries. This section reviews some of the issues associated with the proposals emerging from the Doha Round. In particular, the reduction of MFN tariff rates will lead to the erosion of the preference margins currently benefiting the exports of the least developed countries under various non-reciprocal market access preference schemes.

Also, the reduction of tariffs has serious fiscal consequences for many developing countries. Over thirty countries—mostly small

---

[7] Among the costs that should be calculated are those associated with relocating labor, the loss in the value of the housing capital stock, and the value of the associated infrastructure.

[8] See Shapiro and Stiglitz (1984) for a calculation of the relationship between the level of unemployment and the cost of losing one's job.   [9] For a survey of these studies, see Kletzer (2001).

and poor—derive more than 25 per cent of their public budgets from tariff revenue. For these countries, trade liberalization will necessitate massive reform of the taxation system to avoid fiscal crises.

Finally, developing countries face disproportionately high implementation costs from the proposals related to the Singapore Issues. Regulatory agreements in areas such as trade facilitation and competition policy require public expenditure on new laws, systems, administration, and enforcement. Estimates of the costs of implementing the regulatory changes in the Uruguay Round are high. For developing countries, whose institutions are weakest and in greatest need of reform to meet international standards, these implementation costs are disproportionately high. Thus, seemingly symmetric rules may have asymmetric costs.

For these reasons, Doha Round agreements should offer equitable market access rules as well as addressing differences in adjustment costs in order to achieve a fair deal for developing countries.

Erosion of LDC trade preferences

Several developed countries offer non-reciprocal preferential market access which reduces the tariff rates on the goods of least developing countries below MFN rates. Almost 12 per cent of US imports subject to MFN tariffs enter the US from LDCs under lower tariff rates through such non-reciprocal preference programs. Many LDCs fear that reductions in MFN tariff rates through multilateral trade liberalization would harm their exports by eroding their preferential margins.

Preferential tariffs for LDCs have formed an important part of global trade architecture since the inception of the Generalized System of Preferences (GSP) in 1968. Recently there have been a number of initiatives in OECD countries to discriminate further in favor of LDCs. Most notable among these are the EU's Everything but Arms (EBA) initiative and the US's African Growth and Opportunity Act (AGOA).

The net effect on LDCs of preference erosion through reduction in MFN tariffs depends on whether the loss of trade diversion (the negative switching or substitution that occurs as the margin of their preferences declines) exceeds the gains from trade creation (the increase in global trade resulting from improved market access). The evidence below suggests that favorable trade diversion resulting from preferences has had only a limited effect on most LDCs.

However, large effects on a small group of countries and a small group of sectors cannot be ignored. The net effects of reductions in MFN tariffs could be summarized as being positive and significant for most industries in most countries (particularly developing countries outside the preferential schemes for least developed countries) but large and negative for a small number of producers. The policy implication of these results is straightforward: preference erosion is not a consideration that should impede multilateral liberalization, but it does suggest that compensation and adjustment programs for the small group of net losers should be an integral part of any liberalization program.

The benefits of trade preferences for LDCs

Preference schemes have been adopted in an effort to support the development of poor countries and assist them to integrate into the global trading system. Preferences increase the exports of beneficiaries, partly by diverting trade from countries that do not receive preferences. This competitive advantage may help LDCs to develop through increased investment, employment, and growth. Additionally preferences may encourage industrial diversification in countries that have relied on the production of primary goods.

However, analysis of preferential schemes on LDC exports shows only limited impact. Brenton (2003) studies the impact of the EBA initiative, which the EU has argued will 'significantly enhance export opportunities and hence potential income and growth' for LDCs (CEC 2002). In 2001 the EBA initiative granted duty-free access to imports of all products from the least developed countries (except arms and munitions).[10] Total exports from these LDCs to the EU increased by 9.6 per cent in 2001. However, in practice, as noted

[10] However, not all the preferences were implemented immediately; some will be delayed until 2009. The calculations here ignore these future impacts.

earlier, the EBA was only relevant to the 919 products (of the EU's 10,200 tariff lines) which had not previously been granted duty-free status under either the GSP or the Cotonou Agreement.[11] Of these 919 products, imports from LDCs were recorded in just 80 products in 2001. Brenton (2003) notes that total exports of these products actually fell from   3.5 million in 2000 to   2.9 million in 2001.[12] Moreover, trade in these goods in 2001 amounted to just two-hundredths of one per cent of the total value of LDC exports to the EU. Thus it appears that the direct impact of the EBA initiative has not been significant in the short term and, given the small size of trade in affected products, it is not likely to be large in the medium term. (Supporters of the EBA initiative are more optimistic; they focus on the fact that its provisions are being implemented only gradually over time. But as the discussion above indicates, the devil is often in the detail, and this provides some grounds for skepticism.)

Analysis of the long-run effects of trade preference systems including many countries requires general equilibrium analysis. Laird, Safadi, and Turrini (2002) evaluate the effects of the GSP scheme by analysing the welfare consequences of replacing GSP with MFN tariff rates. Their computable general equilibrium (CGE) simulations identify the costs and benefits of the GSP to a range of countries. Table 13.1 reports the percentage change in exports associated with the removal of the GSP (i.e. negative values indicate benefits resulting from the GSP). The trade effects are quite small, with the largest effect in South Asia, which is estimated to have had an increase in exports of 1.58 per cent as a result of preferences. There are also negligible effects on donor countries, among whom Europe alone suffers a very small export decline.[13] Table 13.1 also indicates that trade effects are concentrated in a small number of sectors, particularly textiles and processed agriculture. The smaller effects in agriculture for some of the LDCs

[11] Forty-four of these tariff lines were products such as bananas, rice, and sugar, for which liberalization was delayed for up to 8 years.

[12] The actual decline was even larger, but Brenton removes the effect of the large drop in EU imports of Sudanese grain sorghum in 2000–1. These numbers do not include trade in the 44 products for which liberalization was delayed. There may, of course, be other factors affecting trade, and it is clearly possible that the declines would have been even larger but for the EBA initiative. The analysis above simply demonstrates the limited scope of the agreement.

[13] Note that this study only considers the GSP scheme and does not include the effects of other schemes such as the EU's Cotonou Agreement, which offers the largest gains to African countries.

Table 13.1. Export changes resulting from the replacement of GSP with MFN tariffs (GCE results, %)

| Exporting region | Sectors | | | | | | | | Total |
	Mining	Transportation equipment	Machines	Metal	Other manufacturing	Agricultural primary	Agricultural processed	Textiles, apparel	Services	
Asian NICs	−0.05	−0.89	−1.03	−0.53	−1.2	0.33	−1.57	−2.07	1.02	−0.70
China	−0.13	1.09	−0.31	−0.53	−1.0	0.21	−1.45	−2.67	0.91	−0.8
South Asia	1.01	−1.29	−1.46	−2.12	−1.98	−0.79	−2.44	−3.50	2.28	−1.58
Western Europe	−0.60	−0.20	0.13	−0.36	0.23	0.01	0.62	1.40	−0.67	0.001
North America	−0.70	0.03	0.06	−0.11	0.05	−0.62	0.06	0.14	−0.49	−0.12
CEED	−0.15	−3.37	−1.51	0.07	−1.31	0.25	−1.54	0.68	0.70	−0.54
Sub-Saharan Africa	−0.06	1.78	−1.00	2.27	−1.70	−1.43	−9.40	−5.96	1.77	−0.75
Oceania	−0.68	0.50	0.17	−0.31	0.01	−0.49	−0.02	1.13	−0.09	−0.16
North Africa/Middle East	−0.10	−0.71	−3.74	−0.62	−1.51	−0.34	−2.18	−2.99	1.26	−0.48
South America	−0.13	1.11	0.62	−0.19	−1.83	−0.56	−2.51	−0.44	0.49	−0.39
Japan	−1.47	−0.67	−0.40	−1.13	−0.79	−1.37	−1.33	−4.34	−0.63	−0.64
Rest of world	0.145	−1.83	−2.88	−0.24	−2.80	−0.48	−6.90	−7.02	1.58	−1.46

Source: Laird, Safadi, and Turrini (2002).

Table 13.2. Welfare effects from the replacement of GSP with MFN tariffs (GCE results, US $m)

	Allocation component	Terms-of-Trade component	Total	% change
Asian NICs	−405	−1,950	−2,317	−0.23
China	−360	−1,613	−1,855	−0.15
South Asia	−327	−594	−964	−0.19
Western Europe	−722	4,634	3,719	0.05
North America	85	1,866	2,252	0.02
Transition economies	−317	−941	−1,297	−0.17
Sub-Saharan Africa	−173	−512	−701	−0.22
Oceania	1	−22	−11	−0.003
North Africa and Middle East	−474	−1,315	−1,816	−0.23
Latin America	−226	−789	−1,043	−0.05
Japan	−246	1,466	1,189	0.033
Rest of world	−107	−256	−446	−0.17
Total	−3,275	−27	−3,293	

Source: Laird, Safadi, and Turrini (2002: table 5).

suggest that the GSP might play an important role in diversifying the industrial base of those economies. Table 13.2 reports the effects of the GSP on welfare. The largest beneficiaries in percentage terms are Africa and the Asian NICs. Overall the effects are quite small, amounting to approximately 0.2 per cent of real income in any region. The implication of these results, if correct, is that there is likely on average to be little difference between the impact of trade liberalization measures (which undermine the benefits of preferences) on countries that are the beneficiaries of preferences and those that are not.

Why are the benefits so small?

In practice LDCs are often not able to realize much of the benefit promised by market access preferences. This is evident in the low degree of utilization of preference schemes. Table 13.3 illustrates the utilization of preferences offered by Canada, the EU, Japan, and the US. The table separates the underutilization of preferences into a component relating to the generosity of the scheme itself (the

Table 13.3. Utilization of non-reciprocal preferences granted by the Quad countries to LDCs, 2001

	Total imports (1)	Dutiable imports (2)	Imports eligible for GSP (3)	Imports receiving GSP (4)	Product coverage percentage	Utilization percentage ((4)/(3))	Utility percentage ((4)/(2))
Canada	243.2	94.6	11.4	8.0	12.1	70.2	8.5
EU	4372.4	3958.1	3935.7	1847.4	99.4	46.9	46.7
Japan	1001.3	398.1	278.3	228.4	69.9	82.1	57.4
US	7221.3	6716.3	2960.1	2836.1	44.1	95.8	42.2
Total	12838	11167.1	7185.5	4919.9	64.3	68.5	44.1

Source: UNCTAD (2003).

product coverage ratio) and a component relating to the take-up rate (utilization ratio).

Interestingly, Table 13.3 shows that the EU has a high product coverage percentage and a lower than average utilization percentage and the US seems to have the reverse. In the case of the EU, over 50 per cent of eligible exports are not getting preferential access. Part of the reason for this is stringent rules of origin which are designed to prevent trade deflection, whereby products from non-beneficiary countries are routed through LDCs to exploit the preferences. Brenton (2003) suggests that one reason for the lack of take-up is that it can often be difficult or costly to acquire the required documentation to satisfy rules of origin.

Recent literature suggests that rules of origin are a main reason for the under-utilization of trade preferences (see Estevadeordal 2000), and preference-receiving countries themselves consistently identify rules of origin as a problem for their exporters.[14] Rules of origin often require exporters to devise and operate a new accounting system, which in most cases differs from existing systems designed to deal with domestic legal requirements. In many cases the additional expenditure incurred in operating a parallel accounting

[14] The shortcomings of the origin system and consequent obstacles to the utilization of preferences identified by preference-receiving countries were discussed in the context of the UNCTAD Working Group on Rules of Origin and in the Special Committee on Preferences. See 'UNCTAD, Compendium of the work and analysis conducted by UNCTAD Working Groups and Sessional Committees on GSP Rules of Origin, Part I' (UNCTAD/ITD/GSP/31) of 21 February 1996.

system may outweigh the benefit conferred by tariff preferences. This possibility is supported by evidence suggesting that under-utilization is strongest in sectors where the preference margin is lowest and therefore less likely to be greater than the administration costs of complying with rules of origin.[15] Another cost imposed by rules of origin is that they may disqualify LDC exporters from preferences if they avail themselves of cheap imported intermediate inputs. UNCTAD (1996) finds evidence of this by relating peaks in Bangladeshi and Cambodian imports of fabrics from China to low utilization rates of preference schemes by textile exporters in those countries. This can be assumed to be a strong indication that the manufacturers have chosen to give up tariff preferences because they cannot comply with rules-of-origin requirements.

Another problem with preference schemes is that they are not particularly generous when rates are weighted across goods. Table 13.4 shows the benefits of GSP rates against MFN rates. When simple averages are taken the GSP rates are more favourable in all countries. However when weighted across goods average MFN rates are even lower than average GSP rates in the EU, Canada, and Japan. This occurs because the GSP rates in those countries are set as a margin under the MFN rates which are typically higher on imports

Table 13.4. Tariff averages for imports under MFN and GSP, 1999

		Simple tariff average	Weighted tariff average
Canada	MFN	4.49	1.27
	GSP	2.89	4.18
Japan	MFN	5.28	1.97
	GSP	2.2	3.47
US	MFN	5.59	2.56
	GSP	0.0	0.0
EU	MFN	7.07	3.56
	GSP	5.23	4.54

Source: Laird, Safadi, and Turrini (2002)

[15] UNCTAD (1996): 58.7 per cent of those Mexican exports to the US that were eligible for preferences but were not imported under them constituted goods whose preference margin was less than 5 per cent. Evidently, the cost of establishing that one is qualified to receive preferential treatment exceeds the benefits.

from developing countries. That means that MFN rates are so much higher on the goods exported by developing countries that even after GSP discounts, LDCs face higher average tariff rates. In a sense, the GSP only partially compensates for the discrimination by developed countries against the goods produced by the developing countries.

Figures 13.1*a* and 13.1*b* show the import duties paid to the US on high-value agricultural products. Figure 13.1*a* indicates that the US tariff system already discriminates against both low-income and middle-income countries in these products. Whereas high-income countries account for 75 per cent of dutiable imports in 2001 they paid only 56 per cent of duty. By contrast middle- and low-income countries paid higher duty as a proportion of dutiable imports. The reason is that (even allowing for preferences) US tariff peaks tend to concentrate on goods exported intensively by developing countries. Figure 13.1*b* calculates an 'effective tariff rate' as the ratio of duties collected to the value of imports. The effective tariff rate paid by middle-income countries is almost twice as much as that paid by developed countries. Trade preferences often further discriminate against middle income countries.

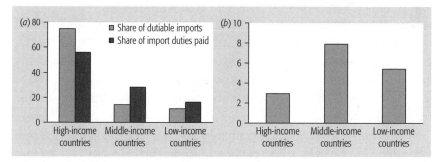

Figure 13.1. **Agricultural import protection in the US**
(*a*) **Share of dutiable high-value agricultural products imports to the US and share of duty paid, 2001 (% of total)**
(*b*) **Effective US import tarrifs on high-value agricultural products by source, 2001 (% *ad valorem*)**

Source: Wainio and Gibson (2003).

*The impact of the erosion of the benefit of trade preferences
as a result of lower MFN rates*

Estimates of the benefits of preferences for LDCs (often calculated
as the costs LDCs would experience if they were eliminated) are
different from estimates of the costs of preference erosion through
reduced MFN tariff rates. The chief difference is that in the case of
preference erosion LDCs are compensated for the loss of competitive
advantage in donor countries by increased market access in all other
countries. As a result the costs to LDCs of preference erosion
through MFN tariff reductions are likely to be smaller than the costs
of preference elimination.

Waino and Gibson (2003) use a partial equilibrium model to
estimate the effects of tariff-cutting liberalization on developing
country exports. Their study focuses on the US and considers only
a range of high-value agricultural products, including fresh fruits
and beverages and processed food and beverages. Table 13.5 reports
the results of an experiment in which all tariffs are eliminated. In
particular it reports the trade creation effects (derived from the
price reductions following tariff cuts) and the trade-shifting effects
(from domestic consumers switching to those goods whose
protection—and price—has declined most) for countries receiving
non-reciprocal preferences, free-trade partners, and countries subject to MFN tariff rates.[16] The table indicates that the magnitude of
trade effects is small. It also indicates that the beneficiaries of
non-reciprocal trade preferences suffer no net loss from loss of preferences. Their market share is reduced but this is offset by capturing
additional market share in those commodities for which they face
(the now-lower) MFN tariffs, but also compete with exporters in free
trade agreements.

Waino and Gibson's study probably understates the net benefits of
liberalization because they do not include the gains to LDCs from
increased market access in countries where they were not previously
receiving benefits. Since 28 per cent of LDC exports go to developing
countries, and developing countries have higher average MFN tariffs

---

[16] Quite simply the model assumes that tariff reductions flow through to price reductions and increase
the level of US domestic demand. However, the trade creation effects in their model may be overstated
since they assume an infinite elasticity of supply.

Table 13.5. **Effect of full tariff liberalization on high-value agricultural imports to US (US $m)**

	Preference beneficiaries	FTA partners	MFN partners	Global total
Pre-liberalization imports	4,503	9,709	7,551	21,762
Effect of liberalization				
Trade created	194	92	391	679
Trade shifted	−23	−153	176	0
Total effect	171	−61	567	679
Total effect as percentage	3.8%	−0.6%	7.5%	3.1%

Source: Waino and Gibson (2003).

than developed countries, the lowering of these tariffs is a potentially significant source of trade creation.

Waino and Gibson (2003) offer the example of Peruvian asparagus, US$26.7 million of which was exported to the US at preferential rates and US$5.9 million at MFN rates. Peru is a low-cost exporter of asparagus and thus the reduction in its margin of preference caused only a small loss of market share, which would be more than offset by increased MFN exports under lower rates.[17] Moreover, if liberalization includes reductions in quotas, countries receiving preferences may even experience an increase in their exports to donor countries.

Vulnerable industries

The results above indicate that the average effect of preference erosion on LDCs is unlikely to be large. However, this is not true for all industries in all countries. Industries that are particularly reliant on preferences could be seriously damaged by preference erosion.

In general the higher the dependency of countries on preferences, the larger the potential loss from MFN tariff cuts. Table 13.6 gives a useful insight into developing countries' levels of EU preference dependence. The penultimate column gives the share of exports newly liberalized under the EBA in 2001 as a percentage of total

[17] In a situation such as that just depicted, the *marginal* export is at MFN rates; the impact on trade is thus determined solely by the change in the MFN rate. Peruvian exporters, however, lose a rent equal in value to the value of the preference.

Table 13.6. **Importance of Products Liberalized under the EBA (monetary values in US$ 000)**

	Total exports to EU (1)	EBA exports (products liberalized in 2001) (2)	Sugar, bananas, and rice (3)	EBA exports share (%) ((2)/(1))	Sugar, bananas, and rice export share (%) ((3)/(1))
ACP countries					
Angola	1,944,630	91	0	0.00	0.00
Congo	941,784	7	50	0.00	0.01
Equatorial Guinea	754,865	0	0	0.00	0.00
Liberia	736,973	10	0	0.00	0.00
Madagascar	600,912	72	8,500	0.01	1.41
Guinea	579,518	41	0	0.01	0.00
Mozambique	530,174	248	991	0.05	0.19
Tanzania	395,283	35	6,648	0.01	1.68
Sudan	303,550	778	13,982	0.26	4.61
Mauritania	258,568	6	6	0.00	0.00
Uganda	242,524	116	55	0.05	0.02
Malawi	194,903	0	22,617	0.00	11.60
Ethiopia	159,389	12	968	0.01	0.61
Zambia	158,375	1,359	6,675	0.86	4.21
CAR	152,804	0	0	0.00	0.00
Niger	119,613	6	0	0.00	0.00
Benin	63,698	69	0	0.11	0.00
Burkino Faso	63,052	52	0	0.08	0.00
Djibouti	61,494	38	0	0.06	0.00
Togo	58,591	26	26	0.04	0.02
Chad	57,638	1	0	0.00	0.00
Mali	45,726	67	0	0.13	0.00
Sierra Leone	38,420	72	0	0.19	0.00
Rwanda	21,782	6	78	0.03	0.36
Comoros	20,770	3	0	0.00	0.00
Gambia	20,679	41	0	0.00	0.00
Burundi	19,474	19	0	0.10	0.00
Lesotho	12,797	0	0	0.00	0.00
Haiti	16,356	158	0	0.97	0.00
Vanuatu	13,653	0	0	0.00	0.00
Cape Verde	11,803	10	0	0.11	0.00
Sao Tome	8,009	0	0	0.00	0.00
Eritrea	6,737	1	0	0.01	0.00
Solomon Islands	4,975	0	0	0.00	0.00
Guinea Bissau	4,542	0	0	0.00	0.00
Somalia	3,047	0	0	0.00	0.00
Samoa	2,206	0	0	0.00	0.00
Kiribati	728	0	0	0.00	0.00

Table 13.6. *continued*

	Total exports to EU (1)	EBA exports (products liberalized in 2001) (2)	Sugar, bananas, and rice (3)	EBA exports share (%) ((2)/(1))	Sugar, bananas, and rice export share (%) ((3)/(1))
Tuvalu	390	0	0	0.00	0.00
Non-ACP countries					
Bangladesh	3,318,865	69	5	0.00	0.00
Cambodia	482,480	0	0	0.00	0.00
Laos	143,716	74	42	0.05	0.03
Nepal	135,119	0	0	0.00	0.00
Yemen	83,596	169	0	0.20	0.00
Maldives	37,377	1	0	0.00	0.00
Afghanistan	23,813	0	0	0.00	0.00
Bhutan	552	0	27	0.00	4.89
Total	12,859,883	3,658	60,670	0.03	0.47
Total-ACP	8,634,365	3,344	60,596	0.04	0.70
Total Non-ACP	4,225,518	313	74	0.01	0.00

Source: Brenton (2003).

exports to the EU for a range of developing countries. The average is 0.03 per cent, and no country is higher than one per cent. This indicates that the amount of products involving preferences is a small fraction of total exports and that the erosion of preferences is unlikely to have a significant affect on these countries.

The table also reports the proportion of exports in a group of vulnerable industries, including bananas, rice, and sugar (final column). The share of these goods in total exports is quite large for a small group of countries, reaching a peak of 11.6 per cent in Malawi. Unfortunately, tariffs on these goods were not eliminated immediately under the EBA in 2001, but they will gradually be phased out by 2009. In these critical goods, the increased preference margin potentially has a large effect on exports and, conversely, the erosion of these preferences by MFN tariff reduction could have a large negative effect on these countries.

Addressing the problems of adjustment in critical industries in vulnerable countries should be a key component of any multilateral reform proposal. There are many examples of critical industries—particularly in small countries—which face highly negative consequences from preference erosion.

Assistance for critical industries and their workers is a preferred solution to the maintenance of preference margins. There are two reasons to prefer assistance to delayed MFN liberalization. First, delayed liberalization discriminates against developing countries which do not benefit from preferences. The second reason for preferring assistance is that the maintenance of long-term preferences induces beneficiaries to specialize in activities in which they may never be competitive once preferences are removed. This discourages industrial diversification and increases adjustment costs when the preferences are eventually removed.

At the same time, it should be recognized that sometimes, providing even temporary preferential access can provide long-term gains. By excluding some critical products (particularly bananas, rice, and sugar) from immediate zero tariff under the EBA in 2001, the EU may be missing the opportunity to provide these industries with a foothold in their markets in advance of MFN liberalization.[18]

Fiscal effects

In some countries tariff revenues make up a substantial part of total government revenue. Many of these countries are concerned that trade liberalization will have a significant adverse effect on public revenue and the ability to fund public expenditure.

Taxes on international trade account for around one per cent of government revenues in developed countries and around 30 per cent in the least developed countries. Small countries are the most reliant on tariffs. For example, tariffs make up 62 per cent of tax revenue in the Bahamas, 54 per cent in the Solomon Islands, and 75 per cent in Guinea (Ebrill, Stotsky, and Gropp 1999). Figure 13.2 shows the ratio of tariff revenue to GDP for five country groups. African governments are most reliant on revenue from tariffs, followed by Middle

---

[18] Though, to be sure, for some of these products, it is unlikely that there will be MFN liberalization any time soon. Moreover, market 'loyalty' is likely to be less important in 'commodity' trade than in trade in manufactures.

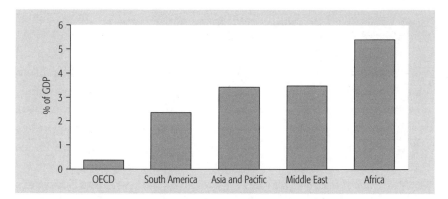

Figure 13.2. **Average tariff revenue, 1995 (% of GDP)**
Source: Ebrill, Stotsky, and Gropp (1999).

Eastern and Asia/Pacific countries. Table 13.7 shows tariff revenue as a proportion of GDP for 8 countries. The table demonstrates that changes in tariff revenue resulting from trade reform have wildly disproportionate effects on developing countries.

The complete elimination of tariffs would, of course, reduce tariff revenue to zero. This scenario would require developing countries to change fundamentally the structure of their taxation systems in order to raise revenues from other sources.

However, in practice the effect of less ambitious trade liberalization on government revenues is more complex. If government replaces tariffs with, for instance, a uniform VAT imposed at the point of production—and for imported goods, at the point of importation—then the only difference is that tariffs would be taxed at a uniform rate (and domestic production would be taxed at the same rate). Typically, governments also provide an export rebate, so that the import content of exported goods is effectively tax-exempt. Moreover, trade liberalization often involves a range of reforms other than tariff reductions, such as the elimination of trade-related subsidies and the 'tariffication' of non-tariff barriers. Many of these reforms could increase government revenues (see Table 13.8).

For these reasons the effect of trade liberalization on government revenues is difficult to predict. Senegal pursued trade liberalization in the mid-1980s, following which there were large revenue shortfalls. Lost tariff revenue combined with slow growth in trade volumes and

Table 13.7. **Tariff revenue for selected countries, 1995 (% of GDP)**

OECD		Asia/Pacific		South/Central America		Middle East		Africa	
Average	0.37	Average	3.42	Average	2.36	Average	3.48	Average	5.39
Australia	0.65	Fiji	4.95	Argentina	0.70	Bahrain	2.79	Botswana	5.85
Austria	0.14	India	2.76	Bahamas	8.32	Egypt	3.59	Burundi	2.51
Belgium	0.52	Indonesia	1.03	Bolivia	1.05	Iran	2.34	Cameroon	2.56
Canada	0.42	Korea	1.32	Brazil	0.46	Israel	0.19	Congo, Democratic Republic of	1.33
Denmark	0.20	Malaysia	3.04	Chile	2.20	Jordan	7.74	Côte D'Ivoire	6.17
Finland	0.23	Myanmar	0.89	Colombia	1.43	Kuwait	0.95	Ethopia	2.30
France	0.13	Nepal	3.00	Costa Rica	2.97	Morocco	4.27	Gabon	4.47
Germany	0.21	Papua New Guinea	3.85	Dominican Republic	3.80	Oman	0.95	Gambia	8.76
Greece	0.23	Philippines	4.96	Ecuador	1.64	Pakistan	4.88	Ghana	3.37
Iceland	0.38	Singapore	0.35	El Salvador	2.12	Syria	2.48	Kenya	3.94
Ireland	0.51	Solomon Islands	11.43	Guatemala	1.87	Tunisia	8.14	Lesotho	32.27
Italy	0.15	Sri Lanka	3.68	Nicaragua	5.25			Malawi	3.02
Japan	0.21	Thailand	3.15	Panama	2.62			Mauritius	6.74
Mexico	0.61			Paraguay	1.75			Rwanda	3.22
Netherlands	0.59			Peru	1.54			Senegal	4.81
New Zealand	0.92			Uruguay	0.96			Sierra Leone	3.62
Norway	0.30			Venezuela	1.39			South Africa	0.18
Portugal	0.28							Zambia	3.06
Spain	0.19							Zimbabwe	4.30
Sweden	0.27								
Switzerland	0.33								
Turkey	0.76								
UK	0.35								
US	0.27								

Source: Ebrill, Stotsky, and Gropp (1999).

weaknesses in economic management led to dire fiscal consequences. To raise more revenue, the tariff reductions were quickly abandoned and the liberalization process delayed. By contrast, trade liberalization in Morocco was accompanied by programs to broaden the domestic tax base, including the introduction of a VAT in 1986. As a consequence, Morocco was able to reduce its reliance on trade taxes while maintaining a stable ratio of public revenue to GDP.

The desirability of replacing revenue from trade taxes with domestic revenue sources raises the issue of relative efficiency of alternative

Table 13.8. **Summary of effect of trade liberalization on revenue**

Trade reform	Expected revenue effect
Replace NTBs with tariffs	Positive
Eliminate tariff exemptions	Positive
Eliminate trade-related subsidies	Positive
Reduce tariff dispersion	Ambiguous/Positive
Eliminate state trading monopolies	Ambiguous/Positive
Reduce high average tariffs	Ambiguous
Lower maximum tariff	Ambiguous
Eliminate export taxes	Ambiguous/Negative
Reduce moderate or low average tariffs	Negative

Source: Sharer *et al*. (1998).

forms of taxation. There is some theoretical research suggesting that reducing trade taxes and replacing them with a consumption tax is welfare-enhancing (Keen and Lightart 1999) on the basis that they are broader and less distortionary. More recently, however, Emran and Stiglitz (2004) have shown that in developing countries with an informal sector in which, say, a VAT cannot be imposed, it is desirable to retain some trade taxes, e.g. to tax imports at a higher rate than domestic production.

The issues of complementary policies to minimize the fiscal effects of trade reforms will be taken up later in the chapter.

The main point in this section is that global trade reform has significant consequences for the fiscal structures of developing countries, whereas developed countries are by and large immune. Developing countries are likely to suffer either a loss of total tax revenue or, at best, a large administrative cost—and even more economic distortions—associated with the implementation of a new taxation system.

Implementation costs

While traditional market access agreements such as tariff and quota reductions incur small implementation costs, the 'new' trade agenda embodied in the Uruguay Round and even more in the

Singapore Issues may impose a much larger implementation burden. Implementation costs are another example of how WTO agreements may have different impacts on poor and rich countries. Compliance with WTO agreements is harder for developing countries, whose administrative systems usually require larger reform to meet agreed standards. In addition, developing countries have the weakest government institutions and the greatest constraints on public resources. Implementation of an agreement incorporating the Singapore Issues would require expenditure on system design and drafting of legislation; capital expenditure on buildings and equipment; personnel training; and the ongoing costs of administration and enforcement.

Finger (2000) points out that the implementation of regulatory agreements will often draw money from the development budgets of poor countries. For this reason such agreements should be analysed in terms of their rate of return and compared to the alternative development priorities on which the same money could be spent. Finger estimated the implementation of three of the Uruguay Round's six agreements that required regulatory change (customs reform, intellectual property rights, and sanitary and phytosanitary (SPS) measures). His analysis suggests that the average cost of restructuring domestic regulations in the twelve developing countries considered could be as much as US$150 million. In eight of these countries this figure is larger than the entire annual development budget.

Many developing countries have been unable to meet their Uruguay Round obligations because of these high costs. By January 2000, up to 90 of the WTO's 109 developing country members were in violation of the SPS, customs valuation, and TRIPS agreements. Estimates of the cost of compliance with the Uruguay agreements vary widely depending on the quality of the existing systems and the strength of institutions in each country. Hungary spent more than US$40 million to upgrade the level of sanitation of its slaughterhouses alone. Mexico spent more than US$30 million to upgrade intellectual property laws. Finger (2000) suggests that for many of the least developed countries in the WTO compliance with these agreements is a less attractive investment than expenditure on basic development goals such as education.

The costs of implementing the regulatory agreements that could potentially emerge from the Doha Round will vary widely across countries. However, many of the proposed reforms within the Singapore Issues could be costly. For example, were there to be new competition regimes (which seems unlikely), such regimes would be difficult to implement. Competition law is technical and requires institutional skills and resources that are in short supply in many developing countries. In addition, competition law enforcement is expensive. OECD and national sources indicate that the annual budget of the antitrust office in OECD countries is in the US$15–50-million-plus range. For developing countries with enforcement agencies the budgets are lower but still significant (Hoekman and Mavroidis 2002).[19]

Similarly the costs of trade facilitation could be large for some countries. For example, the World Bank assisted Tunisia in its program of streamlining and modernizing its customs procedures. The total value of World Bank loans to Tunisia for this purpose was US$35 million in 1999. Similarly the World Bank lent US$38 million to Poland for upgrading the physical and managerial infrastructure of its port facilities (Wilson 2001). Projects to implement the WTO Agreement on Customs Valuation, which also includes broader customs reform, have been estimated to cost between US$1.6 million and US$16.2 million. For example, a six-year program in Tunisia to computerize and simplify procedures cost an estimated US$16.2 million (Finger and Schuler 2000). However, Bolivia implemented a broad customs reform programme that cost US$38.5 million.

The size of the implementation costs associated with the Singapore Issues raises questions about the appropriateness of their inclusion in the Doha agenda. The important lesson from the Uruguay Round is that regulatory changes imposed a large and (in the case of the many non-compliant countries) unacceptable burden on developing countries. The rules seemed to be constructed with little awareness of development problems and little appreciation for the institutional capacities of least developed countries.

---

[19] Note, for example, the costs of antitrust offices in Mexico (US$14 m), Poland (US$4.1 m), Hungary (US$2 m), and Argentina (US$1.4 m). There are doubts about whether these sums provide adequate enforcement.

Poverty and labor markets

It is not an easy task to identify social groups who systematically suffer as a result of trade liberalization. Heterogeneous trade patterns and factor endowments across countries mean that similar reform scenarios would have different effects on similar social groups in different countries, and hence the consequences of reform are often masked in cross-country data.

Predicting which social groups in which countries will be detrimentally affected by trade reform is a task that defies generalizations about the consequences for 'the poor'. Instead, identifying the losers from trade reform requires analysis of the particular effects on different groups stratified by income source and expenditure patterns.

There are a variety of effects on workers—both wages and unemployment rates may be affected; and the effects in the short run may differ markedly from the effects in the long run. In the short run, there are a number of reasons that markets do not adjust quickly, so that the impact of liberalization is that workers lose jobs; this job loss occurs faster than job creation. This is especially the case in developing countries where financial markets are weak (so that firms cannot quickly take advantage of any new opportunities that a new trade agreement opens up), or when the country has a tight monetary policy (e.g. as part of a so-called structural adjustment program). But even if job creation matches job destruction, the new jobs may require different skills, and may be created in different locales. Typically, dislocated workers, even in advanced industrial countries with low unemployment rates, suffer marked reductions in their wages (part of which, but only a part, may be explained by a loss of rents from being in a protected sector).

Economic theory suggests that if the economy manages to remain at full employment then trade liberalization will tend to lead to factor market price equalization, i.e. higher wages for unskilled labor in less developed countries and lower wages in developed countries. Incomes on average may increase, as countries are able to exploit their comparative advantage. But even this conclusion has been questioned, as attention has focused on the consequences of market imperfections, such as imperfect competition or incomplete risk markets. For instance, as Newbery and Stiglitz (1982) showed, trade liberalization may make everyone worse off when risk markets are limited.

Even when trade liberalization leads to increased efficiency, it is a one-off effect. It does not necessarily lead to sustained increases in the rate of growth of productivity, and indeed, if trade liberalization is associated with greater volatility, there is the possibility that it will actually lead to slower productivity growth.

A number of empirical studies have, nonetheless, tried to argue that trade openness leads to increased productivity growth (e.g. Sachs and Warner 1995; Sala-i-Martin 1997), and there is also evidence that increased productivity growth leads, in the long run, to increased wages (though there may be differential effects on the wages of particular groups, even negative effects). However, both of these relationships are controversial (Rodriguez and Rodrik 2000). Part of the problem with the studies focusing on the relationship between trade openness and productivity growth is that they are beset by a host of econometric and interpretive problems. Openness itself, for instance, is an endogenous variable, particularly as it is often measured (e.g. as ratio of trade to GDP).

An example of the problems in interpretation is provided by a recent study by Rama. Rama (2003) classifies seventy countries into three groups: rich countries, non-globalizers (not yet fully integrated into the international market), and recent globalizers.[20] Figure 13.3 reports the growth rate of the average wage between the 1980s and the 1990s for a set of common occupations. He suggests that this implies that openness is good for workers, at least at an aggregate level. But the countries that are not integrated into the international market include those with a host of other problems—African countries, for instance, facing civil strife or the AIDS epidemic. These other circumstances (inadequately controlled for in the statistical analysis) may provide more of an explanation for the poor performance—in trade, growth, productivity, and wages—than 'trade openness'.

Francois, van Meijl, and van Tongeren (2003) use a general equilibrium framework to analyse the effects of three alternative

---

[20] Rama uses the three-group classification proposed by Dollar and Kray (2001).

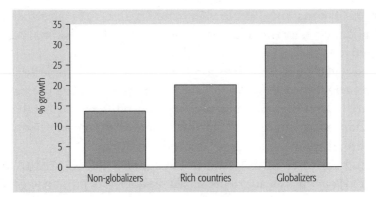

Figure 13.3. **Wage growth by country groups, 1980s–1990s**
Source: Freeman, Oostendorp, and Rama (2001).

liberalization scenarios, representing a range of possible outcomes from the Doha Round.[21] The pattern of unskilled wage changes across countries is illustrated in Figure 13.4. Wages increase for all countries with the exception of China and some Central and Eastern European countries. China is hurt because the authors build China's full accession to the WTO into their baseline. Further global liberalization increases competition for exports and reduces world prices for low-skill manufactures. The effect of liberalization increases over time and the more ambitious the reform scenario, the larger the benefits. But as we noted earlier, these general equilibrium models need to be used with caution. They typically do not incorporate a host of market imperfections that characterize developing countries, and they almost never incorporate dynamic changes (e.g. those associated with the adoption of new technologies). China may be in a better position to grab and maintain market share than other developing countries, in which case the results could be quite the opposite.

Average wage data may conceal more complex effects of trade liberalization. Disaggregated analysis reveals that workers in some sectors may gain while others lose. If inequality rises sufficiently,

---

[21] Experiment 1 models a linear 50% reduction in all forms of protection, including agricultural and industrial tariffs, export subsidies,. OECD agricultural domestic support, and tariff-equivalent barriers. Experiment 2 models a 'Swiss formula' reduction in which the maximum tariff is reduced to 25% (see Francois and Martin 2003). Experiment 3 models a complete elimination of protection.

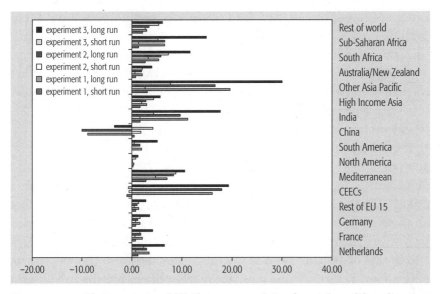

Figure 13.4. **Changes in unskilled wages resulting from three liberalization alternatives within the Doha Round**

Source: Francois, van Meijl, and van Tongeren (2003).

the poor's gain from overall per capita income may be offset. Certainly there are many well-known cases of countries where inequality has risen as they have become more integrated into the world economy. Inequality increased in Argentina, Chile, Colombia, Costa Rica, and Uruguay after they liberalized trade at different times (World Bank 2000). The decade following the signing of NAFTA saw real wages in Mexico fall, even as trade increased.[22]

These results seem to contradict standard economic theory (the Samuelson–Stolper theorem), which predicts that in countries with a relative abundance of unskilled labor, trade liberalization should result in a reduction in inequality. But this re-emphasizes the points made earlier—the importance of market imperfections, including the absence of risk markets, and dynamic effects. In some cases, trade liberalization has exposed countries to more risk, and the poor often bear the brunt of such risk. In other cases, greater global

[22] Such data does not, of course, address the counterfactual: what would have happened *but for* the trade agreement? But it certainly shows clearly that trade liberalization by itself is no guarantee of improved living standards for workers.

integration leads to an increased transfer of technology, and if these include unskilled-labor-saving innovations, they may well lead to a lowering of unskilled real wages.

As Figure 13.5 indicates, while there does not appear to be a strong relationship between income and wage inequality and openness,[23] different types of liberalization shocks have different effects on different income groups. For example, there is considerable evidence that financial liberalization can expose an economy to shocks which are particularly pernicious for the poor. Levinsohn, Berry, and Friedman (1999) examine how the 1997–8 Indonesian economic crisis affected the poorest households. Through a cost-of-living analysis they concluded that the lowest-income households tended to be hurt the most. By contrast, Minot and Goletti (2000) analyse the effects of another kind of liberalization shock on the well-being of the poor. They examine how rice market liberalization in Vietnam (principally the removal of quota restrictions) may affect poverty

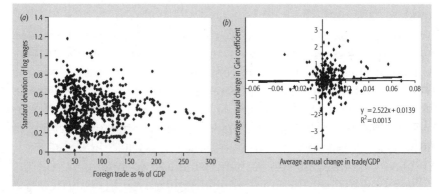

Figure 13.5. **Liberalization and inequality**
(*a*) **Wage dispersion and openness to trade**
Source: Rama (2003).

(*b*) **Change in trade and inequality**
Source: Dollar and Kray (2001).

---

[23] Rama (2003) argues that wage inequality across occupations does not increase with openness. Others (e.g. Dollar and Kray 2001) have suggested that there is no discernible relationship at the country level between trade openness (measured by trade volumes) and inequality (measured by the Gini coefficient). However, as noted earlier, openness (as measured) is an endogenous variable, so that the results have limited value in providing inferences concerning the effects of a change in policy, such as liberalization.

levels. They find that liberalization raises prices and that since rice production is relatively labor-intensive in Vietnam, a rise in prices increases the demand for agricultural labor and consequently the agricultural wage rate. They find that the net effect on real incomes in rural areas is generally positive and reduces most measures of poverty. These examples serve to indicate that different liberalization programs may have different effects on poverty which are masked in cross-country data.

These examples make clear that a full analysis of the impact on poverty must look at impacts on unemployment, factor prices, and goods prices. As previously noted, computable general equilibrium (CGE) models are frequently used to analyse the effects of trade liberalization on factor and consumer prices across countries. Unfortunately, they seldom incorporate risk and unemployment, which play an important role in generating poverty. In addition, most of these models consider the welfare change for a single representative household in each region, making them a poor tool for the analysis of poverty. Hertel, Ivanic, Preckel *et al.* (2003*a*) augment the standard type of CGE analysis by adding several different types of households categorized by their income source into households whose primary source of income is from (1) transfers, (2) agriculture, (3) non-agricultural business, (4) wages, or (5) diversified sources. They use survey data for several countries to include information on the income and expenditure profile of each group. This framework allows them to look at the effects of trade liberalization at a sub-national level to discover vulnerable populations within countries whose plight might have been masked in national-level data.

They find that poverty rates do not fall uniformly within countries. Table 13.9 shows the model's price change predictions for Indonesia (Hertel, Ivanic, Preckel *et al.* 2003*a*). Increased demand for Indonesia's exports bids up their price relative to the world average. The home price of commodities rises (see the short run total column) as other countries reduce their protection and the EU and US reduce the supply of subsidized exports (see the Liberalization by DCs column). The price rise is not offset by the cuts in the relatively modest Indonesian agricultural tariff rates (Own-country liberalization column). By contrast the prices of manufactured goods (durables and

Table 13.9. Effect of global trade liberalization on market prices in Indonesia (% change)

	Short run							Long run	
	Own-country liberalization		Liberalization by DCs		Liberalization by LDCs		Total		Total
	Agricultural	Non-agricultural	Agricultural	Non-agricultural	Agricultural	Non-agricultural			
Factors									
Agricultural Profit	−0.8	−1.7	3.9	2.0	0.1	0.0	3.5	Land	5.3
Non-Agricultural Profit	−0.3	−0.1	1.5	3.2	0.1	−0.3	4.1	Capital	5.0
Unskilled labor	−0.4	0.0	2.1	3.4	0.1	0.1	5.3	Unskilled wages	6.1
Skilled labor	−0.4	0.1	1.6	3.3	0.1	0.1	4.8	Skilled wages	5.3
Public transfers	−0.5	−0.2	2.0	3.1	0.1	−0.2	4.4	Public transport	5.7
Private transfers	−0.5	−0.2	2.0	3.1	0.1	−0.2	4.4	Private transport	5.7
Producer prices									
Staple grains	−0.5	0.1	3.4	2.6	0.1	−0.3	5.4	Staple grains	7.1
Livestock	−1.4	0.2	2.5	2.3	−0.3	−0.3	3.0	Livestock	5.3
Other food	−1.3	0.8	5.0	1.7	0.5	−0.7	6.1	Other food	6.3
Non-durables	−0.1	−3.7	0.7	2.8	−0.1	−0.7	−1.2	Nondurables	0.7
Durables	0.0	−9.8	0.1	1.3	−0.1	−0.4	−8.8	Durables	−9.7
Services	−0.2	0.8	1.3	2.4	0.0	−0.1	4.2	Services	5.8
Margin services	−0.2	0.8	1.3	2.4	0.0	−0.1	4.2	Margin services	5.8
Consumer prices									
Staple grains	−0.4	0.2	3.1	2.5	0.1	−0.3	5.2	Staple grains	6.8
Livestock	−1.2	0.3	2.3	2.3	0.1	−0.6	3.2	Livestock	5.4
Other food	−1.1	0.8	4.5	1.8	0.2	−0.3	5.9	Other food	6.2
Non-durables	−0.1	−3.0	0.8	2.8	0.0	0.7	−0.3	Non-durables.	1.6
Durables	−0.1	−2.2	1.0	2.1	0.1	−0.2	0.5	Durables	1.4
Services	−0.2	0.8	1.3	2.4	0.1	−0.1	4.2	Services	5.8

Source: Hertel, Ivanic, Preckel et al. (2003a: table 5).

non-durables) fall as a consequence of liberalization by other LDCs and tariff cuts, leading to a large change in the relative prices of food and manufactures.

Turning now to the effects of these price changes on poverty, Table 13.10 shows both the short-run and long-run consequences of these price changes on the head–count ratio for each income group. The total column indicates that poverty falls by 1.5 per cent in the short run and 1.1 per cent in the long run. However, the changes are not uniform across social groups. The increase in the relative price of agricultural goods causes a sharp decline in poverty (2.8 per cent) in poverty among the group deriving its income from agricultural goods. By contrast the poverty headcount among the non-agriculture group (perhaps this could represent the urban poor) actually increases. The table indicates that a major cause of this is the liberalization of agriculture by developed countries, the effect of which is

Table 13.10. **Effect of global trade liberalization on poverty in Indonesia (% change in headcount across social strata grouped by primary income source)**

Short-run effects of		Primary income source					
		Agriculture	Non-agriculture	Labor	Transfer	Diverse	Total
Own-country liberalization	of agricultural goods	1.3	−0.9	−0.7	−0.3	0.3	0.5
	of non-agricultural goods	1.7	0.7	−0.4	0.3	10.9	1.1
Liberalization by DC's	of agricultural goods	−4.1	3.5	2.9	1.6	−0.7	−1.1
	of non-agricultural goods	0.1	−1.5	−2.4	−1.0	−0.8	−0.7
Liberalization by LDC's	of agricultural goods	−1.7	0.4	0.3	0.0	−0.7	−0.8
	of non-agricultural goods	−0.1	−0.3	−1.3	−0.4	−0.4	−0.3
Total short-run change in poverty		−2.8	1.8	−1.6	−0.2	−1.4	−1.5
Long-run change in poverty		−0.9	−1.1	−1.5	−0.3	−1.2	−1.1

Source: Hertel, Ivanic, Preckel *et al*. (2003*a*: table 6).

to increase poverty by 3.5 per cent as a consequence of the relative
price changes described above. For Indonesia, the population in the
two income categories that lose (transfer and non-agricultural)
makes up just 14 per cent of the poor. Consequently national poverty
falls as a result of global trade liberalization in Indonesia.

Table 13.11 shows Hertel, Ivanic, Preckel *et al.*'s (2003*b*) findings
for several countries. They suggest that multilateral trade liberalization will increase the poverty headcount in Thailand, Peru, and
Venezuela and reduce it in all the other countries except Zambia,
which experiences no change. In Brazil, for example, poverty rises for
the non-agricultural and labor strata, which together accounts for
more than 45 per cent of the poverty headcount, but poverty falls
amongst the agriculture group, which comprises 25 per cent of the
poor population. However, since the gains in agriculture are so large
a high proportion of the group leaves poverty, causing an overall
reduction in national poverty.

While, for reasons already explained, computable general equilibrium models need to be used with considerable caution, the detailed

Table 13.11. **Effect of global trade liberalization on poverty for 14 developing countries (% change in number of poor, relative to total population)**

| Country | Primary income source | | | | | |
	Agriculture	Non-agriculture	Labor	Transfers	Diverse	Total
Bangladesh	−0.4	−0.4	0.1	−0.1	−0.1	−0.1
Brazil	−11.4	2.9	1.2	0.1	−2.2	−2.4
Chile	−25.0	3.4	2.3	0.7	−2.4	−3.9
Colombia	−8.9	0.5	1.0	−0.1	−2.1	−2.2
Indonesia	−2.8	1.8	−1.6	0.2	−1.4	−1.5
Malawi	−2.6	0.4	−0.7	−0.2	−2.5	−2.0
Mexico	2.5	−0.8	−0.7	−0.2	0.2	−0.2
Peru	2.2	1.1	3.9	0.6	1.8	1.4
Philippines	−5.2	1.1	−0.9	0.0	−3.0	−3.1
Thailand	−0.2	13.6	8.8	6.9	4.9	5.7
Uganda	−0.2	−0.8	−0.7	−0.2	−0.5	−0.5
Venezuela	−9.1	0.6	0.8	0.1	0.5	0.3
Vietnam	10.9	−16.0	−11.1	−3.8	−6.1	−5.6
Zambia	0.0	−0.1	0.2	0.0	−0.1	0.0

Source: Hertel, Ivanic, Preckel *et al.* (2003*b*: table 8).

analysis provided by Hertel *et al.* highlights the differential effects on different groups, and the fact that, while some individuals may be lifted out of poverty, others will be forced into it. Certainly, the distributional impacts cannot be ignored.

Policies to minimize the costs of adjustment

Trade liberalization can contribute to increased economic growth in the long run. However, in the short run some social groups in developing countries may be negatively affected by changes in the prices of the goods they consume and produce. Trade reform must therefore be designed in conjunction with a range of complementary polices to protect vulnerable social groups.

This section provides a brief survey of some of the main policies that have been proposed to mitigate the effects of adjustment on developing countries.

Social safety nets and credit markets

Even if the adjustment costs are quite small and short-lived, the extremely poor in many LDCs may be incapable of sustaining themselves for short periods because of a lack of savings and the unavailability of credit and insurance. For this reason one of the most important components of trade reform is an effective social safety net.

Workers in industries which experience a negative shock through lower foreign demand from lost exports, or lower domestic demand as a result of increased competition from imports, may require funding if they lose their jobs in the adjustment process. Unemployment benefits can enhance adjustment by giving workers the funds necessary to search for alternative employment in different industries or locations. Many developed countries already have comprehensive safety nets, but developing countries will require assistance.[24]

---

[24] Such assistance can also increase economic efficiency, by allowing workers to continue searching until they find a job which better matches their skills.

Figure 13.6. **Expenditure on social security and welfare (% of GDP)**
Source: Besley, Burgess, and Rasul (2001).

Figure 13.6 shows the average social security expenditure for several regions. The poorest countries are not able to spend enough to make their programs effective and will require international assistance to meet the adjustment needs of trade reform.

Firms may also require assistance. Companies may need to make adjustment-related investment in order to cope with new market forces. In developing countries where capital markets are less sophisticated, firms may be credit-constrained[25] even if they would be able to pay back the loans. The World Bank (1997) has reported that lack of access to finance for new investments was the most severe constraint small firms in Ghana faced after trade reforms in 1983. Changes in relative prices resulting from liberalization will have short-run effects on cash flows that will differ across firms, with the result that even if *on average* these cash flows improve, the adverse effects on the losers can more than offset the positive effects on the winners (See Greenwald and Stiglitz 1993).

Technical assistance

The Uruguay Round Decision on Measures in Favor of Least Developed Countries called for 'substantially increased technical assistance in the development, strengthening and diversification of

---

[25] Even in developed countries, small and medium-sized businesses often face severe credit constraints.

their production and export bases including those of services, as well as in trade promotion'.

If the global gains from trade liberalization are as large as some researchers suggest—the World Bank estimates that further liberalization could yield an increase in real income by 2015 of more than US$500 billion[26]—then it is reasonable to enshrine a principle of compensation whereby those countries that suffer significant adjustment costs relative to welfare gains should receive offsetting assistance.

A principle of compensation is important for at least two reasons. First, if the 'development focus' of the Doha Round is to have any meaning, then WTO members must be mindful of the fact that the cost of adjusting to their agreements will have serious consequences for development. Not only do adjustment costs fall particularly harshly on the poorest people in the world because they are least able to afford them, but the costs also consume resources that would otherwise be spent on alternative development priorities. For many people, the impact of trade reform will overwhelm the effects of other economic development programs.

The second motivation for the provision of compensation for adjustment costs is the pragmatic need to win political support for reform. High adjustment costs give some groups a vested interest in the status quo. Identifying and compensating those groups may be an effective way of removing impediments to welfare-improving global policy changes.

The purpose of technical assistance is to improve the trade performance of developing countries through policy and strengthening of institutions. A systematic review of technical assistance efforts is beyond the scope of this chapter. In this section we note some of the trends and limitations of existing programs and the need for more wide-ranging support.

The responsibility for technical assistance has fallen largely on international organizations. Both the World Bank and the WTO have increased their technical cooperation activities. However, as much

---

[26] The World Bank estimates that further liberalization of trade can generate up to US$500bn in static and dynamic gains by 2015 (World Bank 2003). These estimates assume the elimination of agricultural export subsidies and domestic support, a tariff ceiling of 10% for agricultural products and 5% for manufacturing in OECD countries, and a 15% ceiling for agricultural products and 10% for manufacturing in developing countries.

as 90 per cent of financing for these activities comes from trust funds provided by two or three bilateral donors, while the WTO itself has typically allocated for technical cooperation activities less than one per cent of its total annual budget—less than half a million US dollars (see Michalopoulos 2000).

Trade-related technical assistance is often provided to assist governments to implement existing agreements. This assistance is often conceived by the provider and 'supply-driven' and is not related to the overall priorities of the beneficiary (Prowse 2000). In addition, technical assistance needs to be pro-active. It should strengthen the recipient country's ability to determine its own development priorities and influence the outcome of WTO agreements.

A third useful expansion of technical assistance would extend its scope towards ensuring that developing countries have access to equal protection under the WTO's dispute settlement system. Lack of institutional capacity limits developing countries' ability to present and defend cases in the dispute systems, making those systems manifestly unfair in practice. Developing countries are disadvantaged in complex and expensive legal proceedings. An expansion of existing legal assistance schemes will be an important prerequisite for institutional fairness.

The WTO Singapore Ministerial Conference in 1996 mandated a more 'integrated approach to assisting LDCs to enhance their trading opportunities'. In 1997, the Integrated Framework for Trade-related Technical Assistance (IF) was launched with a view to building trade capacity in developing countries (see Table 13.12). The IF attempts to pull together the resources of several international agencies to increase the scope and value of trade-related technical assistance. It also attempts to redress some of the common criticisms of such assistance by ensuring that such assistance is demand-driven, that it matches the specific needs of each LDC, and that it enhances rather than undermines each LDC's ownership of trade-related technical assistance (UNCTAD 2002). Trade-related technical assistance activities are broadly defined as:

- enhancing government institutions to manage trade policies
- assistance to create supportive trade-related regulations and policy

- strengthening export supply capabilities
- strengthening trade support and trade facilitation capabilities

Table 13.12. **Trade-related assistance provided by multilateral agencies**

Organization	Activities
IMF	Trade policy advice provided in the context of country surveillance and/or program support, and considered in a broader economic and social framework. Normally will include an assessment of the key complementary policy requirements to support in-country trade reform— notably in fiscal policy and the adequacy of social safety nets. Trade-related technical assistance focused primarily on trade facilitation issues (customs administration) but also on collation of data on external trade.
ITC	Emphasis on enterprise-oriented aspects of trade policy and trade promotion such as business implications of multilateral and regional agreements, private sector involvement in trade policy, and management of regulation-related issues by businesses. Hands-on training, assistance in data collation, analysis, and institutional matters to favor private sector capability in trade policy-making, managing of regulatory issues in trade, and compliance.
UNCTAD	Policy analysis on trade and investment—advocacy of developing country interests. Analysis of trade policy options in the context of economic development. Trade-related technical assistance includes training and support in trade negotiations and implementation of commitments, accessions advice, and customs administration.
UNDP	Trade policy options considered in the broader context of economic and social development. Complementary policy analysis to support trade reform. Sector-specific trade assistance in areas such as agriculture, fisheries, tourism, and textiles. Private sector engagement in trade policy-making.
World Bank	Trade issues are considered in a broader economic and social context of development and investment-related policies. Creation and dissemination of a core knowledge base that combines policy-relevant research, advocacy, capacity-building, training, and operational support for trade at the country level, including networking to link think tanks and trade policy makers within a country.
WTO	Emphasis on the WTO agreements. Factual information on WTO rights and obligations of developing countries and progress in trade negotiations. Training and consultation to assist developing country members in applying the WTO agreements and using the WTO mechanisms.

Source: Prowse (2002).

In the initial phase of the implementation of the IF, the trade assistance needs of forty LDCs were advanced. After limited success several problems were identified with the IF approach. There had been a substantial failure to put trade-related development issues at the centre of national, agency, and donor priorities. At the country level, national needs were selected without sufficiently broad consultation. At the donor and agency level, insufficient attention was given to integrating trade issues into the wider development agenda.

In 2001 an enhanced IF program was adopted with a view to embedding trade-related capacity building into countries' overall development strategies through their national Poverty Reduction Strategy Papers (PRSPs). For this purpose, 'trade integration studies' were commenced for a group of pilot countries. This strategy has the distinct advantage of increasing the level of 'ownership' by LDCs.

The above list of trade-related assistance activities, however, is inadequate in scope compared to what is needed. For instance, monetary policies or structural adjustment programs advocated by the IMF may adversely affect the flow or affordability of finance to facilitate the restructuring of the economy in response to liberalization. While much of the technical assistance is designed to enhance the ability of countries to design their own programs aimed at adapting and responding to a new trade agreement, conditionalities associated with various forms of financial assistance may give them less scope for doing so. Moreover, advice concerning how to cope with the reduction of tariff tax revenues arguably reflects an inadequate understanding of the nature of developing countries (e.g. the importance of the hard-to-tax informal sector) and, as a result, leads to tax structures which have adverse effects on growth and development.

Capturing the benefits of liberalization for LDCs

Market access on its own is not sufficient to bring the benefits of trade to developing countries. The UN Secretary General noted in response to the European Union's 'Everything but Arms' initiative that 'the LDCs have neither the surplus of exportable products nor the production capacity to take immediate advantage of new trade opportunities. They will need substantial investment and technical assistance in order to expand their production'.[27] Certainly, the limited increase in exports in the affected commodities from the least developed countries to Europe is consistent with these concerns.

There can be no doubt among WTO members that tariff reductions must be accompanied by concerted efforts to ensure that poor producers are able to capitalize on new trading opportunities. In particular, the Development Round faces the challenge of dealing with two of the largest impediments to LDC export growth: supply constraints and product standards.

Supply constraints

Increased market access might generate a disappointing supply response from many LDCs. In the context of low productive capacity, a deficient policy environment, poor infrastructure, poor access to technology, and missing/imperfect markets (especially financial markets), liberalized markets will not stimulate the required development to take advantage of new trading opportunities.

There has been some attention given to this issue within the WTO. The final Declaration of the WTO Doha Ministerial meeting—which was warned by the G77 countries about the lack of technical assistance in recent years—reiterates the importance of technical assistance and 'reaffirms...the important role of sustainably financed technical assistance and capacity-building programmes' (para. 41).

Easing supply constraints requires a broader interpretation of the responsibilities covered by technical assistance, i.e. more than bolstering public institutions. While public sector capacity-building is an important objective, it is not a substitute for programs to enhance the capacity of the private sector to develop into new markets.

A key component of private sector development is improved access to finance—to take advantage of new opportunities for exports, there

---

[27] Quoted in *The Financial Times*, 5 Mar. 2001.

must be export finance. In countries with underdeveloped financial sectors, inadequate finance is a major constraint inhibiting exports. To the extent that the poor are involved in trading activities, they may face special difficulties in obtaining access to the trade credit they need because of particular difficulties in assessing the credit-worthiness of traders and because traders do not have sufficient collateral.

Where there is an absence of private credit, there may be a role for publicly funded institutions to increase access to finance for low-income producers. For example, the Development Bank of Mauritius (DBM) played a key role in providing finance for the expansion of existing business and the establishment of new firms in Mauritius. Among its several activities the DBM was involved in building industrial estates to encourage development in export processing zones (EPZs), setting up foreign exchange schemes for small and medium-sized enterprises, providing working capital through micro-credit, and extending preferential credit schemes.

Inadequate infrastructure is also an important source of supply constraints. In particular, poor transport infrastructure can prevent local farmers from getting access to large domestic markets and international ports.

Another barrier to full participation in international trade is the difficulty of establishing new industries in countries with poorly diversified industrial bases. As noted earlier, when the EU introduced its 'Everything but Arms' initiative in 2001, it extended duty-free access to imports from LDCs in 919 product categories, but the following year, imports were recorded in just 80 (Brenton 2003). Failure to diversify is particularly evident in Africa, where the share of agricultural value added in the GDP increased from 22 per cent to 25 per cent over the 1980–97 period while it fell from 18 per cent to 16 per cent over the same period for the developing countries as a group.

Figure 13.7 traces the long-term trends in the commodity structures of Tanzania and Malaysia. Malaysia, like most South-East Asian countries, was primarily agricultural in the 1960s and 1970s. These countries pursued a successful pattern of industrialization through import substitution followed by export-oriented growth. As

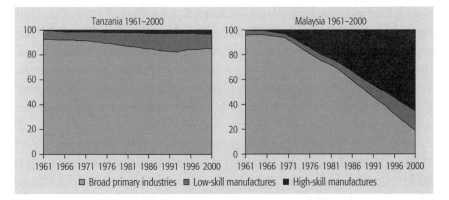

Figure 13.7. **Commodity structure of exports, Tanzania and Malaysia (% of total exports)**

Source: Bonaglia and Fukasaku (2002).

the ASEAN countries developed, they pursued a range of policy measures to offset the anti-export bias resulting from local protection under the import-substitution policy. These policies included incentives for private and foreign investment (particularly investment in new industries), EPZs, investment in infrastructure, and duty drawbacks for exporting firms.

Product standards

As well as supply constraints, developing countries might suffer from structural bottlenecks. Product standards—which require that exported goods comply with a wide range of technical standards and regulations set by the importing markets—are often a barrier to developing country exporters. There are currently over 100,000 standards and technical rules in use around the world (UNIDO 2002). These standards are designed with the intention of facilitating exchange and safeguarding health and safety. However, developing countries may find compliance difficult or prohibitively expensive.

The potential for standards to have a detrimental effect on LDC exports was recognized in the Uruguay Round. The Technical Barriers to Trade (TBT) Agreement and the Agreement on the Application of Sanitary and Phyto-sanitary Standards (SPS), both negotiated as part of the Uruguay Round, were meant 'to ensure that technical regulations and standards do not create unnecessary obstacles to trade'.[28] Article 12.7 of the TBT Agreement specifically states: 'Members shall...provide technical assistance to developing country members to ensure that the preparation and application of technical regulations, standards and conformity assessment procedures do not create unnecessary obstacles to the expansion and diversification of exports from developing country Members'.

In spite of these agreements many developing countries do not have the ability to assist their producers to meet product standards. There are serious deficiencies in infrastructure, processing technologies, and national regulatory bodies. As a consequence, significant assistance from developed countries is required to build up their capabilities to conform to these product standard requirements if trade liberalization is to have its intended impact on the poorest countries.

UNIDO recommends a number of priority areas for international assistance to the institutional development of developing countries, including:

- A national/regional standards/standardization body: standards are essential for production and trade, but also for consumer protection. To ensure that international (and national) standards are set in a balanced manner, developing countries need to participate in the drafting of such standards.

- A national/regional metrology system: a system that ensures that the measurements and tests required for all production, quality, and certification activities are consistent and correct. This includes operational laboratories for primary and secondary physical standards as well as certified reference materials for chemical and microbiological purposes.

- A certification/conformity assessment system: a system including internationally recognized testing facilities that are able to test products and certify that products and management/production processes comply with applicable requirements and standards.

---

[28] Preamble to the TBT Agreement.

- An accreditation system: a system which evaluates calibration and testing laboratories and other bodies involved in certification of products, systems, and processes, with a view to ensuring that testing facilities and methodologies, and thereby the certification activities, satisfy international standards.

Conclusion

Trade liberalization creates adjustment costs as resources move from one sector to another. This chapter has described several sources of adjustment costs (broadly defined) and concludes that adjustment to a post-Doha trading regime will be disproportionately costly and difficult for developing countries because of the loss of preference margins, the loss of revenue from trade taxes, institutional weaknesses including the absence of adequate safety nets, large implementation costs, lack of the finance required to restructure the economy, and the limited ability of poor populations to manage short-term unemployment.

The effect of adjustment can be mitigated by effective national and international policies to reduce the costs and facilitate the adjustments. For instance, economies facing a new onslaught of imports as a result of trade liberalization must find mechanisms to provide credit for the creation of new enterprises and the expansion of existing enterprises to take advantage of the new export opportunities, and macro-economic policies must be sensitive to these needs, ensuring that (real) interest rates are kept appropriately low. In the past, international institutions advising developing countries have not been sufficiently sensitive to these needs. But more than good policies will be required. There is a need for assistance, for instance to develop the required physical and institutional infrastructure and to provide compensation to alleviate the suffering of adversely affected groups. This in turn will require a coordinated and well-financed international effort. In the absence of a significant increase in international assistance, responsibility for these policies will fall on resource-constrained domestic governments, and trade reform (if it is pursued at all) will come at the expense of other development priorities. As a result, even a development-oriented round of liberalization may fail to produce the growth benefits promised by the advocates of a new trade agreement.

APPENDIX 1

Empirical review of market access issues

The 'Doha Development Agenda' of November 2001 puts poverty-reducing economic growth at the center of the WTO's considerations. If the development focus of the Doha Round is to be a meaningful operating principle, then the overriding task of the Round must be to ensure that the liberalization agreements promote development in poor countries. In practice this means giving priority to reforms which yield the largest benefits to developing countries, helping governments move towards good trade policies, and dealing effectively with the implementation constraints faced by poor members.

A key theme of this book is that the WTO's agenda should be driven by economic analysis rather than the momentum of powerful interest groups. This appendix supports the conclusions in the main part of the book by reviewing the empirical evidence on the potential benefits and costs of liberalization across various trade and factor flows. This type of analysis is a crucial step to ensuring that priority is given to those elements of the agenda that deliver the largest gains to developing countries.

This appendix is a brief survey of the effects of different liberalization programs on global welfare. The bulk of useful regional-level empirical studies use computable general equilibrium (CGE) models. Such studies are based on simple models of the entire economy that, as the name suggests, are developed in a computable form. These models enable us to observe the effects of various liberalization experiments on trade volumes, prices, and incomes. Simulations can separately determine the effects of reform on different sectors and on different countries and regions. CGE models have several limitations. They require a large amount of data (to estimate accurately all the demand and supply functions which underlie them) and rely on a few crude assumptions. Most importantly, they do not incorporate key features of developing countries, such as the high level of unemployment. Most assume away the problems posed by uncertainty, but the absence of risk markets makes risk of central concern in developing countries. Most assume perfect competition, while markets in developing countries may be highly non-competitive. We present these models not because we believe that they provide accurate assessments of the costs and benefits of trade liberalization, but because they call attention to some of the key issues—and because they have become a point of reference.

Where possible, the specific effects of reform on Commonwealth developing countries has been included. However, the empirical evidence in this regard is thin and most global CGE studies do not disaggregate the effects on small countries beyond the regional level.

This appendix analyses the potential gains and costs from liberalization in four areas: agricultural trade, services, the temporary movement of natural persons, and trade in manufactured goods.

To some extent the results of the survey give cause for a re-evaluation of the current focus of negotiations. The estimated welfare gains from those negotiating areas which attract considerable attention are estimated to yield smaller benefits than other reforms on which there has been less focus, and less progress.

Three conclusions which we believe are relatively robust emerge from the empirical survey below:

- Liberalization of labor markets—in particular, allowing an increased quota of workers from developing countries to work temporarily in developed countries—offers large welfare gains.

- There are significant gains to be realized from the reductions in tariff barriers to South–South trade. In both agriculture and manufacturing the gains to developing countries from liberalization of trade between themselves are estimated to be greater than those from liberalization of trade with the OECD. (This may be both because tariff barriers between developing countries are higher—implying greater benefits from reductions—and because of the extensive use of non-tariff barriers by developed countries.)

- There is considerable evidence that poorly implemented liberalization, especially in the service sector, can have negative effects on the poor. Carefully managed implementation, effective regulation, and substantial assistance will be a necessary part of any reform agenda.

The literature surveyed identifies ambiguous effects of agricultural and investment liberalization on developing countries. The reason for the ambiguity will be detailed in the discussion below.

A1.1 **Agriculture**

In the Doha Ministerial Declaration, WTO members committed themselves to reform of the main instruments of agricultural protection, including 'substantial improvements in market access; reductions of, with a view to phasing out, all forms of export subsidies; and substantial reductions in trade-distorting domestic support'. They also agreed that 'special and differential treatment of developing countries shall be an integral part of all elements of the negotiations'.

This vision combines wide-ranging reform of the distorted agricultural trade policies of developed countries and gradual liberalization in developing countries.

This section surveys the (at times thin) empirical evidence on the potential costs and benefits associated with the kind of reform envisioned by the Doha Declaration. It focuses specifically on the welfare effects of liberalization for developing countries.

Developing countries face the benefits of increased market access and the (potential) costs of higher prices for domestic consumers. The fundamental point is that consumers benefit from lower prices which result from large agricultural subsidies, and producers lose. The net effect of wide-ranging agricultural reform varies across developing countries depending on the composition of their exports and imports of different commodities and the price sensitivity of those commodities to liberalization. As a result, the conclusions of the empirical evidence give cause for caution.

A reform agenda which maximizes the welfare of developing countries must also recognize the specific effects of different protection instruments on different commodities.

Furthermore, developed countries have a large number of instruments by which they can redistribute income and alleviate poverty. In less developed countries, by contrast, the set of instruments is far more circumscribed. Since agriculture producers are among the poorest people in developing countries, increasing the prices they receive may be one of the few instruments for alleviating rural poverty. But such policies are, at the same time, likely to increase urban poverty. Tariffs on imports (especially when they countervail subsidies by more advanced industrial countries), with some of the proceeds used to provide targeted food subsidies, may accordingly increase welfare.

Reform should focus on maximizing market access benefits and identifying ways of offsetting the terms-of trade-impact on consumers. This requires

(1) a rapid elimination of the most damaging protection instruments: export and production subsidies on commodities that compete with developing countries and which are not consumed extensively by developing countries, or in which the effect of liberalization on prices paid by consumers in developing countries is likely to be small; (2) increased market access, particularly for the goods exported by developing countries; (3) a gradual reduction of production subsidies on sensitive commodities (those imported by developing countries with, say, substantial negative price effects on poverty); and (4) assistance for the poorest countries.

While average manufacturing tariffs have fallen significantly in recent decades, agricultural protection has remained stubbornly high. The average level of agricultural producer support in OECD countries ranges from less than 5 per cent of gross farm receipts in Australia to 20 per cent in the US and 35 per cent in the EU (see Fig. A1.1). Developing countries face high tariff barriers on many of their agricultural exports—the average tariff on agricultural goods exported to developed countries was 15.1 per cent in 2000 (Hertel *et al.* 2000).[1]

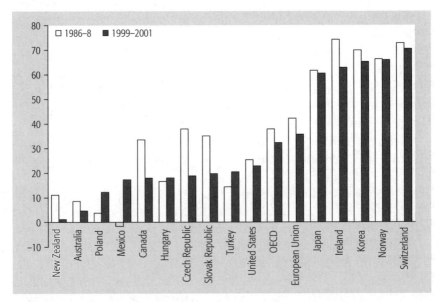

Figure A1.1 **Agricultural producer support, 1986–1988 and 1999–2001 (% of value of gross farm receipts)**

Source: Anderson (2003).

---

[1] There are also large non-tariff barriers for some commodities, e.g. sugar quotas.

Table A1.1. **Average protection in agriculture and food, 2005**

This table shows the average protection (% *ad valorem*) for food and agriculture by sector. The figures are worldwide averages in 2005. Subsidy equivalents are aggregated across all regions and divided by exports at domestic market prices.

	Import tariff (1)	Export subsidy (2)	Production subsidy (3)
Food grains	23	1	6
Feed grains	97	4	11
Oilseeds	4	0	9
Meat and livestock	17	8	2
Dairy	23	27	2
Other agriculture	11	0	0
Other food	1	0	0
Beverages and tobacco	18	0	0

Source: Hertel, Anderson, Francois *et al.* (2000: 26).

Table A1.1 shows the (projected) levels of farm support in 2005 after the Uruguay Round agreements are fully implemented (Hertel, Anderson, Francois *et al.* 2000). Tariffs are particularly high in the feed grains, dairy, and food grains sectors. Column 2 shows that dairy products are the world's most subsidized exports, followed by meat and livestock. Producer payments are highest for grains and oilseed sectors and lowest for meat, livestock, and dairy (col. 3).

Average levels of subsidies (or protection) do not necessarily provide a good indicator of how distorted the market is. For instance, most cotton production may be totally unsubsidized, but America provides large subsidies, which has a substantial *marginal* effect. The price effect of large subsidies to even a limited group can be quite large, given the inelasticity of demand for agricultural goods.

Table A1.2 shows the average tariffs on agricultural goods by importing and exporting region. Developing countries face even higher tariffs on exports to other developing countries (18.3 per cent) than on exports to developed countries (15.1 per cent).

A second important determinant of the welfare effects of liberalization is the agricultural trade balance across countries. Table A1.3 reports the average trade specialization indices for several countries and regions over the course of three decades. These indices give a measure of the trend of agricultural trade balances through time. The value of the index ranges

Table A1.2. **Average agricultural tariff rates (%)**

This table reports the average tariff rates faced by high- and low-income countries on their own and each other's goods.

Exporting region	Importing region	
	High-income countries	Developing countries
High-income countries	15.9	21.5
Developing countries	15.1	18.3
World	15.6	20.1

Source: Hertel and Martin (2000).

from −1 for a country that imports and does not export a particular commodity, to +1 for a country which only exports it.

Table A1.3 shows a division between temperate products (program crops and livestock), where developing countries are largely net importers and developed countries are largely net exporters, and tropical products, for which developing countries are largely net exporters. Many of the most developed countries—the including the EU, the US, Australia, and New Zealand—have increased their food trade balance over the last thirty years. Most of the developing countries and regions—Sub-Saharan Africa, Latin America (excluding Argentina and Brazil), Indonesia, Mexico, the Middle East, and North Africa—have actually become more dependent on imports in program crops and meat/livestock.

Table A1.4 gives an indication of developing countries' trading relationship with the developed world. It shows developing countries' exports to, and imports from, OECD countries as a share of each country's total. As a group, the OECD countries are big exporters of commodities to countries like China, India, and the rest of South Asia (RSoAsia), and the Middle East and North Africa (MENA). These countries are likely to be affected by liberalization, which alters the price of OECD exports. Indonesia, Sub-Saharan Africa (SSA) and China also rely on the OECD countries as export markets for most of their products.

For countries like these, which are heavily integrated into OECD markets, liberalization brings risks and rewards. Producers gain from greater market access, while consumers may lose through higher prices. These effects are discussed in more detail in the next section. However, Table A1.3 gives us some indication of their relative importance across countries: many developing countries are net importers of most commodities.

Table A1.3. **Trade specialization indices, 1965–1998**

The trade specialization index is calculated as $(X - M) / (X + M)$, where X is exports and M is imports for each country. A country that only exports has an index value 1. A country that only imports has an index value -1. Program commodities are composed of paddy rice, wheat, cereal grains, oilseeds, raw sugar, processed rice, and refined sugar. 'Livestock and meat' includes livestock, wool, animal products, meat, and dairy. 'Other' agriculture and food includes vegetables and fruits, plant-based fibers, other crops, vegetable oils and fats, and other processed food.
n.a.: not available.

Years	Program commodities			Livestock and meat products			Other agriculture and food		
	1965–75	1976–85	1986–98	1965–75	1976–85	1986–98	1965–75	1976–85	1986–98
Aus/NZ	0.95	0.97	0.94	0.99	0.98	0.98	0.13	0.10	0.32
Japan	−0.94	−0.96	−1.00	−0.96	−0.96	−0.96	−0.60	−0.67	−0.82
Korea	−0.90	−0.82	−0.90	−0.14	−0.73	−0.85	−0.23	−0.23	−0.21
USA	0.59	0.78	0.81	−0.04	0.16	0.24	−0.08	−0.04	0.00
Canada	0.55	0.72	0.76	0.13	0.32	0.40	−0.18	−0.18	−0.09
Mexico	0.19	−0.87	−0.83	0.03	−0.41	−0.54	0.66	0.56	0.36
EU15	−0.74	−0.56	−0.27	−0.49	−0.05	0.13	−0.48	−0.37	−0.17
EFTA	−0.91	−0.89	−0.76	−0.08	−0.02	−0.04	−0.27	−0.27	−0.08
CEU	−0.51	−0.71	0.03	0.57	0.44	0.50	−0.20	−0.28	−0.15
Turkey	−0.54	0.25	−0.51	0.04	0.55	−0.32	0.86	0.79	0.43
China	−0.17	−0.55	−0.18	0.87	0.69	0.38	0.22	0.36	0.28
Indonesia	−0.57	−0.88	−0.88	0.13	−0.11	−0.30	0.74	0.71	0.52
Vietnam	n.a.	−0.37	0.85	n.a.	−0.65	−0.01	n.a.	−0.10	0.48
ASEAN4	0.58	0.49	0.20	−0.74	−0.30	−0.34	0.48	0.55	0.38
India	−0.58	−0.15	0.43	−0.40	−0.24	−0.10	0.43	0.24	0.44
RoSoAsia	−0.59	−0.16	−0.40	−0.43	−0.70	−0.67	0.45	0.13	−0.02
Argentina	0.97	0.99	0.96	0.99	0.92	0.75	0.64	0.71	0.78
Brazil	0.58	0.15	0.29	0.51	0.47	0.35	0.79	0.85	0.66
RLatAm	0.36	0.07	−0.08	−0.17	−0.23	−0.23	0.56	0.56	0.57
FSU	n.a.	n.a.	−0.63	n.a.	n.a.	-0.59	n.a.	n.a.	−0.31
MENA	−0.91	−0.97	−0.94	−0.80	−0.94	−0.87	−0.01	−0.54	−0.45
Tanzania	n.a.	n.a.	−0.40	n.a.	n.a.	0.18	n.a.	n.a.	0.69
Zambia	−0.35	−0.40	−0.40	−0.88	−0.78	−0.59	−0.38	−0.15	0.34
RoSSA	0.39	−0.13	−0.17	0.37	−0.05	−0.25	0.68	0.54	0.53
RoWorld	−0.10	−0.43	−0.66	−0.27	−0.50	−0.45	−0.16	−0.25	−0.43

Source: Dimaranan, Hertel, and Keeney (2003).

These results, however, have to be taken with some caution. They reflect the pattern of trade flows that result *given the highly distorted trade regime*. Many developing countries simply cannot compete against the huge subsidies, say, to dairy. If these subsidies were not there, these countries would become exporters rather than importers.

Table A1.4. **Share of developing country trade with OECD, 1997 (%)**
Commodity categories as for Table A1.3.

	Program commodities		Livestock and meat		Other Agriculture and food	
	Exports	Imports	Exports	Imports	Exports	Imports
China	52	76	60	85	55	44
Indonesia	78	58	69	95	27	44
Vietnam	13	56	74	82	24	40
ASEAN4	40	48	54	71	47	44
India	27	75	52	85	31	24
RSoAsia	23	66	61	81	62	18
Argentina	23	58	38	35	57	36
Brazil	48	21	71	33	50	36
RLatAm	47	63	77	69	47	51
FSU	37	23	50	80	48	63
MENA	43	66	73	80	66	60
Tanzania	89	31	54	60	54	25
Zambia	86	7	69	93	65	43
RoSSA	63	49	77	82	69	62
RoWorld	62	73	59	66	62	61

Source: Dimaranan, Hertel, and Keeney (2003: table 4).

Moreover, agricultural markets are global markets, and so even if developing country A imports wheat from developing country B, the price it pays is greatly affected by the subsidies provided by the developed world or by trade barriers that A might impose against the imports of the commodity.

The (national) real income effects of liberalization are dominated by two factors: (1) the change in allocative efficiency, and (2) the change in terms-of trade. Gains from allocative efficiency are realized when market distortions are removed, permitting the economy to reallocate its resources to the most productive use. These benefits accrue largely to the liberalizing region itself. They are partially reflected in the huge budgetary savings that accrue to the government of the liberalizing country.

The terms-of-trade effect comes from changes in a country's export prices relative to its import prices. The impact of global liberalization on national terms of trade is usefully decomposed by McDougall (1993) into three separate effects—the world price effect, the export price effect, and the import price effect.

Export and import restrictions mean that there is a wedge between the international price and the price that may be received by producers or paid by consumers in each country. A country with an export subsidy faces a higher producer and consumer price than the world price. A country with a production subsidy faces a higher producer price (inclusive of the subsidy), but the consumer price is the world price. A country with an import quota or tariff faces both a higher consumer and higher producer price. Full liberalization entails eliminating all of these restrictions. Since there are huge subsidies at present for the production of temperate agriculture products, the world price of these crops would go up. The consumer price would go up less in the EU,[2] which has an export subsidy, than in the United States. Developing countries that protect agriculture would see consumer and producer prices go down relative to the world price, but since the world price has gone up, the net effect is ambiguous.

Making matters more complicated are cross-commodity movements. Not all agricultural crops are equally subsidized. The elimination of subsidies would lead to a reallocation of resources within the agricultural sector. It is possible, for instance, that with the elimination of the dairy subsidy, the output of beef cattle could rise, and thus the price of beef might fall, even though the consumer price of milk products might rise. In general, vegetables are less subsidized than grains, and hence there would be a shift away from grains towards vegetables. Shipping costs are, however, less for grains than for vegetables, and vegetable markets tend to be localized. Thus, even if vegetable prices in developed countries fall, it will have little impact on developing countries.

For a few crops, like sugar, there are quotas. The elimination of the quota would lower producer and consumer prices in those developed countries imposing quotas, and raise international producer and consumer prices. The overall impact on developing countries depends on who receives the quota rents. Even when the rent goes to those in developing countries, it does not seep down to producers.

Differences between production and export subsidies are often exaggerated. A production subsidy of t_p per cent in an economy producing x_p raises output by approximately $t_p \eta_s$, where η_s is the elasticity of supply. The output impact per dollar of subsidy is $t_p \eta_s / t_p px = \eta_s / px$, and the impact on exports is $\eta_s / px\alpha$, where α is the ratio of exports to total production. On the other hand, an export subsidy raises both the production price and the consumption price, so that output is increased and consumption reduced. The impact on exports is thus $\eta_s / px\alpha + (1/\alpha - 1)\eta_d / pc$, where c is consumption. While the impact on developing countries per dollar of subsidy is

---

[2] Consumer prices could even fall.

greater, the difference is small if the elasticity of demand is small, which is the case for many agricultural commodities.

It is important to recognize that among the 'consumers' of agricultural goods is agro-business. While the higher price discourages direct consumption, it also discourages agro-business, shifting it to other countries, including developing countries. Thus, while there remains a presumption that export subsidies are worse than production subsidies for developing countries, there is some question not only about the magnitude, but even about the sign.

There are several additional concerns about the effects of agricultural liberalization on developing countries. The effects of Uruguay Round liberalization were noted at the Marrakech Meeting, where the Ministerial Decision on 'Measures Concerning the Possible Negative Effects of the Reform Program on Least Developed and Net Food-Importing Developing Countries' addressed the need to provide adversely affected countries with assistance.

The effect of liberalization on poverty is difficult to determine, largely for the same reasons that we noted that there was an ambiguity in the impact on developing countries as a whole: consumers lose while producers gain. One problem is that the limited resources of small farmers could prevent them from taking advantage of liberalized markets unless credit facilities are improved.

One of the most significant effects of liberalization on the poor is felt through changes in the price of food. Anderson, Dimaranan, Francois *et al.* (2000) model a general equilibrium framework and find that full liberalization of OECD farm policies would have a large effect on the volume of international food trade (a 50 per cent increase) but only a small effect on prices (a 5 per cent increase on average). Beghin, Roland-Holst and vander Mensbrugghe (2003) find that the price rise is larger for some commodities. However, this does not include the effects of reform to non-farm trade and so may misstate the effect in a multisector agreement. But even in this study, the expected price increases are not large—the smallest increases (about 4–6 per cent) are in the wheat, rice, and coarse grains sectors. The effect of price increases on poverty is hard to generalize across developing countries and within countries. This is because the relationship between liberalization and poverty depends on the shares of household income from different factors (land, labor, capital)—the prices of which will change. The size of these changes depends on factor substitutability, factor intensities, and factor mobility. The impact of price changes on welfare depends on the relative shares of different goods in the production bundle. Additionally, liberalization could have effects on net transfers, including increased welfare, remittances from distant relatives, or changed taxation levels (Anderson 2003).

Despite these difficulties, Anderson (2003) argues that *since most of the poorest people are net sellers of food (or at least sellers of agricultural labor) liberalization would reduce poverty.* Increases in the price of food would stimulate production and increase the demand for unskilled farm labor. Because unemployment (both open and disguised) is chronic in developing countries, this in itself would have enormous benefits.

Another concern is food self-sufficiency. Some fear that cuts to protection by OECD countries will lead to unaffordably high international food import bills (see e.g. Sharma, Konondreas, and Greenfield 1996).

Table A1.5 shows the proportion of the population that is undernourished in several developing countries. The last two columns show the value of food imports as a percentage of total exports and total agricultural exports. Interestingly, however, net food importer status (greater than 100 per cent in the last column) is not highly correlated with the FAO's category 'Low-income food-deficit country' (LIFDC). Botswana, Jamaica, and Peru are all net importers but are not classified as food-deficient. Also Côte d'Ivoire, Malawi, and Kenya all import less than 20 per cent of their export volume, but are classified as food-deficient.

An additional concern is that the liberalization of agricultural trade would prevent countries from managing external price shocks. However, Zwart and Blandford (1989) argue that liberalization could lead to less volatile food prices, since trade can even out surpluses and deficits across countries with heterogeneous production shocks.

But governments may want to intervene to stabilize either producer or consumer prices, especially in developing countries, where means for risk absorption are limited. Thus, initiatives at agriculture liberalization should leave scope for developing countries to implement such stabilization schemes.

A final concern is that many of the least developed countries already receive preferential access to OECD country markets. Some of the beneficiaries of these agreements are concerned that their advantages might be eroded under a broader multilateral agreement.

However, there are several reasons why multilateralism should be preferred. First, preferential agreements harm those countries that are not in the agreement, including many which are very poor. Borrell (1999) discusses this point in the context of the banana dispute of the 1990s, for which one study showed that for every dollar of benefit to producers of

Table A1.5. **Income category and food trade status**

LI, LMI, and UMI refer to the World Bank classifications of low-income, lower-middle-income and upper-middle-income countries; LDCs are least-developed countries, as recognized by the UN; LIFDCs are low-income food-deficit countries, defined by the FAO as those countries with a GNP per capita less than $1,445 in 2000 and which are net importers of food defined on a calorie basis; NFIDCs are net food-importing developing countries, as defined by the WTO Committee on Agriculture.
n.a.: not available

	Population under-nourished (%)	Income/food trade status groupings		Food Imports	
				(% of total exports)	(% of agricultural exports)
Bangladesh	35	LDC	LIFDC	21	829
Botswana	25	UMI	NFIDC	14	256
Brazil	10	UMI		7	30
Costa Rica	5	UMI		6	19
Côte d'Ivoire	15	LI	NFIDC	LIFDC	9	17
Egypt	4	LMI	NFIDC	LIFDC	20	542
Fiji	n.a.	LMI		9	52
Guyana	n.a.	LMI		7	23
Honduras	21	LMI	NFIDC	LIFDC	13	48
India	24	LI		LIFDC	5	42
Indonesia	6	LI		LIFDC	6	56
Jamaica	9	LMI	NFIDC		12	111
Kenya	44	LI	NFIDC	LIFDC	13	32
Malawi	33	LDC		LIFDC	13	16
Morocco	7	LMI	NFIDC	LIFDC	12	146
Pakistan	19	LI	NFIDC	LIFDC	15	134
Peru	11	LMI	NFIDC		14	152
Philippines	23	LMI		LIFDC	6	123
Senegal	25	LDC		LIFDC	26	357
Sri Lanka	23	LMI	NFIDC	LIFDC	12	68
Thailand	18	LMI		2	14
Uganda	21	LDC		LIFDC	20	41
Zimbabwe	38	LI		5	13

Source: Anderson (2003: table 4).

bananas in ACP countries, the regime harmed non-ACP developing country producers by a similar amount and reduced the welfare of EU consumers by 13 dollars. This type of scheme does not seem to be a very efficient means of assisting banana producers in ACP countries, who could be directly compensated by gains from the removal of the preference.

Second, if developing countries only sell part of their production in preferential markets, then they are selling the rest of their output at lower than

Table A1.6. **Welfare and efficiency gains expected from a 40% liberalization in agriculture, 2005**
Column (1) reports the efficiency changes as a share of food and agricultural value added. AgrMkt40
(col. (5)) excludes reductions in production subsidies whereas Agr40 covers all forms of protection.

Region	Agr40 experiment ratios (percentages)				Total EV by experiment (US$m)			
	Eff/$VA (1)	Eff/EV (2)	EV/Exp (3)	Agr40 (4)	AgrMkt40 (5)	Manufact40 (6)	BusFinSvces (7)	T&Tsvces (8)
NAmerica	9	11	0.035	3,401	1,436	3,310	4,517	52,532
WEurope	6	104	0.369	36,959	27,810	8,180	8,532	128,593
Aus/Nzl	6	−12	0.377	1,786	1,348	207	209	8,421
Japan	6	120	0.253	12,552	13,461	6,607	2,564	33,358
China	6	1,067	0.012	172	753	22,593	826	8,710
Taiwan	4	143	0.060	265	295	3,288	83	6,072
Other NICs	3	115	0.333	2,672	2,996	5,270	612	23,228
Indonesia	2	1,183	0.002	6	26	792	270	1,474
Other SEAsia	2	101	0.465	1,931	1,247	2,631	393	11,092
India	1	137	0.200	1,058	927	3,084	19	3,989
Other SoAsia	1	118	0.852	1,176	1,181	1,645	9	2,213
Brazil	1	64	0.245	1,988	1,683	4,491	457	3,625
Other LatAm	1	48	0.360	3,055	2,366	1,449	652	8,611
Turkey	1	123	0.142	338	332	619	70	3,524
Other MENA	0	−15	−0.202	−1,506	−718	1,074	231	16,667
EIT	0	142	0.033	301	282	1,391	1,865	10,265
SoAfrCU	0	46	0.080	129	54	283	128	1,897
Other SSA	0	31	0.194	436	529	249	30	4,496
RoWorld	−1	115	0.741	2,601	2,611	2,399	137	3,798
World				69,320	58,619	69,564	21,604	332,565

Source: Hertel, Anderson, Francois *et al*. (2000: table 8).

normal prices because of the depressing effect of OECD protection on prices
in the rest of the international market.

The empirical results below come largely from CGE (computable general
equilibrium) models.

Hertel, Anderson, Francois *et al.* (2000) report simulation results from a
40 per cent liberalization of all types of protection (including production
and export subsidies). The impacts of these changes on real income are dominated by efficiency and terms-of-trade effects.

There are significant gains from increases in allocative efficiency. The
first column in Table A1.6 reports the efficiency gains as a share of food and
agricultural value added. Large gains accrue to countries with the most
distorted policies, such as Europe, the US, and Japan. In Western Europe the

efficiency gains from liberalization amount to more than 8 per cent of the entire sector's value added.

Hertel, Anderson, Francois *et al.* (2000) add these efficiency gains to the terms-of-trade effects to calculate a measure of welfare gains, the 'equivalent variation' (EV)—which represents the amount of money that would make consumers equally well off had there been no liberalization. The second column in Table A1.6 shows the ratio of efficiency gains to total gain (EV). Where this is greater (less) than 100 per cent the terms-of-trade effects are negative (positive). For example, India experiences a terms-of-trade loss. Sub-Saharan Africa, Brazil, and Latin America experience a terms-of-trade gain because they are net exporters of food.

Table A1.7. **Change in world trade volume from agricultural liberalization (%)**

Change in world trade resulting from a 40% reduction in protection across 3 sectors: agriculture, manufactured goods, and services. AgrMkt40 excludes reductions in production subsidies whereas Agr40 covers all forms of protection.

	AgrMkt40	Agr40	Manufac40	Services40
food grains	1.9	−7.2	1.2	0.5
feed grains	4.1	1	0.7	0.5
oilseeds	0.6	5.8	0.1	0.3
meat & livestock	5.6	4.9	1.1	0.3
dairy	−6.7	−6.9	0.1	0.7
other agriculture	8.3	8.1	0.9	0.4
other food	12.1	11.8	0.5	−0.1
beverages & tobacco	27.5	27.6	0	0.8
extract	0	−0.1	1.8	0.3
textiles	0.2	0.2	16.3	0.3
wear & apparel	0.7	0.4	22.3	0.6
wood & paper	0	0	3.6	0.4
chemical & universal	0	−0.1	4.6	0.6
metals	0	0	5.5	0.4
autos	0.3	0.5	9.4	0.9
electronics	0.1	0.1	4.1	−0.1
other manufactures	0.1	0.2	5.2	0.2
house utilities	0	0	0.1	1
trade & transport	0.5	0.5	1.5	59.8
construction	0.3	0.5	0.4	18.3
business & finance	0.1	0.1	0.5	10.8
government & service	−0.1	−0.1	0.8	39.2

Source: Hertel, Anderson, Francois *et al.* (2000: table 6).

The total global welfare increase from a 40 per cent liberalization of agricultural protection is US$70 billion in this study. The distribution of these gains across countries is regressive. By far the largest absolute gains (col. (4)) accrue to developed countries, Western Europe, and Japan, who benefit from the reduction in their own subsidies. However, col. (3) shows a measure of relative welfare which accounts for the importance of food in GDP in each region. Although the benefits of liberalization to Western Europe are large, the food sector only represents 5 per cent of GDP. Column (3) shows the total gain (EV) as a percentage of expenditure on food in that region. This is one way of representing the benefits of liberalization relative to the importance of agriculture in the economy. On this category, the largest gains are realized in Other South Asia (non-India), Rest of the World (RoWorld), Other South-East Asia (non-Indonesia), the Other NICs, and then Western Europe.

For comparison, Table A1.8 shows the results of a second CGE study by Anderson, Dimaranan, Francois *et al.* (2001). They estimate that the total welfare gain from the liberalization of all (i.e. 100 per cent) of agricultural protection is US$164 billion.[3] The Anderson study reports the impact of liberalization by different regions on other regions. It concludes that the farm policies of the OECD countries—after the Uruguay reforms have been accounted for—reduce welfare in developing countries by US$11.6 billion.

Table A1.8. **Welfare gains from global removal of trade barriers, 2005 (US$bn)**

Liberalizing region	Benefiting region	Agriculture and food	Other primary	Textiles & clothing	Other manufactures	Total
High-income	High-income	110.5	−0.0	−5.7	−8.1	96.6
	Low-income	11.6	0.1	9.0	22.3	43.1
	Total	122.1	0.0	3.3	14.2	139.7
Low-income	High-income	11.2	0.2	10.5	27.7	49.6
	Low-income	31.4	2.5	3.6	27.6	65.1
	Total	42.6	2.7	14.1	55.3	114.7
All countries	High-income	121.7	0.1	4.8	19.6	146.2
	Low-income	43.0	2.7	12.6	49.9	108.1
	Total	164.7	2.8	17.4	69.5	254.3

Source: Anderson, Dimaranan, Francois *et al.* (2001).

[3] This study is roughly consistent with Hertel, Anderson, Francois *et al.* (2000), whose predicted US$70bn gain was based on a 40% reduction of barriers.

This is a small number in comparison to the gains realized by developing countries as a result of liberalization in other developing countries (US$31.4 billion), and the gains realized by developed countries as a result of their own liberalization (US$110.5 billion). It is also a small number in comparison to the gains predicted from liberalization in the temporary movement of natural persons. The reason many developing countries do not gain more is not difficult to understand given the structure of these models. Their gains from more efficient resource allocation are offset by an adverse change in the region's terms-of-trade.

Moreover, these models simply add up the gains and losses. No note is made of the fact that rural producers may be far poorer than the average person in society; or that those who buy *imported* food (say wheat) are far richer than those who live off locally grown crops, like millet. Nor does it take into account any multiplier effects, e.g. the losses in income to producers may have a larger effect on GDP than corresponding gains in income to consumers (e.g. because of differences in marginal propensities to consume). With unemployment rampant in most developing countries, aggregate demand is often a constraining variable. Nor do these models take into account the effects of credit constraints: higher prices allow poor rural farmers to buy more fertilizer and higher-quality seed, thus providing a further boost to their income. The higher incomes, in turn, may allow other forms of high-return investment—including temporary migration into higher-paying urban areas. Finally, there is considerable evidence that at very low incomes, productivity depends on nutrition, and the higher incomes accordingly will have a direct impact on agricultural productivity—another effect not incorporated into these models.

For further comparison, we look at studies which focus on the effects of specific protection mechanisms. Dimaranan, Hertel, and Keeney (2003) examine the effect of domestic support (not including market access restrictions) in industrialized countries on developing countries. The terms-of-trade effect dominates welfare outcomes in their simulations, leading them to conclude that a cut in OECD production subsidies would lead to welfare losses in most developing regions. The first column in Table A1.9 reports the average world price impacts of cutting domestic support in all industrialized countries for all agricultural commodities by 50 per cent. The table shows that domestic support has the largest effect on price for program crops (wheat, corn, barley, rice) and ruminant livestock (beef). Sugar and dairy, which are mainly protected by tariffs, show small price declines, and land and labor shifts out of program crops. The remaining columns in Table A1.9 decompose the world price effects by type of domestic

Table A1.9. **Change in average world prices due to comprehensive OECD domestic support**

Commodity	World price change	Contribution by tax/subsidy to world price change			
		Output	Int.Input	Land	Capital
pdrice	0.26	0.12	0.34	0.05	−0.23
wheat	4.91	1.03	1.68	1.11	1.09
crsgrns	5.5	1.42	1.79	1.02	1.27
oilsds	3.53	0.92	1.21	0.79	0.6
rawsgr	−0.58	0.09	0.14	−0.33	−0.48
othcrops	−1.5	−0.01	−0.03	−0.69	−0.77
ruminants	4.3	0.48	0.95	−0.38	3.25
nonrumnts	0.54	0.26	0.45	−0.14	−0.02
rawmilk	0.21	0.14	0.81	−0.33	−0.4
pcrice	0.27	0.13	0.12	0.06	−0.03
vegoilfat	0.97	0.2	0.34	0.24	0.2
refsgr	−0.06	0.05	0.06	−0.03	−0.15
rummeat	2.21	0.31	0.56	−0.11	1.44
nrummeat	0.43	0.17	0.28	−0.06	0.04
dairy	−0.19	0.14	0.36	−0.27	−0.43
othprfood	0.22	0.06	0.11	0.07	−0.03
mnfc	0.12	0.01	0	0.1	0.01
srvc	0.11	0.01	0	0.1	−0.01

Source: Dimaranan, Hertel, and Keeney (2003: table 10).

instrument: output subsidies, intermediate input subsidies, land-based payments, and capital subsidies (including livestock-based payments).

As shown in Table A1.10, the welfare impacts of domestic support reduction arise from allocative efficiency, output stimulus, and terms-of-trade effects. The two largest agricultural exporters, Argentina and Brazil, gain considerably in each of these categories. For these countries the terms-of-trade effects are large and positive. However, for most developing countries the terms-of-trade effects are negative and exceed the allocative efficiency gains. A 50 per cent reduction in OECD domestic support results in a decline in aggregate developing-country welfare of US$357 million.

Turning our attention to another experiment in partial liberalization, Hertel, Anderson, Francois *et al.* (2000) analyse the effect of reductions in border protection (leaving production subsidies unchanged). They report that, not surprisingly, the global gains from this partial liberalization are smaller than when liberalization also includes production subsidies: US$59

Table A1.10. **Welfare impacts of domestic support reform ($m)**

Region	Equivalent variation				Terms-of-trade components region		
	Total	Allocative efficiency	IS effect	Terms of trade	World price	Export price	Import price
China	−69.1	−69.6	−18.0	18.5	−51.8	137.1	−66.8
Indonesia	−13.6	0.8	−1.9	−12.4	−54.5	35.5	6.6
Vietnam	−8.2	−1.9	0.3	−6.6	−10.0	5.8	−2.4
ASEAN4	−15.2	4.9	−4.3	−15.9	−47.4	113.4	−81.9
India	35.9	15.2	−2.1	22.8	−22.9	38.6	7.1
RoSoAsia	−44.2	−3.3	−1.2	−39.7	−57.2	17.2	0.3
Argentina	157.3	26.2	10.6	120.5	183.1	−53.1	−9.5
Brazil	200.2	73.3	31.9	94.9	1.1	88.5	5.3
RoLatAmer	−214.3	−29.9	−1.0	−183.4	−244.7	101.8	−40.5
MENA	−270.1	−50.6	−1.8	−217.7	−315.9	83.1	15.1
Tanzania	−7.0	−1.2	−1.0	−4.9	−7.1	1.8	0.4
Zambia	0.0	0.2	0.0	−0.3	−1.4	0.4	0.7
RoSSA	−126.1	−16.0	−2.1	−108.0	−149.7	31.1	10.6
RoWorld	17.1	27.7	−1.1	−9.4	−221.4	285.9	−73.9
LDC total	−357.3	−24.2	8.4	−341.6	−999.7	887.0	−228.9

Source: Dimaranan, Hertel, and Keeney (2003: table 11).

billion rather than US$70 billion (see Table A1.7). However, the additional benefit from including production subsidies accrues entirely to developed countries, which reap allocative efficiency gains. Western Europe alone gains an additional US$9 billion when production subsidies are included. By contrast, many developing countries are worse off when production subsidies are liberalized because of the terms-of-trade effect. The Middle East and North Africa and Sub-Saharan African countries outside the customs union are significantly worse off as a result of the reduction in production subsidies (Table A1.7).

The quantitative studies above indicate that the effect of agricultural liberalization on developing countries is complex. Competing efficiency and price effects have different effects across heterogenous countries.

For the reasons explained earlier, these results should not be taken too seriously. The underlying assumptions of the computable general models do not provide a good description of the economies of developing countries. The results are highly sensitive to assumptions about elasticities and cross-elasticities of supply and demand.

Still, there are three lessons that emerge from these admittedly highly restrictive studies. The first is that in the process of liberalization, many developing countries will find themselves worse off, especially urban workers. But these adverse effects can be mitigated by adjustment assistance from the more developed countries, *which at the same time leaves the more advanced industrial countries better off*. This is because of the large allocative inefficiencies associated with the distorted patterns of production.

The second is that, while a true Development Round has to go well beyond agriculture, it must include agriculture, for three reasons: it is too important to some of the developing countries; there can be no principled trade agreement without including agriculture; and, not surprisingly, as a consequence, it has taken on enormous symbolic value.

Third, the potential for losses does not suggest that multilateral reform should be abandoned. Instead, it suggests that to share benefits among all countries, reform must accommodate differences across countries. The case for liberalization is particularly strong for those commodities, like cotton, the elimination of whose subsidies would have little direct bearing on the standard of living of those in developing countries.

The empirical results surveyed above indicate that uniform elimination of all agricultural protection would result in negative terms-of-trade effects for many developing countries and sharp declines in farm incomes in Europe and North America. The latter are in a position to bear the costs; the former may not be. A reform agenda must carefully discriminate between liberalization instruments. Such an agenda would have three key components.

First, a significant reduction in border protection in developed countries (particularly the EU), including tariff cuts and the elimination of export subsidies. Tariffs on the goods produced primarily by developing countries, as well as those consumed primarily in developed countries, should be reduced most rapidly. For example, the elimination of US and EU quotas and tariffs on sugar and tropical products would increase the price received by developing world producers but only have a small effect on consumer prices in developing countries.

Second, domestic production support for price-sensitive necessities that are widely consumed in developing countries should be reduced gradually, with some of the savings in developed country subsidy budgets being directed at ameliorating the adjustment costs of those in the developing world. Many developing countries in North Africa, Sub-Saharan Africa and Latin America (though not Brazil, Argentina, or Mexico) rely on imports of subsidized grains and oilseeds from OECD producers. The empirical evidence reviewed above suggests that these countries are particularly exposed to agricultural reforms which might increase the price of some commodities.

Third, domestic support should be shifted from market price support to alternative payment systems. Reinstrumentation of protection in OECD countries towards the least trade-distorting instruments (such as land-based payments) is one possible means of compensating OECD farmers while minimizing the impact on developing world producers. But many of the so-called non-trade-distorting subsidies do in fact lead to increased production, and too much has been made of the distinction between export subsidies and production subsidies.

This type of program is similar to the thrust of the OECD in its 'Positive Reform Agenda' for agriculture (OECD 2002) and is supported by a series of recent research contributions.[4]

A1.2 **Services**

This section analyses the potential gains from the liberalization of services. Services represent an increasingly large share of GDP in both developed and developing countries—but a much larger share in developed countries. Indeed, the area of focus of trade negotiations during the past fifty years, manufacturing, is increasingly becoming the province of developing countries. It is natural, then, that the developed countries like the United States should shift their focus towards liberalization of services.

The bulk of the empirical studies surveyed below suggests that the liberalization of services could yield significant welfare gains—much larger than the gains from agricultural or manufactured goods. The estimates of global gains are as high as US$400 billion. The estimates are large because protection levels are high in the service sector, and services make up a large (and growing) share of world trade. Additionally, services are key inputs into the production of almost all goods.

The enthusiasm in the cross-country empirical literature is tempered by negative experiences at the national level. Opening up markets has been

---

[4] Rae and Strutt (2003) use a CGE framework to compare the welfare gains of liberalization in border measures and domestic support. They find that improved market access generates far greater trade and welfare gains than reductions in domestic support. They conclude that the WTO should focus primarily on achieving reductions in border restrictions and give a lower priority to the elimination of domestic support. Hoeckman, Ng, and Olarreaga (2002) focus on the effect of OECD agricultural reform on developing countries. They reach the same conclusion—that developing countries' interests are better suited through tariff cuts rather than cuts in domestic support. It is still the case, however, that the elimination of domestic subsidies for certain commodities (like cotton) is likely to have a small effect on consumers in a developing country, and a large benefit to producers. There are other crops for which this is also likely to be true. The critical distortion differs markedly across commodities. Their results are highly dependent on assumptions concerning demand and supply elasticities, and therefore results may differ markedly across commodities. In the case of sugar, it is trade restrictions which dominate; in the case of wheat, it is almost surely production and export subsidies which dominate.

accompanied at times by a reduction in competition, and an increase in prices.[5] In the case of financial services, there are even allegations that the supply of credit to medium-sized and small domestic enterprises has been reduced. Financial and capital market liberalization has been associated with greater instability, not higher levels of economic growth. These adverse consequences, in turn, help to explain the unhappiness of many countries about efforts to force further opening up of the service sector.

It is easy to explain the discrepancy between the models and the outcomes. It is partly that, deficient as the models used to analyse the consequences of agricultural liberalization are, those in the area of services are far worse. They model trade in services in exactly the same manner as they model trade in goods, and thus the models have *all* the problems we noted earlier. But in addition, there are several further problems. There are some formal barriers to trade: the United States, for example, does not allow coastal shipping by ships of another nationality. There are restrictions on media ownership. Foreigners may not buy spectrum in the US, and if they cannot buy spectrum they cannot provide broadcasting services except by selling services to Americans who own stations. But many of the barriers to trade are more subtle and are typically hard to quantify. Because the estimates of government-created trade barriers are unreliable, so are the resulting estimates of the benefits that would accrue from eliminating them. Worse still, debates about liberalization in services do not center around discussions of lowering the effective barrier from, say, 40 per cent to 20 per cent. Rather, they center around particular *measures*, such as privatization and elimination of particular regulations. In each of these cases, the ramifications of the particular measure extend well beyond the impacts on trade; in many cases, these are incidental. Inevitably, then, debates about service sector liberalization devolve into fundamental debates about national economic and social policy. Should the media, for instance, be controlled by a few rich, foreign firms, who are able to use their wealth to control the flow of information to the citizenry? This is an issue which is fundamental to the functioning of democracy and should not be relegated to trade negotiators. (At the same time, we should recognize that there are certain service sector liberalizations which are little different in their impact than a standard trade liberalization; such is the case for construction and maritime

---

[5] For example, privatization of utilities—such as South Africa's experience of granting its newly privatized telecommunications utility Telekom a 5-year monopoly—can lead to inefficient services (OECD 2002). Similarly the poor regulation of financial sectors across South-East Asia contributed to instability prior to the crises of the late 1990s. Poor electricity deregulation has led to problems in many countries.

services—areas which were not included in the Uruguay negotiations and which are of some concern to developing countries.)

Part of the reason that the standard models are unpersuasive arises from the fact that they fail to take account of the highly differentiated nature of services and the large 'local information' content. There are other ways in which trade in services is *obviously* different from trade in goods. For the most part, services have to be consumed at the point of production. In the case of haircuts, the point is obvious. But the same is true for retail sales, hotels, and electricity. Thus, the issue of trade in services in inextricably linked (as already noted) to the movement of capital and labor. Without these, there can be little trade in services.

But movements of labor and capital introduce a host of other considerations, quite different from those associated with trade in goods. The issues of labor—which are of vital concern to developing countries—are dealt with in the next section. The central issue of concern for capital flows is investor protections. What the investors would like, of course, is a world without regulation or taxation, but that would compromise the general well-being of the developing world. Indeed, most of the failures of liberalization have been because of failures to put into place an adequate regulatory environment (including one which ensures competition).

Economic theory, of course, says that, under certain idealized circumstances (e.g. constant returns to scale), full global efficiency can be gained either through the free mobility of capital or the free mobility of labor. But in the general case, equating the marginal returns to capital will not suffice to equate the marginal returns to labor.

What do international firms provide when they provide services? Why might an American company have a competitive advantage in financial services over a domestic company? Presumably, this relates to *knowledge* and *information*, e.g. about how to organize the provision of the services.

There are, in fact, a variety of ways besides direct investment by which such services are sold. Hotels and restaurants issue franchises, which have been enormously popular. Firms may contract out management services.

Of increasing concern in recent years in the United States is the problem of 'contracting out' services through the Internet. This is one area in which production of a service can occur at a place different from that where the service is consumed. Such services are, in many ways, very much like traded goods. It is of importance to developing countries that this nascent industry not be impaired by the creation of new trade barriers by the developed countries.

A further concern is that many service sector liberalizations increase poverty, by increasing prices of essential services or reducing access for the poor. Private firms may be less willing to engage in cross-subsidization of market segments in poor and rural areas. Even if liberalization leads to lower average costs through increased competitiveness and efficiency, prices for some end-users may rise. Mosely (1999) estimates the impact of financial liberalization on access to rural credit in four African countries—Uganda, Kenya, Malawi, and Lesotho. The study found that liberalization expanded credit where it was accompanied by innovative reforms with regulation focused on rural access and poverty reduction. However, merely privatizing government micro-credit agencies had a negative effect on rural areas, as witnessed by the consequences of reform in Malawi.

There is also a concern that some service sector liberalizations, even if they increase economic welfare, narrowly defined, have an adverse effect on community life. Each individual in the community values having the local store. The local store owner, like other local businessmen, provides essential services for the community. But these are services that are not 'priced'. It pays each consumer to buy the goods for the lowest price. Walmart is thus able to drive the local store out of business. But there are fundamental questions: 'Is the community better off with the local businessman replaced by a hired manager that is rotated in and out of the community in three years' time?'

The Services sector account for half of GDP in developing countries (60 per cent in developed countries) and are some of the fastest-growing industries in many economies. The performance of the services sector is critical to growth. For example, the strength of a country's financial sector is a determinant of growth (see Levine 1997; Carlin and Mayer 2003). Well-managed and well-regulated banks lead to an efficient transformation of savings to investment, ensuring an appropriate allocation of resources. Similarly, efficient business services reduce transactions costs, and telecommunications capabilities are an important prerequisite for development in many sectors.

The GATS framework provides for four modes of service delivery:

- Mode 1, *cross—border supply*, which is analogous to trade in goods, arises when a service crosses a national frontier, for example, the purchase of software or insurance by a consumer from a supplier located abroad.

- Mode 2, *consumption abroad*, occurs when the consumer travels to the territory of the service supplier, for example, to purchase tourism, education, or health services.

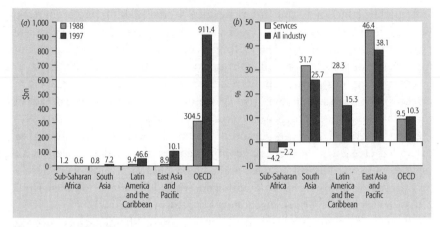

Figure A1.2. **Foreign direct investment in services**
(a) Regional FDI stock
(b) Compound annual growth rate
Source: OECD (2002).

- Mode 3, *commercial presence*, involves foreign direct investment, for example, when a foreign bank or telecommunications firm establishes a branch or subsidiary in the territory of a country. Figure A1.2 indicates that the stock of service-sector foreign direct investment (FDI) in developing countries is small relative to OECD countries. However, as Fig. A1.2*b* indicates, service, sector FDI is growing more rapidly in developing countries, with the exception of Sub-Saharan Africa.

- Mode 4, *movement of individuals*, occurs when independent service providers or employees of a multinational firm temporarily move to another country.

These four elements of the General Agreement on Trade in Services (GATS) encompass the movement of both capital and labor for services provision. This broad approach enables countries to bargain to exploit their comparative advantage. For example, developing countries might exchange greater market access for capital for more fluid movement of unskilled workers to developed countries. Figure A1.3 shows that the existing commitments have been lopsided, with the development of Mode 4 proceeding most slowly.

International service transactions remain heavily protected in many countries. Table A1.11 estimates the tariff-equivalent protection levels for the construction services, business and finance, trade and transport, and government services sectors across various countries and regions. These are taken from estimates by Francois (1999) based on predictions of the level of

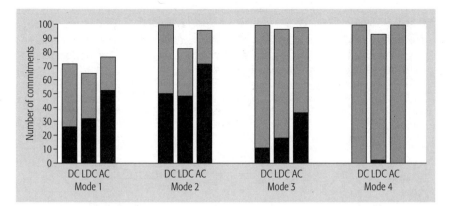

Figure A1.3. **Full and partial market access commitments under GATS**

DC = Developed countries; LDC = Developing and transition economies; AC = Acceding countries

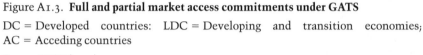

Source: OECD (2002).

bilateral services trade with the US. Discrepancies between the actual level of bilateral trade (from US trade data) and the predicted level are assumed to result from protection. The estimates for the trade and transport and the government services sectors are taken from Hoekman (1995).

Table A1.11 indicates that impediments to trade are quite high in trade and transport, government services, and construction and that barriers to trade in services are much larger than barriers to trade in manufactures and extraction industries. Findlay and McGuire (2003) report that impediments to international services tend to fall as income rises, except in some professional service activities. This is indicated in Fig. A1.4.

One has to be careful, however, about interpreting these data, which refer primarily to Mode 1 impediments. There are some service sectors—like haircuts—that are typically small businesses. Without Mode 4 liberalization, there is likely to be little cross-border sale of these services, even though standard economic theory would suggest that there would be large gains to trade. Services are highly individualized, often requiring large amounts of localized information. Thus, even with no artificially created barriers, individuals in one country may prefer to deal with those from their own community; those from their own community may be able to provide the services that individuals want. Local banks may have a competitive advantage in knowing who the good borrowers are (an advantage which may more than offset the problem of correlated risk). Large multinationals, geared to providing services to those in advanced industrial countries, may

Table A1.11. **Estimated average rates of protection by region and sector, 2005**
Note that figures for services are tariff-equivalent rates. For example, in China, the figures below suggest that import prices in the construction industry must be 41% above their free trade level to explain the relatively low share of imports in this market.

Region	Food	Manufactures	Services			
			Construction	Business & financial	Trade & transport	Government services
NAmerica	5	3	10	8	69	34
WEurope	8	1	18	9	84	40
Aus/Nzl	4	7	24	7	91	31
Japan	58	2	30	20	71	32
China	18	20	41	19	96	42
Taiwan	41	4	5	3	93	36
Other NICs	21	2	10	2	82	37
Indonesia	5	8	10	7	85	43
Other SEA	25	12	18	5	88	40
India	40	35	62	13	96	41
Other SoAsia	37	20	46	20	92	41
Brazil	4	16	57	36	71	44
Other LatAm	9	10	26	5	79	43
Turkey	31	6	46	20	92	40
Other MENA	15	14	10	4	92	40
EIT	12	9	52	18	71	35
SoAfrCU	8	8	42	16	58	26
Other SSA	13	9	11	0	94	43
RoWorld	76	33	46	20	97	38

Source: Hertel, Anderson, Francois *et al*. (2000: table 4). Original sources: Francois (1999), Hoekman (1995).

find it difficult to provide the services demanded in poor developing countries. In short, there are reasons to believe that even apart from artificially created barriers to trade in services, such trade might be more limited than trade in manufactured goods. In that case, even though the service sector is today larger than the manufacturing sector in developed countries, potential gains from trade, and the reductions of trade barriers, may be more limited.

Moreover, one has to distinguish *protection* from the legitimate role of government in imposing *regulations* that promote a variety of concerns of general interest, *even when such regulations have the effect of discouraging foreign firms*. For instance, affirmative action requirements might have this effect, yet it is a legitimate objective of government policy to advance the economic well-being of the disadvantaged.

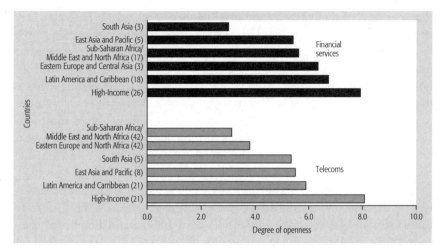

Figure A1.4. **Service sector openness by region: financial services and telecommunications**

The index for financial services captures the restrictions on new entry, foreign ownership, and capital mobility (IMF's Annual Report on Exchange Arrangements and Exchange Restrictions). The openness index for telecommunications captures the degree of competition, restrictions on ownership, and the existence of an independent regulator (ITU-World Bank database for 1998).

Sources: Mattoo, Rathindran, and Subramanian (2001); OECD (2002).

Inefficient service industries operate like a tax on an economy. Since services are essential production inputs for most goods, the price and quality of services provided to other producers have major impacts on the whole economy. This is particularly true in key service industries such as telecommunications, transport, energy, and finance.

For this reason the majority of gains from effectively managed reform accrues to the liberalizing region itself. Domestic firms benefit from access to services at lower prices while consumers gain, and employees in most service industries earn higher wages than in manufacturing (OECD 2002).

This poses two questions. First, if the benefits of liberalization are so great to the liberalizing country, why does one need to include such liberalizations within a trade agreement? Won't countries have an incentive to do that on their own? The answer traditionally put forward is that this is part of the political economy of trade liberalization: one gives up something of value to the other side (refusing at the same time to do something that would be of even greater value to oneself) in order to extract a concession out of the other side. The problem with this argument, in the context of services, is that typically the advanced industrial country *as a whole* has relatively little to gain, though particular firms in the developed country may gain a large amount. Thus, in the area of services, one is pandering to special interests. Pandering to special interests is not only bad economic policy, it is dangerous, because after the foreign firm comes in, the company continues to put pressure on its government to put pressure on the foreign government to pass legislation or regulations that are to its benefit, to renegotiate concessions when they prove unprofitable, or not to abrogate a contract even when there is clear evidence that the contract was only entered into because of corruption.

The reason that particular firms have much to gain, though not necessarily countries as a whole, is associated with the very reason that there are gains to trade in services: these arise not out of the standard differences associated with differences in factor supplies (after all, most of the production actually occurs in the purchasing country) but out of differential *information and knowledge*, including organizational capacity. If that information is widespread within a society, it is more likely that that information can easily flow abroad, especially in our highly interconnected global economy. Walmart, Toys-R-Us, and AIG have certain strengths that may not (or, in some cases, may) be easily imitated. When hard bargaining by the US allowed Toys-R-Us to open up in Japan, Japanese children benefited from the cheaper toys, as did Chinese workers, as China's sales of toys increased. But America benefited only to the extent that Toys—R—Us profits increased. American jobs were essentially unaffected.

The second, related issue is why these liberalizations should be part of an international trade agreement. Such agreements should focus on areas where there is a *global public good* being provided, e.g. through the setting of standards or dealing with global externalities.

For agriculture and manufacturing, most models report results dominated by two main effects—allocative efficiency gains and changes in terms of trade. For services liberalization, movements of capital across borders generate additional effects. First, foreign direct investment inflows and outflows can lead to an expansion or contraction in the capital stock located within a region. Changes in capital endowments affect national output, but since the capital is still *owned* by foreigners, the effect on GNP is less than on GDP.

A second effect on income works through the rents earned on foreign direct investments. Rents are created by barriers to services trade which fall during liberalization. It is conceivable that service sector liberalization could increase GDP but lower GNP, as domestic providers of services lose their rents, foreign firms capture rents associated with their superior knowledge and information.

Unlike agriculture, the modeling which focuses on the benefits resulting from assumed gains in the efficiency of the provision of services suggests that the main beneficiaries of reform in terms of both absolute and relative welfare gains (as a percentage of GDP) are the developing countries.

Dee and Hanslow (2000) use a CGE model called FTAP, to report that the total global gain from liberalizing all post-Uruguay trade restrictions on services is US$130 billion.[6] This amounts to half the total gain (US$260 billion) from total post-Uruguay liberalization—with the other half made up of gains from agriculture (US$50 billion) and manufactures (US$80 billion). These are the projected gains in real income about ten years after the liberalization has occurred. They include the gains from increased trade and more efficient resource allocation.

In a similar exercise by Hertel (1999), world welfare gains were predicted to be smaller than those in Dee and Hanslow (2000). Hertel predicts that the gains from liberalization in agriculture, manufactures, and services are US$164 billion, US$130 billion, and US$55 billion respectively. This variation is largely accounted for by differences in modelling assumptions. In agriculture, Hertel assumes no effective Uruguay liberalization post-1995, leaving much more to be done and more gains to be realized. In manufactures, the difference is largely accounted for by differences in the base year (Dee and Hanslow use 1995, Hertel 2005). Applying the 2005 base to the FTAP model accounts for 90 per cent of the difference. In the service sector, Hertel models only liberalization in the construction and business services sector. He also does not include liberalization of FDI.

Brown, Deardorff, and Stern (2002) use a CGE model to calculate the welfare effects of a 33 per cent reduction to barriers in the service sector. Table A1.12 shows that they expect global welfare to rise by US$413 billion. All of the countries listed experience welfare gains as well as increases in real wages and returns to capital. Developed countries experience large welfare gains—US$142 billion for the EU, US$131.4 billion for the US, and US$57.9 billion for Japan. Brown, Deardorff, and Stern note that their results—which are dependent on the accuracy of the size of barriers they estimated indirectly from trade flow data—show that the liberalization of services is likely to yield significantly larger gains than other reforms.

---

[6] Welfare gains are reported in standard CGE 'real income' terms. Real income is a measure of national income deflated by an index of national prices.

Table A1.12. **Welfare effects of service sector liberalization**

Welfare effects of a 33% reduction in barriers to service trade on imports, exports, terms of trade, welfare, real wages, and the return to capital.

Country	Imports (US$m)	Exports (US$m)	Terms of trade (%)	Welfare (%)	Welfare (US$m)	Real wages (%)	Return to capital (%)
Australia & NewZealand	2,354.4	1,962.3	0.385	1.050	5,379.6	0.694	0.657
Canada	2,244.0	2,136.3	0.083	0.811	5,910.4	0.317	0.316
European Union & EFTA	35,478.1	35,336.8	0.032	1.295	142,003.2	0.553	0.546
Japan	14,797.7	15,501.6	−0.067	0.891	57,875.1	0.247	0.277
United States	32,467.7	32,231.5	−0.033	1.448	131,426.8	0.524	0.534
India	919.2	803.9	0.212	0.552	2,321.6	0.170	0.204
Sri Lanka	121.7	99.1	0.335	1.202	200.4	0.881	0.507
Rest of South Asia	374.3	286.7	0.286	0.689	804.9	0.293	0.453
China	5,660.3	6,210.9	−0.128	1.320	11,959.1	0.840	0.603
Hong Kong	7,587.2	8,058.4	−0.611	4.382	5,643.1	5.638	5.927
South Korea	4,842.2	5,002.5	−0.102	1.339	7,619.5	0.913	0.956
Singapore	3,325.1	3,776.2	−0.297	3.322	2,470.8	4.821	3.972
Indonesia	1,401.3	1,469.4	−0.072	1.256	3,177.0	0.327	0.307
Malaysia	1,487.6	1,466.8	0.049	1.267	1,514.5	1.026	0.928
Philippines	1,986.7	2,195.0	−0.462	2.342	2,067.1	1.739	1.622
Thailand	3,324.2	3,625.3	−0.413	1.401	2,886.4	1.088	0.904
Mexico	863.1	809.1	0.110	0.878	3,099.3	0.204	0.195
Turkey	1,733.3	1,462.9	0.589	1.781	3,745.9	0.695	0.884
Central Europe	3,841.7	3,744.5	0.061	1.409	5,227.2	1.067	0.996
Central & South America	4,199.9	4,442.8	−0.179	1.050	18,363.5	0.256	0.272
Total	129,009.6	130,621.8			413,695.4		

Source: Brown, Deardorff, and Stern (2002: table 4).

Hertel, Anderson, Francois *et al.* (2000) also compare the gains from services liberalization to those for agriculture and manufactures. They report that a 40 per cent cut in protection in the business services and construction sectors yields a US$22 billion gain. Their estimate of the potential gains in the trade and transport sectors is US$332 billion. The trade and transport sectors represent a large share of global trade in services and provide a significant flow on benefits to other sectors of the economy. Table A1.13 shows the wide distribution of these gains across developed and developing countries.

Table A1.13. **Welfare and efficiency gains from liberalization of agriculture, manufacturing, and services**

Column (1) reports the efficiency changes due to a 40% liberalization in agriculture as a share of food and agricultural value added. The second column reports the efficiency gain as a proportion of the total gain in terms of equivalent variation (EV)– where this is larger than 100, the terms-of-trade effect is negative. Column (3) reports the EV as a proportion of total expenditure. Columns (4)–(8) report the EV for 5 different sector liberalization experiments.

Region	Agr40 experiment ratios (%)			Total EV by experiment ($m)				
	Eff/$VA (1)	Eff/EV (2)	EV/Exp (3)	Agr40 (4)	AgrMkt40 (5)	Manuf40 (6)	BusFinSvces (7)	T&Tsvces (8)
NAmerica	9	11	0.035	3,401	1,436	3,310	4,517	52,532
WEurope	6	104	0.369	36,959	27,810	8,180	8,532	128,593
Aus/Nzl	6	−12	0.377	1,786	1,348	207	209	8,421
Japan	6	120	0.253	12,552	13,461	6,607	2,564	33,358
China	6	1,067	0.012	172	753	22,593	826	8,710
Taiwan	4	143	0.060	265	295	3,288	83	6,072
Other NICs	3	115	0.333	2,672	2,996	5,270	612	23,228
Indonesia	2	1,183	0.002	6	26	792	270	1,474
Other SEAsia	2	101	0.465	1,931	1,247	2,631	393	11,092
India	1	137	0.200	1,058	927	3,084	19	3,989
Other SoAsia	1	118	0.852	1,176	1,181	1,645	9	2,213
Brazil	1	64	0.245	1,988	1,683	4,491	457	3,625
Other LatAm	1	48	0.360	3,055	2,366	1,449	652	8,611
Turkey	1	123	0.142	338	332	619	70	3,524
Other MENA	0	−15	−0.202	−1,506	−718	1,074	231	16,667
EIT	0	142	0.033	301	282	1,391	1,865	10,265
SoAfrCU	0	46	0.080	129	54	283	128	1,897
Other SSA	0	31	0.194	436	529	249	30	4,496
RoWorld	−1	115	0.741	2,601	2,611	2,399	137	3,798
World				69,320	58,619	69,564	21,604	332,565

Source: Hertel, Anderson, Francois *et al*. (2000: table 8).

Verikos and Zhang (2001) analyse the sectoral impacts of liberalization in financial and communication services. They estimate that the gain from each sector is US$24 billion. In both sectors, the majority of the gains come from removing restrictions that discriminate against foreign firms.

These gains are not of course divided equally across all countries. In Dee and Hanslow's analysis, their US$133 billion gain accrues disproportionately to developing countries. The service sectors in many developing countries are projected to expand as their relatively large barriers to entry are removed.

For example, the service sector in China (which captures a large part of the welfare gains) is projected to increase by a third when its large barriers to entry are removed. This is predicated, of course, on the assumption that China cannot obtain the requisite knowledge and information to improve its service sector without opening itself more fully, an assumption which is increasingly looking dubious.

Dee and Hanslow report results for only a small number of Commonwealth developing countries. The gain to Malaysia from global service sector liberalization is US$1 billion—equivalent to 0.7 per cent of GDP. The gains to the 'rest of the world' which includes smaller developing countries is US$23 billion or 0.8 per cent of GDP. Australia, China, Mexico, Chile and Indonesia all gain more from tertiary liberalization than from primary and secondary combined.

Service sector liberalization has the potential to deliver large welfare gains to developed and developing countries. But the results of attempts to estimate these benefits need to be taken with even more caution than results in agriculture and manufacturing. The localized nature of the services and the information that leads to success in its provisions means that the elimination of government imposed barriers may not necessarily lead to as much increase in trade as these models predict, and the gains in efficiency may be partially offset as rents are transferred from domestic to foreign producers. Some worry that financial service sector liberalization may even lead to a reduction in national output, as the supply of credit to domestic small and medium size enterprises is reduced. Empirical work estimating these effects is limited, and most of the CGE models simply proceeds by assuming that the production and sales of services is little different than those of agriculture and manufactured goods. Thus to the litany of qualifications to the use of CGE models noted earlier, the additional ones noted here mean that the results need to be taken with circumspection.

Since a large part of the gains from reform in the services sector accrue to domestic policy reforms, it is not obvious why international negotiations are necessary to achieve desirable outcomes. If the main gains could be achieved unilaterally, then what is the utility of multilateral negotiations? Matoo (2002) observes that many developing countries are in a situation where their ability to implement reform is hindered by opposition from domestic lobbies. In this context, it may be useful for some countries to undertake reforms in the context of the momentum of broad international negotiations.

There are however other areas where coordinated reciprocity could yield significant gains in the context of multilateral negotiations. On one hand developing countries have a number of developed country market access interests, particularly in the area of access to labour markets (GATS Mode 4), but also in construction and back-office business services. This suggests the prospect for a deal based on access to labor markets in exchange for a developed country demand such as greater commercial presence by foreign service providers in developing countries (Matoo 2002). But the shape of earlier service sector negotiations undermined this rationale; financial sector liberalization, for instance, *preceded* liberalization in construction and other service sectors that were of interest to developing countries.

Moreover there are several cases in which international cooperation may be valuable. One example is competition policy: a permissible merger in one jurisdiction may have a detrimental effect on competition in a smaller foreign jurisdiction. Fink, Matoo and Rathindran (2001) suggest that the GATS should require domestic competition law to consider the effect of collusive agreements on foreign markets. Second they suggest that foreign consumers should have the right to take action in foreign courts against corporations that abuse their market power.

A1.3 **Temporary migration**

As we noted earlier, the GATS recognises four modes of service delivery. The temporary movement of natural persons (TMNP) is known as Mode 4. It is by far the smallest in terms of trade flows and the volume of scheduled concessions recorded under the GATS (see Fig. A1.3).

The limited commitments that have been made refer to high-skill personnel—business executives etc.—whose mobility is closely linked to foreign direct investment and is an issue of interest to business lobbies in developed countries. Thus far, Mode 4 has not progressed in a way that allows developing countries to use their comparative advantage in low-and-medium skill labor-intensive services.

The empirical studies surveyed below suggest that an expanded Mode 4 could generate enormous welfare gains. The temporary movement of less skilled workers from developing countries (where they are in oversupply) to developed countries (where they are relatively undersupplied) is estimated to increase world welfare by hundreds of billions of dollars, even if the scale of the labor flow is modest.

The movement of natural persons is usefully divided into three categories.

Flows from developed to developing countries

This category represents highly skilled technical or managerial workers who work in developing countries, either providing specialized services such as consulting and legal advice or fulfilling senior management roles in foreign-owned firms. This is a widespread practice which aids the management of multinational firms and supplies useful skills to firms in developing countries.

Skilled flows from developing to developed countries

The emigration of skilled workers from developing countries is actively encouraged by developed countries and provides clear gains to them. Over 30 per cent of all doctors and nurses in the British health care system were born outside the UK. The same is true for more than 12 per cent of academic staff in British universities.

From the perspective of developing countries, this flow is better known as the 'brain drain'. The loss of skilled local workers deprives the country of various economic and non-economic spillovers. The brain drain reduces total output, diminishes the competence of domestic high-skill sectors, and erodes the tax base. To the extent that these skilled workers are complementary to other factors of production, such as unskilled labor, the emigration of these skilled workers leads to lower incomes for these other factors. Desai, Kapur, and McHale (2001) point out that the one million Indians living in the United States account for just 0.1 per cent of India's population but earn the equivalent of 10 per cent of India's national income.

On the other hand, the temporary emigration of skilled persons can benefit developing countries in several important ways. First, the possibility of temporary migration for skilled workers may increase the returns to education in the source country, inducing more investment in human capital. Commander, Kangasniemi, and Winters (2002) argue that this leads to an increase in skilled workers in the domestic economy (even taking account of those that migrate out) which partly offsets the direct effects of the brain drain.

Second, remittances from workers in developed countries back to their families are an additional benefit of migration (Massey, Araugo, Hugo *et al.* 1998). Remittances are an economically significant transfer for LDCs. In 2002, the Inter-American Development Bank reported that US$32 billion in remittances was sent to the countries of Latin America and the Caribbean. This was far greater than total development aid and only slightly less than foreign direct investment (Ellerman 2003). (Though impressive in size, it is worth being circumspect about the potential for remittances to generate sustained development. Martin and Straubhaar (2001) argue that income from remittances is potentially less valuable than income from newly established local enterprises or export earnings because the domestic spillovers may be smaller.)

Additionally there is evidence that national diasporas are an important source of growth. For example, the 50 million Chinese living abroad have been remarkably beneficial to the Chinese economy. They are a source of business experience, network connections, and capital.

Unskilled flows from developing to developed countries

The movement of unskilled workers to developed countries offers the greatest gain because it is associated with the largest difference between factor prices and the largest scope for movement, measured as number of willing people. It is also, however, the subject of the greatest concern in developed countries.

Developed countries experience benefits and costs from unskilled migration. Foreign workers are an important source of labor in developed countries. London's catering industry depends on migrants for 70 per cent of its labor force and a large proportion of seasonal agricultural workers are foreign (Home Office 2001).

Opposition to unskilled labor flows comes from the fear that foreigners displace local workers and contribute to unemployment.[7] A study by the British Home Office (2001) examines the widely held perception that immigration is detrimental to native workers. It concludes that unskilled workers often fill jobs in low-paid and insecure industries. In many cases these are jobs that native workers are unwilling to accept. In these jobs, foreign workers are filling labor market gaps rather than displacing native workers. Where migrants move in to industries with unfilled vacancies, their presence has little effect on either employment or wages of domestic workers.

Even in industries where migrants are competing with domestic workers, the effect is not much different than the impact of labor-intensive imports of foreign goods on domestic manufacturing.

---

[7] Such concerns are, of course, not consistent with the CGE models, which typically are based on full employment.

In an early study, Hamilton and Whalley (1984) suggest that if labor were free to move between countries sufficiently to equalize wages around the world, world output would rise by more than 150 per cent.[8]

Even using the more conservative assumption that part of the cross-country difference in wages reflects productivity differences which persist irrespective of location—e.g. health and education—the gains are large. Winters, Walmsley, Wang et al. (2002) assume that workers from poor countries are naturally only one third as productive as workers in developed countries. They estimate the gain from full labor mobility to be 70 per cent of world GDP.

Obviously full labor mobility is an extreme and impractical assumption. Winters (2000) estimates that even a relatively modest increase in labor mobility would increase world welfare by US$300 billion. This study assumes that 50 million additional workers from developing countries are permitted to work in developed countries. Winters assumes that when workers move from a low-to a high-wage country, they make up one quarter of the wage gap, i.e. three quarters of observed wage gaps are due to persistent differences in productivity.

These rough estimates have been subsequently corroborated by Winters, Walmsley, Wang et al. (2002) using a general equilibrium model. They find that if developed countries allowed temporary workers from developing countries to increase their workforces by 3 per cent (8 million skilled and 8.4 million unskilled workers), world welfare would increase by over US$150 billion. Winters et al. use the GTAP model and database developed by Hertel (1997). They assume that temporary workers make up half the productivity differences between their home country and their host country when they move.

The initial residents of developing countries (which are labor-exporting) gain most from the increase in migration. Their share of the total gain is approximately US$80 billion, more than developed countries and a significantly larger fraction of their income. The largest part of this increase accrues to temporary migrants themselves. In several developing countries Winters et al. find that the remaining residents of developing countries generally experience a loss in welfare. Despite increases in remittances and an improvement in their terms of trade (as the fall in GDP reduces the supply of their goods), the decrease in labor supply leads to a fall in the return to other factors which outweighs these gains.[9] However for many

---

[8] Assuming an elasticity of substitution between factors of 1.

[9] This result is obviously based on the assumption that the migrants are not unemployed unskilled workers, and that there is not an equilibrium level of unemployment.

Commonwealth countries including India and those in South Asia and South Africa, the welfare of permanent residents increases. For these under-developed countries, the increase in remittances outweighs the decline in labor and capital income. Remittance income increases the demand for domestic goods and allows the real wages of both skilled and unskilled workers to rise. The welfare of permanent residents in India and the rest of South Asia increases by US$16 billion and US$350 million respectively. In South Africa, the welfare of permanent residents increases by US$82 million, while the welfare of temporary migrants increases by US$4.4 billion.

The substantial benefits estimated to be available to developing countries from the liberalization of temporary migration for the unskilled—related to the huge differences in wages in developed and less developed countries—suggest that this is a promising area of reform. The global efficiency gains too are probably an order of magnitude greater than those associated with capital market liberalization, which has been the subject of so much atten-tion. Not surprisingly, unskilled workers in developed countries have been worried about the effect of the migration of unskilled labor on their wages, and have so far been effective in limiting the extent of migration. (On the other hand, business interests in developed countries have been successful in allowing migration of skilled workers; this may be partially because unskilled workers have thought that such workers are complements, and thus they too will benefit. But such skilled labor migration is of ambiguous benefit to the developing world.) Winters *et al.* suggest that one possible way forward is to include existing foreign worker schemes under the GATS by scheduling them and subsequently extending them. Many countries already have short-term foreign worker schemes for low-skilled jobs in agriculture, tourism, and construction.

A second approach is to focus on subcontracting schemes in future Mode 4 negotiations. Restricting the movement of people to existing employees of incorporated firms avoids many of the problems of mobility for individual workers (but also limits the scope of benefits). The pre-employment guarantee ensures that the workers will arrive with a job and increases the likelihood of their return after completion of the project. Where firms are responsible for their staff, they can provide housing, health insurance, etc. These services may reduce the costs of mobility for some workers.

However, there are also many disadvantages associated with subcon-tracting. First, many service transactions are not appropriate for subcon-tracting. Limiting mobility to transactions that are suitable for provision by subcontractors obviously diminishes the potential gains from liberalization of migration.

In spite of the huge barriers that developed countries have imposed on the movement of unskilled labor, the economic force leading to such migration is so great that large amounts still occur, in spite of the barriers, and the developing countries have received large benefits, e.g. as a result of remittances. The developing countries have an interest in facilitating the flow of these remittances and in improving the rights and living conditions of the migrants (many of whom are illegal). These issues would be high on an agenda for a Development Round of trade negotiations centered on the concerns of the developing countries.

A1.4 **Manufacturing**

The Doha Ministerial Conference agreed to launch tariff-cutting negotiations on all non-agricultural products. The aim is to 'reduce, or as appropriate eliminate, tariffs, including the reduction or elimination of tariff peaks, high tariffs, and tariff escalation, as well as non-tariff barriers, in particular on products of export interest to developing countries' (Doha Ministerial Declaration, para. 16).

Significant progress on tariff reduction has been made in several sectors. The empirical evidence below suggests that this reform has been accompanied by an increase in the share of manufactured goods in world trade and in the share of manufactured goods in developing country exports.

However, several studies suggest that the potential gains from the Doha Round might be larger than those realized as a consequence of Uruguay Round reform. This may be because the Uruguay Round was tilted against the interests of developing countries. The reduction in tariff peaks on goods of interest to developing countries and the reduction in protection on South–South trade are promising areas for reform.

Figure A1.5 shows that over the same period there has been a shift in the composition of global export towards manufactured products, while the share of agricultural products has fallen.

While the average rate of agricultural protection in OECD countries has risen in the last three decades, manufacturing protection levels have fallen. Average tariffs on industrial goods imported into the OECD countries fell from around 40 per cent in 1950 to 1.5 per cent in 1998 (Hertel 2000). Figure A1.6 shows that in the last forty years, the share of agriculture in total developing country exports has fallen from 45 per cent to less than 10 per cent, while the share of manufactures has risen from 23 per cent to 79 per cent.

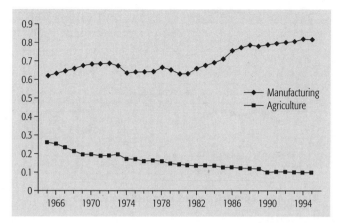

Figure A1.5. **Share of world exports, manufacturing and agriculture, 1965–1995**
Source: Hertel (2000).

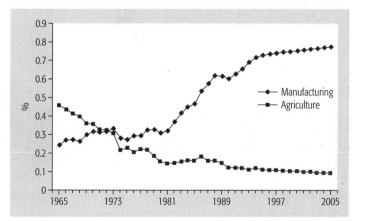

Figure A1.6. **Share of developing countries' exports, manufacturing and agriculture, 1965–2005**
Source: Hertel (2000).

South–North trade

Despite their export shift from agriculture to manufactures (Fig. A1.6) and their increasing share of the world trade in manufactures (Fig. A1.7), developing countries as a group are still net importers of manufactured goods and net exporters of agricultural goods.

Figure A1.8 shows that developing countries have succeeded in increasing the quantity of manufactured goods they provide to major developed

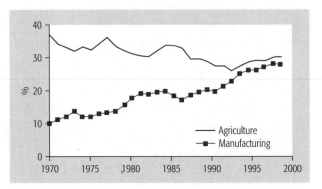

Figure A1.7. **Developing countries' share of world trade, 1970–2000**

Source: World Bank (2002).

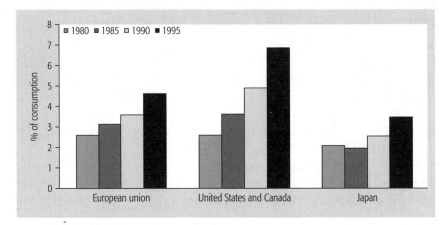

Figure A1.8. **Selected developed country imports from all developing countries, 1980–1995**

Source: UNCTAD (1996).

economies. However, even in the last period reported (1995) the shares were low, ranging from just over 3 per cent in Japan to under 7 per cent in North America.

Aggregate data hides the existence of tariff peaks, which may restrict access to developing countries' products. For example, in the processed food sector, Canadian, Japanese, and EU tariffs on fully processed food are 42, 65, and 24 per cent respectively. By contrast, the least processed products face tariffs of 3, 35, and 15 per cent in the same countries. Partly because of these trade restrictions, the penetration of developing country processed food has been limited (World Bank 2002).

Table A1.14. **Average manufacturing tariff rates**

Average tariff rates faced by high- and low-income countries of their own and each other's goods.

Exporting region	Importing region	
	High-income countries	Developing countries
High-income	0.8	10.9
Developing	3.4	12.8
World	1.5	11.5

Source: Hertel and Martin (2000).

South–South trade

Notwithstanding tariff peaks, developing countries' goods are subject to much higher barriers in other developing countries than in OECD countries. Table A1.14 shows that developing countries face average manufacturing tariffs of just 3.4 per cent in developed countries but 12.8 per cent in developing countries.

Figure A1.9 shows the average MFN tariff on manufacturing by importer in 1995 and 2005. The highest tariffs are in developing countries, particularly India, China, and Other South-East Asia.

Brown, Deardorff, and Stern (2002) use a CGE simulation model to test the effects of trade liberalization in manufactures. In their model domestic consumers respond to reductions in protection by purchasing more imported goods. Industrial sectors in each country expand or contract depending on whether their protection is reduced by more or less than in other countries. Countries with larger than average tariff reductions experience a real depreciation of their currency to maintain a constant trade balance.[10] Welfare in their model is determined by the effect of these changes on allocative efficiency and each country's terms of trade. The authors also incorporate non-tariff barriers. These generate rents to the preferred exporters, which are lost upon elimination. Thus the effect of liberalization may not be positive for all exporters.

Brown *et al.* initially apply their model to the Uruguay Agreement on manufactures. They estimate the welfare gains resulting from a scenario in which all countries reduce their tariffs as per the Agreement. Table A1.15

---

[10] This is the kind of effect which is often ignored in popular discussions of trade liberalization, but is absolutely essential when attempting to appraise the true (general equilibrium) effects.

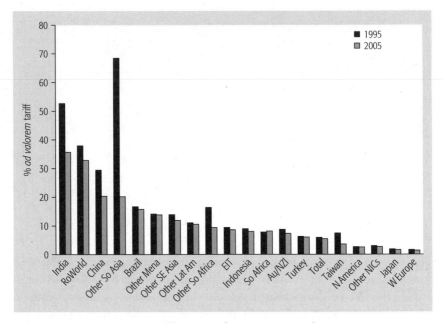

Figure A1.9. **Average MFN tariff on manufactures, 1995 and 2005**
Source: Hertel (2000).

shows that global welfare increases by US$56.5 billion and the gains are shared across all countries. The largest welfare increases in absolute terms accrue to the European Union (US$17.4 billion); however, large relative gains—expressed as a share of GDP—accrue to the Rest of South Asia, the Philippines, and Malaysia.

Brown *et al.* follow this simulation with an estimation of the welfare gains available in the Doha Round (Table A1.16). They present the results of a 33 per cent reduction in post-Uruguay Round tariffs. They estimate that the potential gains from the Doha Round (US$163.4 billion from a 33 per cent reduction) are significantly larger than those realized in the Uruguay Round (Table A1.15). In particular, most developing countries gain significantly more as a share of GDP than they did in the Uruguay Round. The authors suggest that this may be because the Uruguay Round was tilted against developing countries.

Hertel, Anderson, Francois *et al.* (2000) use the GTAP model of global trade to make similar estimates about the welfare gains from a 40 per cent liberalization of post-Uruguay tariffs on manufactures. They find that the global gain is in the region of US$70 billion, roughly the same size as the gains

Table A1.15. Estimated welfare gains from the Uruguay reductions in manufactures tariffs

	Change in imports ($m)	Exports ($m)	Terms of trade (%)	Welfare (%)	($m)	Real wage (%)	Return to capital (%)
Australia & New Zealand	2,848.0	2,527.6	0.347	0.327	1,674.8	0.345	0.300
Canada	1,071.9	1,354.5	−0.086	0.127	926.3	0.137	0.114
European Union and EFTA	16,826.6	15,358.5	0.145	0.159	17,405.6	0.157	0.163
Japan	8,680.6	8,331.3	0.062	0.102	6,608.4	0.092	0.115
United States	12,426.0	13,459.3	−0.133	0.123	11,187.1	0.124	0.122
India	2,585.3	3,628.9	−2.099	0.446	1,875.4	0.316	0.577
Sri Lanka	98.8	106.3	−0.193	0.558	93.0	0.507	0.608
Rest of South Asia	3,454.8	4,820.1	−7.541	2.025	2,366.5	2.224	1.828
China	3,112.6	1,917.7	0.456	0.305	2,762.2	0.347	0.271
Hong Kong	763.5	480.1	0.254	0.360	464.1	0.346	0.373
South Korea	2,858.6	2,733.2	0.068	0.422	2,403.3	0.409	0.435
Singapore	3,539.8	3,647.5	−0.078	2.111	1,570.3	1.943	2.258
Indonesia	936.5	894.5	0.068	0.247	626.0	0.291	0.215
Malaysia	2,790.9	3,411.4	−0.563	1.919	2,293.9	1.816	1.974
Philippines	2,452.6	3,102.1	−1.989	1.917	1,691.7	1.853	1.964
Thailand	1,264.7	1,002.3	0.291	0.366	753.9	0.597	0.283
Mexico	−64.9	1.4	−0.026	0.019	66.3	0.038	0.010
Turkey	319.3	253.9	0.143	0.123	259.1	0.122	0.124
Central Europe	1,871.7	1,846.1	0.020	0.294	1,091.2	0.311	0.270
Central & South America	3,778.8	2,999.5	0.423	0.022	377.1	0.043	0.004
Total	71,616.2	71,876.4			56,496.0		

Source: Brown, Deardorff, and Stern (2002).

they predict from agriculture. Table A1.17 shows that, with the exception of Sub-Saharan Africa, developing countries gain more from the reduction of manufacturing tariffs than they do from reduction of tariffs on agriculture.

A third study, Hertel (2000), using the same GTAP model, estimates that the benefits of full (100 per cent) reduction in post-Uruguay manufacturing tariffs is a global gain of US$130 billion. Again, the author predicts that a large share of this will accrue to developing countries. Figure A1.10 shows the developing country share of the gains from reform in three different sectors (and from combined reform). Manufacturing is the sector most benefited within developing countries (which gain over

Table A1.16. **Estimated welfare gains from manufacturing liberalization in Doha Round**
This table shows simulation results from a 33 per cent reduction in post Uruguay tariffs on manufactures.

	Change in imports (US$m)	Exports (US$m)	Terms of trade (%)	Welfare (%)	(US$m)	Real wage (%)	Return to capital (%)
Australia & New Zealand	3,720.7	3,457.2	0.267	0.545	2,790.6	0.508	0.515
Canada	1,996.0	2,097.3	−0.013	0.347	2,526.2	0.216	0.251
European Union and EFTA	23,184.8	22,840.3	0.050	0.358	39,273.0	0.190	0.199
Japan	19,071.4	15,817.0	0.548	0.696	45,190.9	0.234	0.304
United States	20,454.2	18,337.3	0.167	0.260	23,634.2	0.198	0.224
India	3,280.4	4,054.2	−1.384	0.733	3,084.4	0.439	0.592
Sri Lanka	536.8	592.1	−1.025	3.207	534.5	1.565	2.010
Rest of South Asia	1,892.0	2,018.4	−0.604	1.895	2,214.7	0.889	1.025
China	16,080.3	19,416.3	−1.221	1.199	10,859.3	1.470	1.323
Hong Kong	3,182.8	1,840.3	1.246	1.444	1,859.1	0.947	0.647
South Korea	8,023.4	8,440.7	−0.233	1.515	8,622.9	1.158	1.003
Singapore	4,382.9	4,161.8	0.131	2.276	1,692.5	2.481	2.611
Indonesia	2,362.7	2,336.0	0.053	0.835	2,113.3	0.645	0.447
Malaysia	4,242.8	4,805.2	−0.488	2.555	3,055.1	2.896	2.812
Philippines	3,984.0	4,535.1	−1.192	5.478	4,834.4	3.310	2.461
Thailand	3,406.1	3,970.1	−0.675	0.873	1,798.6	1.664	0.972
Mexico	916.3	1,132.6	−0.166	0.364	1,283.1	0.195	0.204
Turkey	1,421.0	1,558.6	−0.335	0.827	1,740.3	0.349	0.272
Central Europe	3,866.3	4,366.4	−0.428	0.734	2,724.2	0.816	0.722
Central & South America	5,038.9	6,103.2	−0.612	0.206	3,610.0	0.159	0.108
Total	131,043.7	131,880.0			163,441.4		

Source: Brown, Deardorff, and Stern (2002).

70 per cent of the welfare and efficiency dividend). This persistent result in the literature is derived from the fact that developing countries have the highest tariffs on manufacturing goods and thus receive the largest gains from removing the distortions. The studies do not separately analyse 'consumer benefits' (access to goods at lower prices) and 'producer benefits' (the creation of new jobs as a result of access to markets abroad). Another implication of the analysis is that the realization of these allocative efficiency gains will entail significant adjustment costs—a theme we revisit in Appendix 2.

Table A1.17. **Estimated welfare and efficiency gains from a 40% liberalization in agriculture and manufacturing, 2005**

Both columns report the benefits of reform in terms of equivalent variation.

Region	Total EV by experiment (US$m)	
	Agriculture	Manufacturing
NAmerica	3,401	3,310
WEurope	36,959	8,180
Aus/Nzl	1,786	207
Japan	12,552	6,607
China	172	22,593
Taiwan	265	3,288
Other NICs	2,672	5,270
Indonesia	6	792
Other SEAsia	1,931	2,631
India	1,058	3,084
Other SoAsia	1,176	1,645
Brazil	1,988	4,491
Other LatAm	3,055	1,449
Turkey	338	619
Other MENA	−1,506	1,074
EIT	301	1,391
SoAfrCU	129	283
Other SSA	436	249
RoWorld	2,601	2,399
World	69,320	69,564

Source: Hertel, Anderson, Francois *et al.* (2000: table 8).

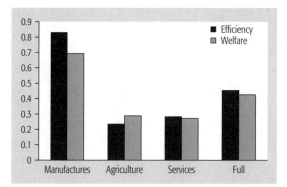

Figure A1.10. **Share of post-Uruguay global liberalization gains accruing to developing countries**

Source: Hertel (2000).

A1.5 **Conclusions**

The purpose of the empirical survey in this appendix is to suggest a prioritization of trade issues that will benefit developing countries. When negotiating parties lobby at the WTO, it is assumed that they do so in their own self-interest. In the case of developing countries and their advocates, it is not always clear what evidence they are using to determine how different reforms will affect them.

The CGE results presented in this appendix are certainly not perfectly reliable estimates of the welfare effects of various WTO proposals—indeed the estimates vary quite widely between different studies. However, they draw attention to the wide range of global effects of WTO proposals.

The results of our empirical survey suggest a different prioritization from the current hierarchy of market access issues receiving attention in the WTO. The evidence we have presented suggests that an alternative market access liberalization agenda might focus on labor market access for unskilled workers, unskilled labor services, market access for agricultural goods exported by developing countries, and tariff peaks for manufactured goods. The empirical work has paid less attention to the non-market access issues like competition policy but, as we noted in the text, here too the agenda that has been pursued, e.g. in the Singapore Issues, is markedly different from that which reflects the interests and concerns of the developing world.

APPENDIX 2

Empirical Review of the Singapore Issues

⚘

The inclusion of a domestic regulatory agenda in WTO negotiations represents a departure from the traditional 'market access' focus of the GATT rounds. The national regulations embodied in the 'Singapore Issues' have become more prominent as the liberalization of traditional trade protection instruments has highlighted the trade impact of remaining differences in national regulatory regimes.

Efforts to harmonize national regulation have commenced in competition law, FDI policy, transparency in government procurement, and trade facilitation. It has been argued that these issues are not priorities for low-income countries and should not form part of a so-called 'Development Round'. In particular, there is significant opposition from developing countries. In the space of a month from early June 2003, 77 developing countries, including over half the WTO membership, made public statements urging that new negotiations should not be launched as part of the Doha Round (CAFOD 2003).

Several developing countries see the Singapore Issues as incursions into their national sovereignty that are not justified by the benefits they bring. Multilateral regulatory disciplines threaten the specter of preventing individual governments from pursuing development policies based on their own national priorities and problems.

In addition there are concerns that the initiatives based on the Singapore Issues may impose a large burden on the administrative capacity of developing countries. There are significant costs associated with both the creation and enforcement of new regimes in competition policy, investment regulations, and trade and customs procedures. Moreover, the required institutional capacity and human expertise may not be available in developing countries. In OECD countries these critical inputs developed gradually over a long period of time. These considerations suggest that the payoff of requiring WTO members to implement rapidly the Singapore proposals may not be large relative to the costs. Furthermore, it suggests that any reform will require significant technical assistance from developed countries.

Finally, there is broad concern that the Doha agenda may be overloaded. The Doha Round has an ambitious work program involving multilateral negotiations on many issues. The inclusion of complex and controversial issues may slow progress on more fruitful initiatives.

As the debate on the Singapore Issues evolved, two other issues became more apparent. The first is that many of the Singapore Issues involve a detailed knowledge of complex public policy issues that goes well beyond the competence of trade ministers to negotiate. The outcomes, accordingly, might not be good even for the developed countries. There was a resonance with what had happened in the intellectual property negotiations (TRIPS) in the Uruguay Round, where both the Council of Economic Advisers and the US Office of Science and Technology Policy raised serious concerns, to which the US Trade Representatives paid little attention in the negotiations. The issues that were being debated under 'Competition' did not attempt to unify treatment of predatory pricing between domestic and foreign firms, a natural part of any attempt at developing a uniform competition code. The United States put highly controversial issues involving capital market liberalization on the agenda of the discussion of investment, which the IMF had revisited almost contemporaneously, raising questions about the potential economic benefits and costs.

This brings us to the second concern: some of the proposals would have actually been adverse to the development of the developing countries. They went against the entire spirit of the Development Round. Such was the case, for instance, with proposals for full capital market liberalization.

In the context of these concerns, we consider four criteria for prioritizing an issue in the current round of negotiations:

- Is the WTO justified by returns to international collective action that are higher than returns to unilateral action, i.e. are there spillovers or externalities which justify multilateralism?
- Are the benefits of the initiative large relative to other proposals? Are the benefits shared between developing and developed countries?
- Are the costs of implementation small relative to the benefits of the initiative?
- To what extent do multilateral commitments impede national development strategies?

Using these criteria, this appendix analyses the merits of including the Singapore Issues in the Doha Development Round. The merits are certainly not uniform across the four issues or even across the different initiatives within each issue.

Significantly more work needs to be done to quantify the potential benefits and costs flowing from the Singapore Issues. Indeed, the paucity of authoritative studies in this area is in itself a reason to advocate caution. Therefore the conclusions of this appendix are preliminary.

Nonetheless, the empirical survey below suggests that the current focus of the WTO's regulatory harmonization agenda is misdirected in some areas.

In the competition and investment arenas, the WTO should move away from imposing uniformity on manifestly different countries and focus its attention on areas where externalities generate returns to multilateralism. In investment policy, reducing the 'race to the bottom' incentive war would be a useful initiative. Similarly, competition policy initiatives should include anti-trust action against cartels which raise prices for developing countries, and a mechanism for analysing the global effects of merger decisions in developed countries. In government procurement and trade facilitation, progress should be made through national efforts aided by technical assistance, rather than through imposing additional obligations in the WTO.

A2.1 **Investment**

At the Singapore WTO Ministerial Meeting in 1996, members agreed to form a working group to study the relationship between trade and investment. Since then, some developed countries have attempted to move towards a negotiated investment agreement within the WTO.

The proponents of such an agreement seek internationally binding rules that would minimize the conditions and regulations on foreign investors entering or operating in host countries and would grant them national treatment. This would involve the removal of performance requirements and the adoption of a range of investor rights.

However, most developing countries are reluctant to agree to this because several believe that an investment regime is inappropriate within a trade organization. Others have concerns about the loss of autonomy over investment policy and the consequent limitations on industrial policy options.

Also, there are broadly expressed concerns that an investment agreement would divert time and human resources from other vital work in the WTO.

The fundamental premise of the argument in favor of a multilateral investment agreement is that it will increase investment flows to developing countries. An agreement which improves investor protections may stimulate domestic investment and alleviate the concerns of foreign investors.

However, there are several reasons to be cautious about the responsiveness of investment to new multilateral protections. First, the current absence of multilateral investment disciplines and the failure of previous attempts to establish them (such as the OECD's ill-fated Multilateral Agreement on Investment, MAI) has not deterred foreign investment. Foreign direct investment has grown rapidly over the last decade, outpacing both trade and output growth.

Additionally, the absence of a multilateral agreement has not prevented substantial unilateral liberalization of investment regimes. UNCTAD reports that between 1991 and 2001, a total of 1,393 changes were made to national investment regulations. More than 90 per cent of these were liberalizing changes. Figure A2.1 shows that in 2001, over 200 regulatory changes were made in 71 countries, only 6 per cent of which were restrictive changes. In this environment there does not seem to be a compelling rationale to force national governments to adopt a uniform multilateral agreement. Idiosyncratic national regimes are sensitive to national development priorities and can be tailored to existing institutional arrangements to minimize implementation costs.

A third reason for caution comes from the historical experience of investment treaties in generating increased investment flows (see Fig. A2.2).

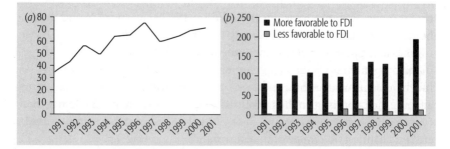

Figure A2.1. **Liberalization of investment regimes, 1991–2001**
(*a*) **Number of countries changing their investment regulations**
(*b*) **Number of liberalizing and restrictive changes to investment regulations**
Source: UNCTAD (2001).

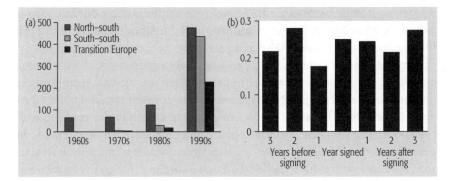

Figure A2.2. **Bilateral investment treaties, 1960s–1990s**
(*a*) **Growth of BITs in developing countries (number of treaties in decade)**
(*b*) **The effect of BITs on FDI (share of annual FDI flow)**
Source: World Bank (2003).

Bilateral investment treaties (BITs) surged in the 1990s to more than 2,000 in 2001. There has been significant activity between developing countries, which accounted for 42 per cent of new BITs in 2001 (UNCTAD 2002). As noted earlier, BITs proscribe a range of investment protections that often go further than many of the realistic proposals before the WTO. Yet there is not much evidence that the signing of bilateral investment treaties increases the flow of investment. An UNCTAD (1998) study found no relationship between the level of FDI and the number of BITs signed by host countries. A more comprehensive study by Hallward-Driemeier (2002) looked at the bilateral flows of OECD countries to 31 developing countries over twenty years. After accounting for trends, they found little evidence that BITs increased investment to developing countries. More research needs to be done on the effects of investment treaties on investment volume, but the existing evidence suggests that the benefits of additional treaties may be small.

Fourthly, the most serious concern, nationalization of foreign investments, has already been addressed at both the national and international level, though national and multilateral agencies providing guarantees against such confiscations of property (MIGA, the Multilateral Investment Guarantee Association, is part of the World Bank Group). Going beyond this entails difficult judgments about what are 'legitimate' and illegitimate restrictions. Most fundamentally, each country has an incentive to develop an investment regime balancing provisions which might serve to attract more foreign investment with those protecting against potential adverse effects on the citizenry. International agreements might help developing countries provide assurances that they will abide by their commitments (which is what MIGA has responsibility for), but they should not dictate how each country should make that balance.

A further difficulty is that in providing further protection, even bilateral agreements negotiated by trade ministers often go too far, intruding on national sovereignty in unacceptable ways. The problem is that it often takes years before the full import is discovered, by which time the possibility of revising the treaty has become difficult and tendentious. The infamous Chapter 11 of NAFTA provides a compelling case in point, where foreign investors were given more rights than domestics (e.g. for compensation for changes in costs or profitability as a result of even fully justified regulations, in what are called regulatory takings). This is arguably having an adverse effect in the development of important regulations in areas like the environment and consumer protection. (The Clinton Administration was opposing attempts to provide such compensation in domestic legislation even as its trade negotiators were putting such a provision into NAFTA, without seeking prior approval of the Cabinet or the National Economic Council. Once such provisions are put into an agreement, it is hard to take them out.) Even judicial protections, such as punitive damages, have come under question.

The attempt to impose restrictions on capital market liberalization illustrates the dangers of these non-trade-related investment agreements. (Trade-related capital flows are already covered within current IMF agreements.) There is compelling evidence that full liberalization has little effect on economic growth, but exposes countries to increased instability—a fact recognized even by the IMF in its recent Board paper.

For these reasons, the current direction of WTO negotiations on investment disciplines seems to offer few advantages to developing countries. An international agreement on investment rules of the type currently being proposed is ultimately designed to maximize foreign investors' rights while minimizing the authority of governments in developing countries. Instead the WTO should focus on improving the investment environment in ways which strengthen the bargaining position of governments *vis-à-vis* foreign investors rather than weakening it.

One area in which there is clear cause for multilateral action is the reduction of 'beggar-my-neighbor' investment incentive competition for foreign investment. Since the mid-1980s the efforts of national and subnational levels of government to attract direct investment to their jurisdictions have increased considerably (Charlton 2003).

Political pressure on governments to be seen as 'job winners' push policymakers to play a race-to-the-bottom game. Oxfam (2000) estimates that developing countries lose US$35 billion per year due to a competitive pressure to reduce corporate tax rates combined with the transfer of profits out of developing countries to low-tax environments.

The potential negative consequences of investment competition are particularly acute in developing nations. The risk of 'overbidding' is exacerbated by institutional weaknesses, poor cost–benefit analysis and, in some cases, corruption. Moreover, the potential consequences of excessively generous incentives might be increased in those developing nations where fiscal positions are already weak.

Agreements to limit the size of incentives seems to be the most obvious approach to pursue within a multilateral framework. The European Union provides a good example of the kind of approach to policy coordination that might benefit developing countries. The EU has been operating state aid guidelines now for several decades. Although grants to foreign direct investment are not explicitly targeted by Commission policy, in practice they are one of the main forms of state aid regulated by it. The EU takes the general view that state aid is incompatible with the common market. The definition of state aid clearly encompasses traditional instruments of investment attraction. Indeed the European Commission classifies state aid as including (1) grants to firms; (2) loans and guarantees; (3) tax exemptions; and (4) infrastructure projects benefiting identifiable end-users. The European Commission claims some success in reducing subsidies in the EU. There is evidence that the Commission has used its guidelines to effectively restrict incentives in some areas. For example, before the introduction of guidelines for the support of small and medium-sized enterprises, it was not rare to find state-aid grants of as much as 20 per cent of an investment project. Under the new framework, the fixed maxima are 7.5 per cent for medium-sized enterprises and 15 per cent for small enterprises.[1]

A2.2 **Competition policy**

Strong competition policy backed by clearly enforced laws is beneficial to developing countries and should be encouraged in international forums. There is a clear concern that the benefits of a liberal trade regime would

---

[1] An example from the Czech Republic provides an illustration of how the Commission uses its power in practice. The Czech Republic planned to offer subsidies to the Volkswagen unit Skoda for an engine plant at Mlada Boleslav. After a year of negotiations with the EU, the government agreed to slash tax breaks and grants that it was offering to Skoda from US$120m to US$22m.

be undermined by domestic or international monopolies and cartels. Liberalization might largely simply transfer rents that had been accruing to the government to private sector monopolies, and not lead to lower consumer prices. However, competition policy disciplines as envisaged by the proponents of a WTO agreement may impinge on the ability of each country to choose a competition policy model which is suitable for its own development priorities, and the proposals under discussion do not address the most important concerns of developing countries. What is required is a paradigm for viewing competition from a development perspective. It is important to ensure that developing country producers receive treatment equal to that of domestic producers (which they currently do not), and to ensure that developing country consumers can be protected from non-competitive actions by global anti-trust action, including anti-trust actions centered in the developed countries. National competition law and policy should complement other national development objectives (such as industrial development). Moreover, such law and policy should not hinder government efforts to minimize adjustment costs resulting from structural change generated by WTO-driven liberalization in other areas. Some sensitive industrial sectors may require protection from advanced foreign firms for the time it takes to create local capacity. In addition, it needs to be recognized that the legal frameworks which have been developed in the advanced industrial countries to promote competition are costly to administer. Early on, there was an awareness of the risk of politicization of competition policy, providing one of the rationales for private enforcement actions. There is some reason to believe that those fears have been justified, and when competition policy is incorporated within a trade regime, there is often more a concern for the promotion of the interests of the country's corporations than on the well-being of consumers. Thus, a failure of a country's firms to do well in a market will be blamed on anti-competitive actions, but the attempt by a foreign government to protect its citizens from the anti-competitive practices of one's own company will be viewed with suspicion. Because of their costs, however, private enforcement actions are often not feasible for those harmed in developing countries.

For these reasons, some of the conventional models of competition enforcement which operate in developed countries may not be appropriate for a developing country. In the discussion below, we identify some policies that might redress the imbalance.

The theoretical benefits of the maintenance of competition are clear. Indeed, the benefits that are associated with free markets are only enjoyed if those markets are competitive. As we suggested before, trade liberalization and privatization will only deliver on their promised benefits in a competitive environment. But imperfections in competition are pervasive, especially in developing countries, where markets are often small. There is an abiding concern that a large multinational can use its economic power to become dominant in certain markets in developing countries—these companies often have global sales that exceed the GDP of the economy.

While the case for strong competition policy is clear, there is regrettably only a small amount of evidence on the welfare effects of competition policy itself. Kee and Hoekman (2002) investigate the impact of competition law on estimated industry mark-ups over cost. They use time series panel data from 28 industries in 42 countries. They conclude that anti-trust legislation has no individual impact on the size of mark-ups. By contrast they conclude that imports and lower entry barriers (which anti-trust policies can lead to) are associated with a larger payoff, a result supported by several studies (Djankov, La Porta, Lopez-de-Silanes et al. 2002; Hoekman, Kee, and Olarreaga 2001; Vandenbussche 2000).

By contrast, Clarke and Evenett (2003) show that in Latin America, Asia, and Western Europe, jurisdictions that did not enforce their cartel laws suffered greater overcharges than those nations that actively enforced them.

New competition enforcement regimes are associated with significant implementation costs. Competition law is technical and requires institutional skills and resources that are in short supply in many developing countries. In addition, competition law enforcement is expensive. OECD and national sources indicate that the annual budget of the anti-trust office in OECD countries is in the range of US$15–50 million plus. For developing countries with enforcement agencies the budgets are lower but still significant (Hoekman and Mavroidis 2002).[2]

Discussions under 'competition' center around two issues: preventing monopolization and anti-competitive practices, and preventing governments from acting in ways which give an 'unfair' competitive advantage to their firms, either by imposing requirements on foreign firms or by subsidizing their own firms.

Under the first rubric, preventing monopolization and anti-competitive practices, there are two important reforms. The first is the adoption of a single standard for predatory anti-competitive behavior between domestic and foreign firms. There is a large literature on the cost of dumping laws, and on their inequities (including those associated with the manner in which they are implemented).[3]

---

[2] For example, 20 noted earlier, the costs of anti-trust offices are large in Mexico (US$14m), Poland (US$4.1m), Argentina (US$1.4m), and Hungary (US$2m).

[3] See for example Martinez-Giralt and Barros (1997).

Another priority should be to protect purchasers in developing countries from paying excessively high prices as a result of monopolies and especially international cartels. National competition policy may ignore collusion by domestic firms to raise prices in export markets since there is no harm to those within the country. Moreover, developing countries without the resources to enforce competition policy effectively on international firms may suffer from international cartels. There is a small amount of (mainly informal) evidence on the effects of international cartels on developing countries (see Figure A2.3). Levenstein, Oswald, and Suslow (2002) analyse sixteen goods whose supply was found to be internationally cartelized by American or European firms. They found that in 1997 developing countries purchased US$36.4 billion of goods from a set of ten industries that had seen a price-fixing conspiracy in the 1990s. This amounts to 2.9 per cent of developing countries' total imports which may have been subject to collusive price-fixing by firms from developed countries. It has been estimated that cartels in developed countries cost consumers in developing countries up to US$7 billion in the 1990s. Some of the worst-offending cartels have been found in the international maritime transport industry. Such cartels are often approved by national competition authorities but have been found to lead to higher prices for consumers. Fink, Mattoo and Rathindran (2001) estimate that collusive practices in the maritime transport industry have cost consumers in the US alone up to US$2.1 billion. If developing countries were to save the same proportion of their shipping costs the savings would be US$2.3 billion.

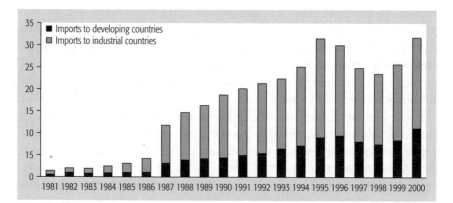

Figure A2.3. **Volume of imports affected by cartels, 1981–2000**
Total imports in sixteen products where cartels have been proved to exist
Source: GEP (2003).

In the mid-1990s, as Russia moved from communism to a market economy, one of the few goods that it could easily sell internationally was aluminum, but its attempts to enter Western markets were hampered as American aluminum companies put pressure on the United States to create an international aluminum cartel that would strictly limit the extent to which Russia could enter Western markets and which would thereby maintain international prices at high levels. This is a case in which both Russia and consumers around the world were injured. But those affected had no recourse to anti-trust laws, especially since governments were involved in the very creation of the cartel.

Almost undoubtedly, the most important international cartel is OPEC, which attempts to control the price of oil. Though several OPEC members are developing countries, most of those in the developing world live in countries which are net importers of oil and therefore are worse off as a result of the oil cartel.

This suggests there might be potential gains from multilateral action to ban export cartels, including those in which governments are a party.

A key issue is how developing countries can respond to anti-competitive actions, including export cartels. No small developing country could force the break-up of a cartel; each would find it expensive to bring a court case, and even if one of them could bring such a case in its own jurisdiction, enforcement of a judgment would be difficult. One option would be to allow governments of detrimentally affected countries to use the court system of OECD countries to prosecute offending firms. Further, adversely affected parties (including governments acting on behalf of citizens) should be allowed to be a plaintiff in civil actions in the courts of the advanced industrial countries, and there should be a provision for class-action suits, with flexible standards for class certification, which would in particular encourage purchasers of products in foreign countries to be able to join in with each other and with other purchasers in the advanced industrial countries. Given the limited resources of developing countries and the high costs of suits, assistance from OECD countries would be desirable. Hoekman and Mavroidis (2002) suggest the creation of a 'special prosecutor' within the WTO with authority to bring cases in the relevant jurisdiction on behalf of developing country consumers.

Merger policy is another area in which national competition policies may have international spillover effects. The concern is that nationalistic approval criteria may allow mergers between domestic firms even when the global welfare effect is negative, so long as the welfare benefits within the country are positive. If these firms have a larger combined market share in some smaller foreign markets than they do in the domestic market, a merger may be domestically acceptable but globally undesirable.

Both from the perspective of developed and less developed countries, there is concern about attempts to harmonize national competition policies, for, in doing so, there is a real risk that the 'least common denominator' will be accepted, that is, one which will provide the least protection for consumers. Even a movement towards a common framework which might be close to a 'least common denominator,' would risk overlooking the differing circumstances of the developing countries *and* encouraging governments to move towards this low standard. This is especially the case because corporate interests tend to be far better represented in trade negotiations than consumer interests.

It would be better to use the discussion of competition issues within the WTO to encourage countries to develop high competition standards and to recognize some of the ways that countries may legitimately do so. For instance, the United States has, on several occasions, recognized that concerns about competition 'trump' intellectual property; standard intellectual property protections, which give temporary monopoly power, have been circumscribed when they lead to excessive monopolization of particular markets. This is a principle which should be more widely recognized: it should be made explicit that such actions are not a violation of the TRIPS Agreement. As a second example, *per se* rules may be easier and less costly to enforce than 'rule of reason' judgments, which require the careful balancing of costs and benefits of certain potentially anti-competitive practices. Strong *per se* rules (such as limiting the share of the country's market that any firm may have) should be allowed, even if they have the effect of limiting entry by international firms (for whom, say, entry into a market would only be worthwhile if they had a dominant position).

On the second rubric, actions taken to give a competitive advantage to a country's own firms (or impose a competitive disadvantage on foreign firms), development concerns should be given priority, and actions which arguably have a development objective should be allowed, at least on a medium-term basis, even if they put foreign firms at a disadvantage. Inevitably, firms from developing and developed countries are in different circumstances—each has some advantages over the others. Firms from advanced industrial countries often have access to lower-cost capital and to government-financed research, especially by-products of the huge expenditures on defense. Local firms may have more local knowledge, and that may give them a competitive advantage. Inevitably, there will be some vagueness in what is meant by 'levelling the playing field'. But approaching the issue from the development perspective provides some guidance into what kinds of policies should be allowed by developing countries. Developing countries should be allowed to provide capital to domestic firms at 'reasonable terms', which may be significantly below the very high interest rates that are imposed on them as a condition of IMF loans, or which they feel they have to maintain in order to prevent a currency crisis. Imposing 'community reinvestment act' requirements on banks to lend a certain fraction of their money to particular groups, e.g. underserved minorities, or small or medium-sized domestic enterprises, is a legitimate restriction. Giving preferences to small and medium-sized enterprises for government contracts (see below) should also be legitimate, *even if in doing so, multinational firms are in effect discriminated against*. At the same time, the standards for judging whether the provision of infrastructure which, in the first instance, may be directed at a particular enterprise is a subsidy or not should be looked at from different perspectives for a developing country than for a developed country. While advanced industrial countries have long been critical of local content requirements, such requirements may in fact facilitate developmental objectives.

A2.3 **Government procurement**

Government purchases of goods and services are a significant proportion of world GDP. Recent analysis by the OECD indicates that total central government expenditure of OECD countries was almost US$2 trillion in 1998.[4] In developing countries this figure was US$300 billion—equal to six times the total annual multilateral and bilateral aid currently given to developing countries (Evenett 2003).

In an attempt to harness this part of the international economy, several WTO members signed the 'plurilateral' (only binding to those members that choose to sign) Agreement on Government Procurement (GPA) at the Uruguay Round in 1994. One of the GPA's primary long-term objectives is to ensure that government decisions to purchase goods and services do not depend on the location of production or the affiliation of the supplier.

Many developed countries, principally the US and the EU, would like to see the GPA develop into a multilateral agreement which in the first stage draws all members into an agreement on transparency, and in the second

---

[4] This figure excludes military expenditure and the payment of state employees.

stage extends the scope to due process and national treatment for foreign firms.

Estimates of the value of a broad multilateral procurement agreement (encompassing both transparency and non-discrimination) depend on the size of the government procurement market, the size of preference margins extended to domestic suppliers, and the general equilibrium gains and losses derived from the elimination of these preferences.

As described above, government procurement accounts for an average of about 10–15 per cent of GDP for developed countries and as much as 20 per cent of GDP for developing countries. National domestic preference margins are estimated by analysing either national policies or the price wedges that explain government purchasing choices. Francois, Palmeter, and Nelson (1997) estimate the margin of preference for OECD countries to be in the 13–50 per cent range.

However, the proportion of government purchases whose prices are inflated by preferential treatment may not be large. In a procurement auction, preferences only raise prices when domestic bidders are not the lowest but are within the preference margin, or when the domestic bidders are the lowest but there is only one of them (in which case the domestic bidder raises its sell price to the lowest foreign price plus the preference margin). However, in other circumstances a preferential procurement policy may actually reduce procurement costs. McAfee and McMillan (1989) show that preferential polices can cause foreign suppliers to reduce their sell price so as to bid under the domestic firms receiving preferences.

Government procurement policies have important economic and social roles in developing countries which would be curtailed if governments were mandated to observe national treatment principles. The level of expenditure and the attempt to direct the expenditure to locally produced materials is a major macroeconomic instrument, especially during recessionary periods, to counter economic downturn (Kohr 2003). If the foreign share increased, there would be a leakage in government attempts to boost the economy through increased spending during a downturn.

Additionally, procurement policies might be used to boost domestic industries or encourage development in specific sectors of national interest. Social objectives could also be advanced by preferences for specific groups or communities, especially those that are under-represented in economic standing.

Finally, while developed countries (and especially, particular firms within developed countries) have much to gain from increased access to government procurement in developing countries, it is not likely that the gains are fully reciprocal. Even the EU has had difficulty making inroads into US government defense procurement. Furthermore, the consequences of procurement liberalization will inevitably depend on liberalization of services and labor flows. If the US government decides to subcontract army meal services, will it allow a foreign firm to provide the service? Almost surely, security concerns will demand that the firm be American. But since defense is a larger portion of expenditures for America, it means that a larger portion of government procurement will be exempt. Some communities in the United States have moved towards contracting out a range of public services, including schools and prisons. It is unlikely that foreign firms have equal access.

In the context of the important government objectives achieved by procurement policy and the lack of any externalities to justify international action, it seems important that developing countries retain their autonomy over this area of policy.[5]

A2.4 **Trade facilitation**

Trade facilitation initiatives hold out the promise of increasing trade and efficiency by reducing onerous trade-related costs.[6] Such costs include: regulatory compliance costs; charges for trade-related services; procedural delays; lack of predictability; and lost business opportunities (Lucenti 2003).

The benefits of improving trade facilitation include: increasing trade in goods and services; promoting competition, which can spur productivity gains as well as lower prices; enhancing efficiency in both the state sector and the private sector; improving the business environment and so encouraging foreign direct investment; and increasing participation of small and medium-sized enterprises in international trade.

---

[5] Moreover, it will be difficult to implement any procurement policy in a way which would be widely acceptable. For example, since a large proportion of American expenditures are for defense, it will almost surely claim a defense exception. Much of government procurement is for services, but the provision of such services requires the temporary movement of natural persons. Contract specification can often be used to give local firms a preference; ascertaining whether the contract specification is 'reasonable' will be extremely tendentious.

[6] The Doha Declaration (para. 27) states that until the Fifth Ministerial Conference, the WTO Council for Trade in Goods shall review and as appropriate clarify and improve relevant aspects of Arts. V, VIII, and X of GATT 1994 and identify the trade facilitation needs and priorities of members, particularly developing and least developed countries. (Article V is on freedom of transit, Art. VIII concerns fees and formalities connected with import and export, and Art. X is on publication and administration of trade regulations.)

The empirical evidence below suggests that many of these benefits may be economically significant but are associated with large implementation costs. Rather than imposing new obligations within the WTO, progress on trade facilitation should be achieved through national efforts aided by technical assistance.

Few studies have explicitly examined the potential gains from trade facilitation. There are dramatic anecdotal stories: e.g. Costa Rica's commitment to trade facilitation was arguably critical in attracting the large Intel plant. Modern manufacturing has increasingly relied on just-in-time inventory methods, and these cannot operate if there are costly delays at borders.

Moreover, the studies presented below differ in terms of the scope of trade facilitation considered and the breadth of countries and commodities analysed. This makes their results difficult to compare meaningfully. However, the results below do highlight the magnitude of potential gains from trade facilitation.

Ernst and Whinney (1987) surveyed EC business costs for the European Commission. The customs compliance costs associated with intra-EC trade were estimated to be 1.5 per cent of the total value of trade between member countries.

The US National Committee on International Documentation (US NCITD) analysed the benefits of trade facilitation in a 1971 study, subsequently updated in the 1990s by Raven (1996). These studies found that the costs of documentation and compliance with export and import regulations (at both ends of the transaction) represented more than 7.5 per cent of the total value of US shipments.

A study by the Swedish Trade Procedures Council (SWEPRO) in 1995 used data from companies and government sources to estimate the cost of compliance with Swedish trade procedures. It concluded that these costs could be as much as 4 per cent of the value of imports and exports.

More recently, a study by Wilson, Mann, and Otsuki (2003) used a computable general equilibrium framework to estimate gains from trade facilitation. They estimated the effect of bringing the below-average Asia Pacific Economic Cooperation (APEC) members halfway to the APEC average in four key areas of trade facilitation (administrative transparency, e-commerce, logistics, and standards harmonization). They estimate this type of facilitation would increase APEC trade by US$280 billion.

Wilson *et al.* compare the relative benefits from trade facilitation with those from traditional market access initiatives. They estimate that a reduction of all tariffs to zero from an APEC average of 6.5 per cent would create a gain of US$27.8 billion. By comparison they find that the improvement in trade facilitation necessary to achieve the same gains is small. Relatively minor improvements in port efficiency, customs procedures, and e-business usage deliver similar-sized gains.

This brief survey suggests that there is a wide span of estimates regarding the costs of trade procedures, ranging from 1.5 to 7.5 per cent of the value of trade flows.

The implementation costs associated with realizing gains from trade facilitation are also significant. Administrative changes are associated with obvious costs to both governments (the creation of new systems and enforcement of new regulations) and business (compliance). For developing countries, a large part of the costs to government should be borne by technical assistance from developing countries.

The costs of trade facilitation depend on the type of reform proposed. For example, as noted earlier, the World Bank assisted Tunisia in its program of streamlining and modernizing its customs procedures. The total value of World Bank loans to Tunisia for this purpose was US$35 million in 1999. Similarly, the World Bank lent US$38 million to Poland for upgrading the physical and managerial infrastructure of its port facilities (Wilson 2001 and WTO 2000). In some cases, streamlining procedures will both facilitate trade *and* save the government money.

Developing countries should therefore put forward the view that improvements in trade facilitation should be made through national efforts aided by technical assistance, rather than through imposing additional obligations in the WTO. If the consideration of the problems in these areas results in some agreements, these should, at best, be adopted only as guiding principles or as flexible best-endeavour provisions, not enforceable through the dispute settlement process (Das 2002).

Discussion here, as elsewhere, has focused more on the concerns of developed countries in gaining access to developing countries than on what should be the concern of the Development Round, i.e. developing countries gaining access to developed countries' markets. Of intense concern in the last few years have been America's visa restrictions. Such restrictions may or may not be justified by legitimate concerns for security. However, it is certainly true that the existence of these security concerns illustrates that the developed countries often put non-trade concerns over trade concerns but often criticize developing countries when they attempt to do the same. Yet the inability to send businessmen to America to market their goods and the long delays and high costs (especially in time) in obtaining a visa are clearly important impediments to trade. This is an issue that would be high on a development-oriented agenda for trade facilitation. The fact that it has not been on the agenda at all is just another illustration of the gap between what has been sold as a Development Round agenda and an agenda that would truly promote the interests of the developing world.

References

ABARE (2001), 'Export Subsidies in the Current WTO Agriculture Negotiations', *ABARE Current Issues* 1:6, 1–8.

Anand, Sudhir, and Vijay Joshi (1979), 'Domestic Distortions, Income Distribution and the Theory of Optimum Subsidy', *The Economic Journal* 89, 336–52.

Anderson, K. (2003), *How Can Agricultural Trade Reform Reduce Poverty?*, Centre for International Economic Studies, University of Adelaide, Discussion Paper 0323 (Adelaide: Centre for International Economic Studies).

——B. Dimaranan, J. Francois, T. Hertel, B. Hoekman, and W. Martin (2001), 'The Cost of Rich (and Poor) Country Protection to Developing Countries', *Journal of African Economies* 10, 227–57.

——and S. Yao (2003), 'How Can South Asia and Sub-Saharan Africa Gain from the Next WTO Round?', *Journal of Economic Integration* 18, 466–81.

APEC Secretariat (1997), 'The Impact of Trade Liberalization in APEC', paper presented at Asia Pacific Economic Cooperation (APEC) Conference, 1988.

Auboin, M., and M. Meier-Ewert (2003), *Improving the Availability of Trade Finance during Financial Crises*, WTO Discussion Papers 2 (Geneva, World Trade Organization).

Baldwin, Robert E. (1969), 'The Case against Infant-Industry Tariff Protection', *Journal of Political Economy*, 77, 295–305.

——John Mutti, and J. David Richardson (1980), 'Welfare Effects on the United States of a Significant Multilateral Tariff Reduction', *Journal of International Economics* 10, 405–23.

Beghin, J. C., D. Roland-Holst, and D. van der Mensbrugghe (2003), *How will Agricultural Trade Reforms in High-Income Countries Affect the Trading Relationships of Developing Countries?* (Paris: OECD).

Ben-David, Dan (1993), 'Equalizing Exchange: Trade Liberalization and Income Convergence', *Quarterly Journal of Economics* 108, 653–79.

Berg, A., and A. O. Krueger (2002), 'Trade, Growth and Poverty', paper presented at the Annual World Bank Conference on Development Economics, Washington, DC.

Bergsten, C. F. (1998), 'Fifty Years of the GATT/WTO: Lessons from the Past for Strategies for the Future', paper presented to the WTO/Graduate Institute of International Studies symposium "Fifty Years: Looking Back, Looking Forward", Geneva.

Besley, T., B. Burgess, and I. Rasul (2000), 'How Much should Governments Spend on Social Safety Nets?', in *Social Protection Anchor* (Washington, DC: World Bank).

Bhagwati, Jagdish (2002*a*), *Free Trade Today* (Princeton: Princeton University Press).

——(2002*b*), 'Intellectual Property Protection and Medicines', *The Financial Times*, Sep. 2002.

Bjornskov, C., and K. M. Lind (2002), 'Where do Developing Countries Go after Doha? An Analysis of WTO Positions and Potential Alliances', *Journal of World Trade* 36, 543–62.

Blackhurst, R., Lyakurwa, B., and Oyejide, A. (2000), 'Options for Improving Africa's Participation in the WTO', *World Economy* 23, 491–510.

Bonaglia, Federico, and Fukasaku, Kichiro (2002), *Trading Competitively: A Study of Trade Capacity Building in Sub-Saharan Africa* (Paris: OECD Development Centre).

Borrell, B. (1999), 'Bananas: Straightening Out Bent Ideas on Trade as Aid', paper presented at the World Bank/WTO Conference on Agriculture and the New Trade Agenda from a Development Perspective, Geneva.

Bouguignon, F., and C. Morrisson (2002), 'Inequality among World Citizens: 1820–1992', *American Economic Review*, 92, 727–44.

Brenton, P. (2003), 'Integrating the Least Developed Countries into the World Trading System: The Current Impact of EU Preferences under Everything But Arms', mimeo, World Bank.

Brown, D. K., A. V. Deardorff, A. K. Fox, and R. M. Stern (1995), 'Computational Analysis of Goods and Services Liberalization in the Uruguay Round', in W. Martin and L. A. Winters (eds), *The Uruguay Round and the Developing Economies*, World Bank Discussion Paper 307 (Washington, DC: World Bank), 365–80.

——————and R. Stern (2002), *Computational Analysis of Multilateral Trade Liberalization in the Uruguay Round and Doha Development Round*, University of Michigan Research Seminar in International Economics, Discussion Paper 489 (Ann Arbor: University of Michigan Research Seminar in International Economics).

Busch, Marc L., and Eric Reinhardt (2003), 'Developing Countries and General Agreement on Tariffs and Trade World Trade Organization Dispute Settlement', *Journal of World Trade* 37, 719–35.

CAFOD Policy Paper, Catholic Agency for Overseas Development.

Carlin, Wendy, and Colin Mayer (2003), 'Finance, Investment and growth', *Journal of Financial Economics* 69, 191–226.

CEC (2002), 'Everything but Arms Proposal: Possible Impacts on the Agricultural Sector', mimeo, European Commission.

Chang, Ha-Joon (2002), *Kicking Away the Ladder: Development Strategy in Historical Perspective* (London: Anthem Press).

Charlton, Andrew (2003), *Incentive Bidding Wars for Mobile Investment: Economic Consequences and Potential Responses*, OECD Development Center Technical Paper 203 (Paris: OECD).

——(2005), 'A Proposal for Special Treatment in Market Access for Developing Countries in the Doha Round', in John M. Curtis and Dan Ciuriak (eds), *Trade Policy Research 2005* (Ottawa: Department of International Trade), forthcoming.

—— and Joseph E. Stiglitz (2004), 'A Development-Friendly Prioritization of the Doha Round Agenda' *The World Economy* 28, 293–312.

Charnovitz, S. (2004), 'The WTO's Problematic "Last Resort" against Noncompliance', mimeo, World Trade Law.

Clarke, J. L., and S. J. Evenett (2003), 'A Multilateral Framework for Competition Policy?', in State Secretariat of Economic Affairs and S. J. Evenett (eds), *The Singapore Issues and the World Trading System: The Road to Cancún and Beyond* (Bern: World Trade Institute).

Commander, Simon, Mari Kangasniemi, and L. Alan Winters (2004), 'The Brain Drain: Curse or Boon?', in R. Baldwin and L. A. Winters (eds), *Challenges to Globalisation* (Chicago: University of Chicago Press).

Corden, W. M. (1957), 'Tariffs, Subsidies and the Terms of Trade', *Economica* 24, 235–42.

——(1974), *Trade Policy and Economic Welfare* (Oxford: Clarendon Press).

Das, Bhagirath Lal (2002), 'The New WTO Work Programme', paper presented at a Third World Network forum, Geneva.

Dasgupta, P., A. Sen, and D. Starret (1973), 'Notes on the Measurement of Inequality', *Journal of Economic Theory* 6, 180–7.

Dasgupta, P., and J. Stiglitz 1972, 'On Optimal Taxation and Public Production,' *Review of Economic Studies*, 39(1), pp. 87–103.

—————— (1974), 'Benefit–Cost Analysis and Trade Policies', *Journal of Political Economy* 82, 1–33.

Dasgupta, P., and J. Stiglitz (1977), 'Tariffs vs. Quotas as Revenue-Raising Devices under Uncertainty', *American Economic Review* 67, 975–81.

————(1985), *Learning-by-doing, Market Structure and Industrial and Trade Policies*, CEPR Discussion Papers 80 (London: Centre for Economic Policy Research).

Deardorff, Alan V. (1994), 'Economic Effects of Quota and Tariff Reductions', in *The New GATT: Implications for the United States* (Washington, DC: Brookings Institution), 7–27.

Dee, P., and K. Hanslow (2000), *Multilateral Liberalization of Services Trade*, Productivity Commission Staff Research Paper (Canberra: Ausinfo).

Desai, Mihir, Devesh Kapur, and John McHale (2001), 'The Fiscal Impact of the Brain Drain: The Fiscal Impact of Emigration from India', paper presented at the NBER-NCAER Conference, Neemrana, India.

Diao, Xinshen, Eugenio Diaz-Bonilla, and Sherman Robinson (2003), *How Much does it Hurt? The Impact of Agricultural Trade Policies on Developing Countries* (Washington, DC: International Food Policy Research Institute).

Diaz-Bonilla, E., M. Thomas, and S. Robinson (2003), 'Trade, Food Security and WTO Negotiations: Some Reflections on Boxes and their Content', in OECD, *Agricultural Trade and Poverty: Making Policy Analysis Count* (Paris: OECD), 59–104.

Dimaranan, B., T. Hertel, and R. Keeney (2003), 'OECD Domestic Support and the Developing Countries', paper for the UNU/WIDER project on the impact of WTO on low-income countries, GTAP Center, Purdue University.

Dixit, A. K., and V. Norman (1980), *The theory of international trade* (Cambridge: Cambridge University Press).

Djankov, Simeon, Rafael La Porta, Florencio Lopez-de-Silanes, and Andrei Shleifer (2002), 'The Regulation of Entry', *Quarterly Journal of Economics* 117, 1–37.

Dollar, David (1992), 'Outward-Oriented Developing Economies Really Do Grow More Rapidly: Evidence from 95 LDCs, 1976–85', *Economic Development and Cultural Change* 40, 523–44.

Easterly, William, Roumeen Islam, and J. E. Stiglitz (2001), 'Shaken and Stirred: Explaining Growth Volatility', in *Annual Bank Conference on Development Economics 2000* (Washington, DC: World Bank), 191–212.

Ebrill, L., J. Stotsky, and R. Gropp (1999), *Revenue Implications of Trade Liberalization*, IMF Occasional Paper 180 (Washington, DC: IMF).

Ellerman, David (2003), *Policy Research on Migration and Development*, World Bank Policy Research Working Papers 3117 (Washington, DC: World Bank).

Emran, M. S., and J. Stiglitz (2004a), 'On Selective Indirect Tax Reform in Developing Countries', *Journal of Public Economics* 89, 599–623.

——— (2004b), *Price-Neutral Tax Reform with an Informal Economy*, Public Economics Working Paper 0407010, (St. Louis: WUSTL Working Paper Archive).

Epstein, S. (1995), *GATT: The Uruguay Round Agreement and Developing Countries* (Washington, DC: Foreign Affairs and National Defense Division).

Ernst & Whinney (1987), 'The Cost of Non-Europe: Border-Related Controls and Administrative Formalities', in *Research on the Cost of Non-Europe: Basic Findings*, vol. 1 (Brussels: Commission of the European Communities), 7–40.

ESCWA (2004), 'Exploring Potential of South–South Agreements including Global System of Trade Preferences (GSTP)', ESCWA report to the UNCTAD forum on 'Multilateralism and Regionalism: The New Interface', São Paulo.

Estevadeordal, A. (2000), 'Negotiating market access: The Use of the North America Free Trade Area Agreement', *Journal of World Trade* 34, 141–66.

FAO (2003), *FAO Papers on Selected Issues Relating to the WTO Negotiations on Agriculture* (Rome: FAO).

Findlay, C., and G. McGuire (2001), 'Restrictions on Trade in Services for APEC Member Economies', mimeo, APEC.

—— and T. Warren, (eds) (2000), *Impediments to Trade in Services: Measurement and Policy Implications* (London and New York: Routledge).

Finger, J. M. (2000), 'The WTO's Special Burden on Less Developed Countries', *Cato Journal* 19:3, 425–37.

—— and P. Schuler (2000), 'Implementation of Uruguay Round Commitments: The Development Challenge', *The World Economy* 23, 511–25.

—— and A. Zlate (2003), 'WTO Rules that Allow New Trade Restrictions: The Public Interest is a Bastard Child', paper prepared for the UN Millennium Project Task Force on Trade.

Fink, C., A. Matoo, and R. Rathindran, (2001), *Liberalizing Basic Telecommunications: The Asian Experience*, World Bank Policy Research Working Paper 2718 (Washington, DC: World Bank).

Fischer, Stanley (2000), lunch address given at the conference on 'Promoting Dialogue: Global Challenges and Global Institutions', American University, Washington, DC.

Francois, J. F. (1999), 'A Gravity Approach to Measuring Services Protection', mimeo, Erasmus University.

Francois, J. F. (2001), *The Next WTO Round: North–South Stakes in New Market Access Negotiations* (Adelaide: Centre for International Economic Studies; Rotterdam: Tinbergen Institute).

—— and W. Martin (2003), 'Formula Approaches for Market Access Negotiations', *The World Economy* 26, 1–28.

—— Bradley McDonald, and Hakan Nordstrom (1995), 'Assessing the Uruguay Round', paper presented at the World Bank Conference 'The Uruguay Round and the Developing Economies', Washington, DC.

—— D. Nelson, and N. D. Palmeter (1997), 'Public Procurement: A Post-Uruguay Round Perspective', in B. Hoekman and P. C. Mavroidis (eds), *Law and Policy in Public Purchasing* (Ann Arbor: University of Michigan Press), 105–24.

—— and A. Strutt (1999), 'Post-Uruguay Round Tariff Vectors for GTAP Version 4', mimeo, Tinbergen Institute, Erasmus University.

—— and I. Wooten (2000), 'Trade in International Transport Services: The Role of Competition', *Review of International Economics* 9, 49–61.

—— H. van Meijl, and F. van Tongeren (2003), *Trade Liberalization and Developing Countries under the Doha Round*, CEPR discussion Paper 4032 (London: Centre for Economic Policy Research).

———— (2004), 'Trade Liberalization in the Doha Round', mimeo, Erasmus University.

Freeman, R., R. Oostendorp, and M. Rama (2001), 'Globalization and Wages', paper in progress, World Bank.

Gallup, John, Jeffrey Sachs, and Andrew Mellinger (1998), 'Geography and Economic Development', paper presented at the World Bank's Annual Bank Conference on Development Economics, Washington, DC.

GATT Secretariat (1993), *An Analysis of the Proposed Uruguay Round Agreement, with Particular Emphasis on Aspects of Interest to Developing Countries*, MTN.TNC/W/W122 (Geneva: World Bank).

Greenwald, B., and J. E. Stiglitz (1993), 'Financial Market Imperfections and Business Cycles', *Quarterly Journal of Economics* 108, 77–114.

Grynberg, R., and R. M. Joy (2000), 'The Accession of Vanuatu to the WTO: Lessons for the Multilateral Trading System', *Journal of World Trade*, 34:6, 159–73.

Hallward-Driemeier, M. (2002), 'Bilatéral Investment Treaties: Do They Increase FDI Flows?', background paper for *Global Economic Prospects 2003: Investing to Unlock Global Opportunities* (Washington, DC: World Bank).

Hamilton, C., and J. Whalley (1984), 'Efficiency and Distributional Implications of Global Restrictions on Labour Mobility: Calculations and Policy Implications', *Journal of Development Economics* 14, 61–75.

Handbury, J. (2005), 'Do Rules of Origin Work? An Empirical Assessment of the Effectiveness of Rules of Origin in NAFTA', mimeo, Columbia University, New York.

Harris, J. R., and M. P. Todaro (1970), 'Migration, Unemployment and Development: A Two-Sector Analysis', *American Economic Review* 60, 126–42.

Harrison, Glenn W., Thomas F. Rutherford, and David G. Tarr (1995), 'Quantifying the Uruguay Round', paper presented at the World Bank Conference 'The Uruguay Round and the Developing Economies', Washington, DC.

Harrison, W. J., and K. R. Pearson (1996), 'Computing Solutions for Large General Equilibrium Models Using GEMPACK', *Computational Economics* 9, 83–172.

Hausmann, Ricardo, and Dani Rodrik (2002), 'Economic Development as Self-Discovery', NBER Working Papers 8952 (Washington, DC: National Bureau of Economic Research).

Hensen, H. T., S. Robinson, and F. Tarp (2002), *General Equilibrium Measures of Agricultural Policy Bias in Fifteen Developing Countries*, TMD Discussion Paper 105 (Washington, DC: International Food Policy Research Institute).

Hertel, T. (1997), *Global Trade Analysis: Modelling and Applications* (Cambridge: Cambridge University Press).

——(1999), 'Potential Gains from Reducing Trade Barriers in Manufacturing, Services and Agriculture', paper presented at the 24th Annual Economic Policy Conference, Federal Reserve Bank of St. Louis.

—— and W. Martin (2000), 'Liberalizing Agriculture and Manufactures in a Millennium Round: Implications for Developing Countries', *World Economy* 23, 455–69.

—— K. Anderson, J. Francois, and W. Martin (2000), *Agriculture and Non-Agricultural Liberalization in the Millennium Round*, Centre for International Economic Studies, University of Adelaide Discussion Paper 0016 (Adelaide: Centre for International Economic Studies).

——M. Ivanic, P. Preckel, and J. Cranfield (2003a), *The Earnings Effects of Multilateral Trade Liberalization: Implications for Poverty in Developing Countries*, GTAP Working Paper 16, version 2 (West Lafayette, Ind.: GTAP).

—————— (2003b), 'Trade Liberalization and the Structure of Poverty in Developing Countries', paper prepared for the Conference on Globalization, Agricultural Development and Rural Livelihoods, Cornell University, Ithaca, NY.

Hoekman, Bernard (1996), 'Assessing the General Agreement on Trade in Services', in W. Martin and L. A. Winters (eds), *The Uruguay Round and the Developing Countries* (Cambridge and New York: Cambridge University Press), 137–68.

Hoekman, Bernard (2003), *More Favorable Treatment of Developing Countries: Toward a New Grand Bargain* (Washington DC: World Bank).

—— (2004*a*), 'Making the WTO More Supportive of Development', mimeo, World Bank.

—— (2004*b*), *Operationalizing the Concept of Policy Space in the WTO*, World Bank Policy Brief 4 (Washington, DC: World Bank).

—— H. Kee, and M. Olarreaga (2001), *Markups, Entry Regulation and Trade*, World Bank Policy Research Paper 2662 (Washington, DC: World Bank).

—— and Michael M. Kostecki (1997), *The Political Economy of the World Trading System: From GATT to WTO* (Oxford: Oxford University Press).

—— and Petros C. Mavroidis (1994), 'Competition, Competition Policy and the GATT', *World Economy* 17, 121–50.

———— (2002), *Economic Development, Competition Policy and the WTO*, World Bank Policy Research Working Paper 2917 (Washington, DC: World Bank).

—— C. Michalopoulos, and L. A. Winters (2003), 'Special and Differential Treatment for Developing Countries: Towards a New Approach in the WTO', mimeo, World Bank.

—— F. Ng, and M. Olarreaga (2002), 'Reducing Agricultural Tariffs versus Domestic Support: What's More Important for Developing Countries?', mimeo, World Bank.

Home Office (2001), *Migration: An Economic and Social Analysis*, Research, Development and Statistics Directorate Occasional Paper 67 (London: Stationary Office).

Horn, H., and P. Mavroidis (2003), '*Which WTO Provisions Are Invoked By and Against Developing Countries*, CEPR Discussion Paper (London: Centre for Economic Policy Research).

Hudec, R. E. (1987), *Developing Countries in the GATT Legal System*, Thames Essays (London: Trade Policy Research Centre).

Ianchovichina, E., A. Mattoo, and M. Olarreaga (2001), *Unrestricted Market Access for Sub-Saharan Africa: How Much is it Worth and Who Pays?*, CEPR Discussion Paper 2820 (London: Centre for Economic Policy Research).

ILO (2002), *Global Employment Trends* (Geneva: International Labour Office).

IMF (1997), *World Economic Outlook* (Washington, DC: IMF).

—— (2002), *Direction of Trade Statistics Quarterly*, March (Washington, DC: IMF).

Isaac, G. E., and W. A. Kerr (2003), 'Genetically Modified Organisms and Trade Rules: Identifying Important Challenges for the WTO', *The World Economy* 26, 29–43.

Johnson, H. (1967), *Economic Policies toward Less Developed Countries* (Washington, DC: Brookings Institution).

Kaul, Inge, Pedro Conceicao, Katell Le Goulven, and Ronald U. Mendoza (eds) (2003), *Providing Global Public Goods* (Oxford: Oxford University Press).

Keck, A., and P. Low (2004), *Special and Differential Treatment in the WTO: Why, When and How?*, Staff Working Paper ERSD-2004-03 (Geneva: Economic Research and Statistics Division, World Trade Organization).

Kee, Hiau Looi, and Bernard Hoekman (2002), 'Competition Law and Market Discipline: A Cross-Country, Cross-Industry Analysis', mimeo, World Bank.

Keen, M., and J. E. Lightart (1999), *Coordinating Tariff Reduction and Domestic Tax Reform*, IMF Working Paper, WP/99/93 (Washington, DC: IMF/World Bank).

Kennett, Maxine, Simon J. Evenett, and Jonathan Gage (2005), 'Evaluating WTO Accessions: Legal Economic Perspectives', draft ms.

Ketkar, Suhas, and Dilip Ratha (2000), 'Development Financing during a Crisis: Securitization of Future Receivables', mimeo, Economic Policy and Prospects Group, World Bank.

Kletzer, Lori G. (2001), *Job Loss from Imports: Measuring the Costs* (Washington, DC: Institute for International Economics).

Krueger, Anne (1997), 'Trade Policy and Economic Development: How We Learn', *American Economic Review*, 87, 1–22.

Kuznets, S. (1955), 'Economic Growth and Income Inequality', *American Economic Review* 45, 1–28.

Lacarte-Muro, Julio, and Petina Gappah (2000), 'Developing Countries and the WTO Legal and Dispute Settlement System: A View from the Bench', *Journal of International Economic Law* 3, 395–401.

Laird, S. (2002), 'Market Access and the WTO: An Overview', in Bernard Hoekman, Aadyita Mattoo and Philip English (eds), *Development, Trade, and the WTO: A Handbook* (Washington, DC: World Bank), 97–104.

—— R. Safadi, and A. Turrini (2002), 'The WTO and Development', paper prepared for the Conference on Policy Reform, Tulane University.

Lall, S. (1992), 'Technological Capabilities and Industrialization', *World Development* 20, 165–86.

Lederman, D., A. Menendez, G. Perry, and J. E. Stiglitz (2000), 'Mexico—Five Years After the Crisis', in *Annual Bank Conference on Development Economics 2000* (Washington, DC: World Bank), 263–82.

Levenstein, Margaret C., and Valerie Y. Suslow (2001), 'Private International Cartels and their Effect on Developing Countries', mimeo, University of Massachusetts.

——— and Lynda J. Oswald (2002), 'International Price-Fixing Cartels and Developing Countries: A Discussion of Effects and Policy Remedies', mimeo, University of Michigan Business School.

Levine, R. (1997), 'Financial Development and Economic Growth: Views and Agenda', *Journal of Economic Literature* 35, 688–726.

Levinsohn, J., S. Berry, and J. Friedman (2003), 'Impacts of the Indonesian Economic Crisis: Price Changes and the Poor', in Michael Dooley and Jeffrey Frankel (eds), *Managing Currency Crises in Emerging Markets* (Chicago: University of Chicago Press).

Lewis, W. A. (1955), *The Theory of Economic Growth* (London, George Allen & Unwin; Homewood, Ill.: Irwin).

Love, James (2001), 'Compulsory Licensing: Models for State Practice in Developing Countries, Access to Medicine and Compliance with the WTO TRIPS Accord', paper prepared for the United Nations Development Programme.

Lucenti, Krista (2003), 'Is There a Case for More Multilateral Rules on Trade Facilitation?', in State Secretariat of Economic Affairs and S. J. Evenett (eds), *The Singapore Issues and The World Trading System: The Road to Cancún and Beyond* (Bern: World Trade Institute), 254–90.

Malcolm, G. (1998), *Adjusting Tax Rates in the GTAP Data Base*, GTAP Technical Paper 12 (Lafayette, Ind.: Center for Global Trade Analysis, Purdue University).

Markusen, J., T. F. Rutherford, and D. Tarr (1999), 'Foreign Direct Investment in Services and the Domestic Market for expertise', paper presented at the Second Annual Conference on Global Economic Analysis, Copenhagen.

Martin, Philip, and Thomas Straubhaar (2001), 'Best Practices to Foster Economic Growth', mimeo, Cooperative Efforts to Manage Emigration (CEME), University of California at Davis.

Martin, W. (2001), 'Trade Policies, Developing Countries, and Globalization', in *Globalization: Policy Research Report* (Washington, DC: World Bank).

—— and D. Mitra (2001), 'Productivity Growth in Agriculture and Manufacturing', *Economic Development and Cultural Change* 49, 403–23.

—— and L. A. Winters (eds) (1996), *The Uruguay Round and the Developing Countries* (Cambridge and New York: Cambridge University Press).

Martinez-Giralt, Xavier, and Pedro Barros (1997), *On the Effects of Anti-Dumping Legislation*, CEPR Discussion Paper 1590 (London: Centre for Economic Policy Research).

Maskus, K. (2003), 'Observations on the Development Potential of Geographical Indications', background paper prepared for the second meeting of the Task Force on Trade and Finance of the UN Millennium Development Goals Project, New Haven, conn.

Massey, Douglas S., Joaquin Arango, Graeme Hugo, Ali Kouaouci, Adela Pellegrino, and J. Edward Taylor (1998), *Worlds in Motion: Understanding International Migration at the End of the Millennium* (Oxford: Clarendon Press).

Mattoo, A. (2001), 'MFN and the GATS', in *Trade Policy for Developing Countries in a Global Economy: A Handbook* Washington, DC: Development Research Group and World Bank Institute, World Bank).

—— R. Rathindran, and A. Subramanian (2001), *Measuring Services Trade Liberalization and its Impacts on Economic Growth: An Illustration*, World Bank Policy Research Working Paper 2655 (Washington, DC: World Bank).

McAfee, R. P., and J. McMillan (1989), *Incentives in Government Contracting* (Toronto: University of Toronto Press).

McDougall, R. (1993), *Incorporating International Capital Mobility into SALTER*, SALTER Working Paper 21 (Canberra: Industry Commission).

Melo, Jaime de, and David Tarr (1990), 'Welfare Costs of US Quotas in Textiles, Steel and Autos', *Review of Economics and Statistics* 72, 489–97.

Michalopoulos, C. (2000), 'The Role of Special and Differential Treatment for Developing Countries in GATT and the World Trade Organisation', mimeo, World Bank.

Minot, Nicholas, and Francesco Goletti (2000), *Rice Market Liberalization and Poverty in Viet Nam* IFPRI Research Report 114 (Washington, DC: International Food Policy Research Institute).

Newbery, David M. G., and Stiglitz, Joseph E. (1984), 'Pareto-Inferior Trade', *Review of Economic Studies* 51, 1–12.

Nguyen, T., C. Perroni, and R. Wigle (1993), 'An Evaluation of the Draft Final Act of the Uruguay Round', *Economic Journal* 103, 1540–9.

Noland, M., and H. Pack (2003), *Industrial Policy in an Era of Globalization: Lessons from Asia* (Washington, DC: Institute for International Economics).

OECD (1993), *Assessing the Effects of the Uruguay Round*, Trade Policy Issues 2 (Paris: OECD).

—— (1998), *Harmful Tax Competition: An Emerging Global Issue*, DAFFE Report (Paris: OECD).

—— (2002a), *Trading Competitively: A Study of Trade Capacity Building in Sub-Saharan Africa* (Paris: OECD Development Centre).

—— (2002b), *Agricultural Policies in OECD Countries: Monitoring and Evaluation* (Paris: OECD).

—— (2003), *Agricultural Trade and Poverty: Making Policy Analysis Count* (Paris: OECD).

—— (2004), *Analysis of CAP Reform*, AGR/CA/APM(2003)16/FINAL (Paris: OECD).

Oman, Charles (2000), *Policy Competition for Foreign Direct Investment: A Study of Competition among Governments to Attract FDI* (Paris: Development Centre Studies, OECD).

Oxfam (2000a), *Submission to the Parliamentary Inquiry into Australia's Relationship with the World Trade Organisation* (Canberra: Oxfam Australia).

—— (2000b), *Tax Havens: Releasing the Hidden Billions for Poverty Eradication* (Oxford: Oxfam).

—— (2003a), *Cambodia's Accession to the WTO: How the Law of the Jungle is Applied to One of the World's Poorest Countries*, Oxfam International Briefing Paper (Oxford: Oxfam).

—— (2003b), *The EU after Cancún: A Way forward*, Oxfam Great Britain (Oxford: Oxfam).

—— (2004), 'Extortion at the Gate: Will Viet Nam Join the WTO on Pro-Development Terms?', Oxfam International Briefing Paper (Oxford: Oxfam).

Page, S., and P. Kleen (2004), 'Special and Differential Treatment of Developing Countries in the World Trade Organization', Overseas Development Institute paper prepared for the Swedish Ministry of Foreign Affairs.

Pauwelyn, Joost (2000), 'Enforcement and Countermeasures in the WTO: Rules are Rules—Toward a More Collective Approach', *American Journal of International Law* 94, 335–47.

Prasad, Eswar, Kenneth Rogoff, Shang-Jin Wei, and M. Ayhan Kose (2003), 'Effects of Financial Globalization on Developing Countries: Some Empirical Evidence', mimeo, IMF.

Prowse, S. (2002), 'The Role of International and National Agencies in Trade-Related Capacity Building', *The World Economy*, 25, 1235–61.

Rae, Allan N., and Anna Strutt (2003), 'Doha Proposals for Domestic Support: Assessing the Priorities', paper presented at the International Conference on Agricultural policy reform and the WTO, Capri, Italy.

Raghavan, C. (1999), 'New Round with an Open-Ended Agenda Advocated', *INFO-SERVICE*, Third World Network, Mar. 1999; available online at <www.twnside.org. sg>.

Rama, M. (2003), *Globalization and Workers in Developing Countries*, World Bank Policy Research Working Paper 2958 (Washington, DC: World Bank).

Ranis, G. (1984), 'Typology in Development Theory: Retrospect and Prospects', in M. Syrquin, L. Taylor and L. E. Westphal (eds), *Economic Structure and Performance* (Orlando, Fla.; Academic Press), 29–37.

Raven, John (1996), *International Trade Procedures: Characteristics and Costing* (London: UK Simpler Trade Procedures Board).

Rodriguez, Francisco, and Dani Rodrik (1999), *Trade Policy and Economic Growth: A Skeptic's Guide to Cross-National Evidence*, National Bureau of Economic Research Working Paper WP/99/7081 (Cambridge Mass.: National Bureau of Economic Research).

Rodrik, Dani (1994), 'Developing Countries often the Uruguay Round', paper prepared for the Group d 24, mimeo.

——(1996), 'Coordination Failures and Government Policy: A Model with Applications to East Asia and Eastern Europe', *Journal of International Economics* 40, 1–22.

——(2001), 'The Global Governance of Trade as if Development Really Mattered', specially invited paper read to the UNDP, New York.

——(2004), 'Industrial Policy for the 21st Century', mimeo, Harvard University.

Rosenstein-Rodan, P. (1961), 'Notes on the theory of the "Big push" ' in H. S. Ellis and H. C. Wallich (eds), *Economic Development for Latin America* (New York: St. Martin's Press), 202–11.

Rothschild, M., and J. E. Stiglitz (1973), 'Some Further Results on the Measurement of Inequality', *Journal of Economic Theory* 6, 188–204.

Sachs, Jeffrey D., and Andrew Warner (1995), 'Economic Reform and the Process of Global Integration', *Brookings Papers on Economic Activity* 1, 1–118.

Safadi, R., and S. Laird (1996), 'The Uruguay Round Agreements: Impact on Developing Countries', *World Development* 24, 1223–42.

Samuelson, Paul A. (1962), 'The Gains from International Trade Once Again', *Economic Journal* 72, 820–9.

Sen, A. (1999), *Development as Freedom* (Oxford: Oxford University Press).

Shapiro, Carl, and J. E. Stiglitz (1984), 'Equilibrium Unemployment as a Worker Discipline Device', *American Economic Review* 74, 433–44.

Sharer, Robert, Nur Calika, Thomas Dorsey, Paul Ross, Clinton Shielis, and Piritta Sorsa (1998), *Trade Liberalization in IMF-Supported Programs*, IMF World Economic and Financial Surveys (Washington, DC: IMF).

Sharma, R., P. Konandreas, and J. Greenfield, (1996), 'An Overview of Assessments of the Impact of the Uruguay Round on Agricultural Prices and Incomes', *Food Policy* 21, 345–50.

South Centre (1996), *Liberalization and Globalization: Drawing Conclusions for Development* (Geneva: South Centre).

Srinivasan, T. N. (1998), *Developing Countries and the Multilateral Trading System*, Boulder, Colo. and London: Westview Press).

—— and Jagdish Bhagwati, (1999), 'Outward Orientation and Development: Are the Revisionists Right?', Yale University Economic Growth Center Discussion Paper No. 806.

Stephens, Malcolm (1998), *Export Credit Agencies, Trade Finance, and South East Asia*, IMF Working Paper WP/98/175 (Washington, DC: IMF).

Stevens, C. (2002), *The Future of Special and Differential Treatment (SDT) for Developing Countries in the WTO*, Institute of Development Studies (IDS) Working Paper 163 (Brighton: IDS).

Stiglitz, J. E. (1987), 'On the Microeconomics of Technical Progress,' in Jorge M. Katz (ed.), *Technology Generation in Latin American Manufacturing Industries* (Basingstoke: Macmillan), 56–77.

—— (1994), 'Rethinking the Economic Role of the State: Publicly Provided Private Goods/Replanteamiento del papel económico del estado: bienes privados suministrados públicamente', Celección els Llibres Dels Fulls *Econòmics* 10, 19–47.

—— (1995), 'The Theory of International Public Goods and the Architecture of International Organizations', Background Paper 7, Third Meeting, High Level Group on Development Strategy and Management of the Market Economy, UNU/WIDER, Helsinki.

—— (1996), 'Some Lessons from the East Asian Miracle', *World Bank Research Observer* 11:2 (Aug.), 151–77.

—— (1997), 'Dumping on Free Trade: The U.S. Import Trade Laws', *Southern Economic Journal* 64, 402–24, repr. in Sir Hans Singer, Neelambar Hatti and Rameshwar Tandon (eds), *Trips, the Uruguay Round and Third World Interests* (New Delhi: BR Publishing, 1999), 711–48.

—— (1999a), 'Knowledge as a Global Public Good', in Inge Kaul, Isabelle Grunberg, and Marc A. Stern (eds.), *Global Public Goods: International*

Cooperation in the 21st Century (New York: Oxford University Press), 308–25.

——(1999b), 'Trade and the Developing World: A New Agenda', *Current History* 98, 387–93.

——(1999c), 'The WTO Millennium Round', *Social Development Review* 3:4, (Dec.), 6–9.

——(2000), 'Capital Market Liberalization, Economic Growth, and Instability', *World Development* 28, 1075–86.

——(2001), 'From Miracle to Crisis to Recovery: Lessons from Four Decades of East Asian Experience', in Joseph Stiglitz and Shahid Yusof, *Rethinking the East Asian Miracle* (Washington, DC: World Bank), 509–25.

——(2002), 'Capital Market Liberalization and Exchange Rate Regimes: Risk without Reward', *Annals of the American Academy of Political and Social Science* 579, 219–48.

——(2003), 'Development-Oriented Tax Policy', paper presented to the 59th Congress of the IIPF, Prague.

Stolper, Wolfgang, and Paul A. Samuelson (1941), 'Protection and Real Wages', *Review of Economic Studies* 9, 58–73.

Sutherland, P. (2005), *The Future of the WTO: Addressing Institutional Challenges in the New Millennium*, Report by the WTO Consultative Board to the Director-General (Geneva: WTO).

SWEPRO (1985), *Data Interchange in International Trade: Uniform Rules for Paperless Open Interchange of Trade Information between Different Computer Systems* (Göteborg: SWEPRO).

Tamms, V. (2000), 'Frontier Cost Estimates of the Impact of Restrictions on Trade in Air Transport Services', in C. Findlay and T. Warren (eds), *Impediments to Trade in Services: Measurement and Policy Implications* (London and New York: Routledge).

TWN (2003), 'US-EC Agriculture Paper Criticised by Developing Countries', Third World Network Info Service on WTO Issues, available online at <www.twnside.org.sg>.

Tyers, R., and K. Anderson (1992), *Disarray in World Food Markets: A Quantitative Assessment* (Cambridge and New York: Cambridge University Press).

UNCTAD (1996a), *Compendium of the Work and Analysis Conducted by UNCTAD Working Groups and Sessional Committees on GSP Rules of Origin*, Part I, UNCTAD/ITD/GSP/31 (New York: United Nations).

——(1996b), 'Strengthening the Participation of Developing Countries in World Trade and the Multilateral Trading System', paper presented at the ESCAP/UNCTAD/UNDP Meeting of Senior Officials, Jakarta.

UNCTAD (1998), *World Investment Report* (New York: United Nations).

——(2000), *World Investment Report 2000: Cross-Border Mergers and Acquisitions and Development*, Geneva: United Nations Conference on Trade and Development.

——(2001), *Duty and Quota-Free Market Access for LDCs: An Analysis of Quad Initiatives* (Geneva: UNCTAD: London: Commonwealth Secretariat).

——(2002), *World Investment Report 2002: Transnational Corporations and Export Competitiveness*, UN publication E.02.II.D.4 (New York and Geneva: United Nations Conference on Trade and Development).

——(2003), 'Main Recent Initiatives in Favour of Least Developed Countries in the Area of Preferential Market Access: Preliminary Impact Assessment' I note by the UNCTAD secretariat for the Trade and Development Board, fiftieth session, Geneva.

——(2004), *The Least Developed Countries Report 2004*, (Geneva: United Nations Conference on Trade and Development).

UNDP (1997), *Human Development Report 1997* (New York and London: Oxford University Press).

UNDP (2003a), *Making Global Trade Work for People* (New York: United Nations Development Program).

——(2003b), *Worker Remittance as an Instrument for Development* (San Salvador: UNDP El Salvador).

UNIDO (2002), *Enabling Developing Countries to Participate in International Trade: Strengthening the Supply Capacity*, UNIDO Strategy Document.

Vandenbussche, Hylke (2000), 'Trade Policy versus Competition Policy: Substitutes or Complements?,' *De Economist* 148, 625–42.

Verikios, G., and K. Hanslow (1999), 'Modelling the Effects of Implementing the Uruguay Round: A Comparison Using the GTAP Model under Alternative Treatments of International Capital Mobility', paper presented at Second Annual Conference on, Global Economic Analysis, Copenhagen.

—— and Xiao-guang Zhang (2001), 'The Economic Effects of Removing Barriers to Trade in Telecommunications and Financial Services', paper presented at the Fourth Annual Conference on Global Economic Analysis, West Lafayette, Ind.

Wainio, J., and P. Gibson (2003), 'The Significance of Nonreciprocal Trade Preferences for Developing Countries', paper presented at the International Conference on Agricultural Policy Reform and the WTO, Capri (Italy).

Walmsley, T., and L. A. Winters (2002), 'Relaxing Restrictions on Temporary Movement of Natural Persons: A Simulation Analysis', mimeo, University of Sussex.

Warner, Andrew M. (2002), 'Once More into the Breach: Economic Growth and Global Integration', mimeo, National Bureau of Economic Research.

Warren, T. (2000), 'The Impact on Output of Impediments to Trade and Investment in Telecommunications Services', in C. Findlay and T. Warren (eds), *Impediments to Trade in Services: Measurement and Policy Implications* (London and New York: Routledge), 1–17.

Wilson, John S. (2001), 'Trade Facilitation Lending by the World Bank— Recent Experiences, Research and Capacity Building Initiatives', draft paper prepared for the WTO Workshop on Technical Assistance and Capacity Building in Trade Facilitation, Geneva.

——(2002), 'Standards, Trade and Development: What is Known and What do we Need to Know?' paper presented at the Roundtable on Informing the Doha Process: New Research for Developing Countries, Cairo.

Wilson, J., C. Mann, and T. Otsuki (2003), *Trade Facilitation and Economic Development: Measuring the Impact*, World Bank Working Paper 2988 (Washington, DC: World Bank).

——— Yuen Pau Woo, Nizar Assanie, and Inbom Choi (2002), *Trade Facilitation: A Development Perspective in the Asia Pacific Region* APEC.

Winters, A. (2003), 'Trade Policy as Development Policy', in J. Toye (ed.), *Trade and Development: Directions for the Twenty-first Century* (Cheltenham: Edward Elgar).

Winters, L. A. (2000), 'Trade, Trade Policy and Poverty: What are the Links?', background paper for the World Bank's *World Development Report 2000/01*.

——(2002), 'Trade Liberalization and Poverty: What are the Links?', *The World Economy* 25, 1339–68.

——and Wendy E. Takacs (1991), 'Labour Adjustment Costs and British Footwear Protection', *Oxford Economic Papers* 43, 479–501.

——T. Walmsley, Z. Wang, and R. Gyrnberg (2002), 'Negotiating the Liberalization of the Temporary Movement of Natural Persons', mimeo, University of Sussex.

World Bank (1993a), *The East Asian Miracle* (Oxford: Oxford University Press).

——(1993b), *Trade Liberalization: Global Economic Implications* (Washington, DC: World Bank).

——(2000), *Does More International Trade Openness Worsen Inequality?*, World Bank Briefing Paper (Washington, DC: World Bank).

——(2002a), *Global Economic Prospects and the Developing Countries: Making World Trade for the World's Poor* (Washington, DC: World Bank).

World Bank (2002*b*), *Trade, Investment, and Development in the Middle East and North Africa*, World Bank report (Washington, DC: World Bank).

——(2003), *Global Economic Prospects*, World Bank, Washington, DC.

——(2004), *Global Economic Perspectives 2004: Realizing the Development Promise of the Doha Agenda* (Washington, DC: World Bank).

WTO (2001*a*), *Doha WTO Ministerial 2001: Ministerial Declaration*, WT/MIN(01)/DEC/1 (Geneva: World Trade Organisation).

WTO (2001*b*), *Market Access: Unfinished Business. Post-Uruguay Round Inventory and Issues*, Special Study 6 (Geneva: World Trade Organization).

——(2003), *Adjusting to trade liberalization: the role of policy, institutions and WTO disciplines*, WTO Special Studies 7 (Geneva: World Trade Organisation).

Zedillo, E. (2001), *Report of the High-Level Panel on Financing for Development*, report presented to the UN Monterrey Conference on Financing for Development (New York: United Nations).

Index

Figures, notes and tables are indicated in bold e.g. **f**, **n**, **t**. More than one figure or table per page is indicated by (**a**) or (**b**)